The River Cottage

Bread Handbook

First published in Great Britain 2009

Text © 2009 by Daniel Stevens
Photography © 2009 by Gavin Kingcome

The quote on p.36 is from *The Tassajara Bread Book*, by Edward Espe Brown, ©1970 by the Chief Priest, Zen Center, San Francisco. Reprinted by arrangement with Shambhala Publications, Inc., Boston, www.shambhala.com

The moral right of the author has been asserted.

Bloomsbury Publishing Plc, 36 Soho Square, London W1D 3QY

A CIP catalogue record for this book is available from the British Library.

ISBN 978 0 7475 9533 5
10 9 8

Project editor: Janet Illsley
Design: willwebb.co.uk
Printed and bound in Italy by Graphicom

MIX
Paper from responsible sources
FSC® C013123

www.bloomsbury.com/rivercottage

While every effort has been made to ensure the accuracy of the information contained in this book, in no circumstances can the publisher or the author accept any legal responsibility or liability for any loss or damage (including damage to property and/or personal injury) arising from any error in or omission from the information contained in this book, or from the failure of the reader to properly and accurately follow any instructions contained in the book.

Notes

Spoon measures are level unless otherwise stated:
1 tsp = 5ml spoon; 1 tbsp = 15ml spoon.

Use fresh herbs and freshly ground pepper unless otherwise suggested.

Use easy-blend (fast-action/quick) powdered yeast, rather than traditional dried yeast.

Oven timings in the recipes relate to fan-assisted ovens.
If using a conventional electric or gas oven (without a fan), increase the temperature by 15°C (1 Gas Mark). Use an oven thermometer to check the accuracy of your oven.

The River Cottage Bread Handbook

by Daniel Stevens

introduced by
Hugh Fearnley-Whittingstall

www.rivercottage.net

BLOOMSBURY
LONDON · BERLIN · NEW YORK · SYDNEY

Contents

Why Bake Bread?	8
Getting Started	14
Bread Making Step by Step	34
The Basic Bread Recipe	72
Beyond the Basic Loaf	84
Bread Made with Wild Yeast	108
Bread Made without Yeast	126
Buns, Biscuits & Batter Breads	138
Using Leftover Bread	174
Building a Clay Oven	192
Useful Things	210

Bread is the staff of life, the saying goes. And in that sense

it is fundamental to our subsistence. But it is also fundamental to our pleasure – because good bread is the founding food of civilisation. So much greater than the sum of its humble parts, it defies all logic: it is the two-plus-two-equals-five of culinary evolution.

Bread is also like humanity itself. We come in many different shapes and sizes, colours and guises, yet underneath the skin/crust, we're all made of the same stuff. And the trick of achieving happiness and harmony is surely to celebrate and enjoy both our similarities and our differences, with equal vigour.

You only have to start reciting the names of the finest breads of the world to begin this process of celebration: cobber, baguette, chapati, sourdough, tortilla, ciabatta, brioche, bloomer... it's a litany of goodness. Wherever you are in the world, is there any better way of making yourself feel at home than breaking bread with the locals? Or, if you're feeling shy, at least going to visit the local baker.

But there's no doubt that for most of us good bread still seems much easier to enjoy than to make. And I must admit that for many years bread making was, for me, something of a culinary blind spot. I largely took the view that the making of bread, like the making of wine, was something best left to the experts. I felt I could enjoy it all the more for not knowing too much about its underlying mysteries. And then I met Dan!

When he first came to work with me in the River Cottage kitchen, Dan wasn't a particularly experienced baker – just a talented young chef long on the two qualities I look for in new recruits: curiosity and enthusiasm. But he soon decided to direct much of his energy and skill towards the blending of flour and yeast, in all its splendid forms. And as I watched him do so, I found myself revising my own rather hands-off approach to baking. His rapid and impressive progress was both engaging and infectious.

I saw that a form of cooking I had previously felt to be something of a dark art, was as ready to reveal itself to the energy of the open-minded, risk-taking enthusiast as any other. It had suited me to leave bread making on the side – I had enough other stuff on my plate. But I began to follow Dan's progress, picking up a few hints and tips even as they solidified in his own mind. And I found myself becoming a better baker, just by virtue of the occasional chat with Dan – and of course frequent sampling of his wares.

I'm not in Dan's league, of course. He has become a truly great baker. And a great teacher too, not least because, like all the best teachers, he is happy to acknowledge that he is still learning. What I love about this book is the irresistible way he passes on his knowledge. Like a nutty professor in his lab, he just can't wait to tell you how it all works. He hasn't lost the sense of wonder that his ingredients can really do the amazing things they do, or that the end results can be as delicious as they are.

This irrepressible enthusiasm now comes with a hefty dose of authority. Dan knows what he's talking about. He believes passionately in using the best ingredients, locally sourced where possible, and will guide you dependably to the right tools, edible and otherwise, for the job. And I can honestly say that I would now rather eat bread baked by Dan than anyone else (except perhaps my wife, who also bakes lovely bread, though sadly not nearly as often as Dan does).

And few, frankly, will be more delighted than I am to have in their hands, at last, the perfect book to help them bake better bread. This simple volume feeds my enthusiasm and knowledge, like a sourdough starter, so that I feel readier than ever to rise to the occasion. That's because Dan's creations, from the simplest flat bread to elaborate, multi-seeded concoctions, via the notoriously temperamental sourdoughs, are achievable and yet consistently delicious. And they are the real deal – about as far from the plastic-wrapped, machine-made monstrosities that shamelessly pass themselves off under the name of 'bread' as it's possible to get.

I'm thrilled that in this handbook, Dan will get to share with you, and with many, his passion and knowledge. Whether you want to know how to bash out a simple white loaf, delight your family with buttery croissants or fling together some Middle Eastern flatbreads to wrap up the meat on your barbecue, you can be sure you're in very safe, if rather floury, hands.

Hugh Fearnley-Whittingstall, East Devon, February 2009

Why Bake Bread?

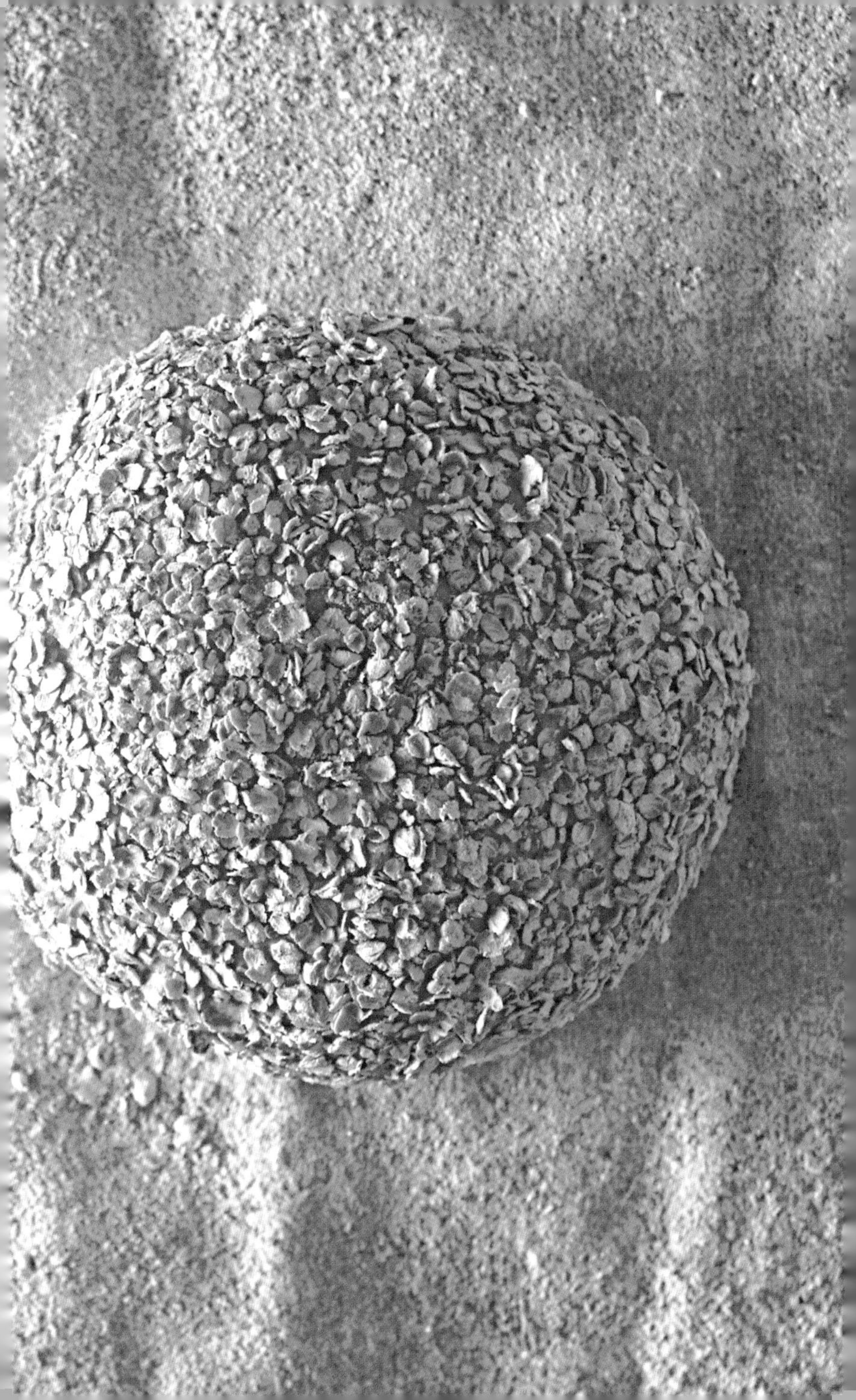

There is nothing in the world as satisfying to eat as home-baked, handmade bread. Of course, technically the artisan baker down the road is much better at it, but no amount of skill and craftsmanship can replace the utter joy of eating and sharing the stuff you make yourself. And it is practical to make bread – exceptional bread – with your own hands, in your own home, on a regular basis.

I know you are busy, so I have given you roti – a flatbread you can make, from cupboard to table, in less than 5 minutes. But I know that you also have free time, and I hope I can persuade you that free time spent in the kitchen – by yourself, with friends or with children, with music in your ears, wine in your glass, flour in your hair and magic in your hands – is time that could not be better spent.

If you are new to bread making, this sense of pleasure might not be immediate, but I am confident that you will reach it more quickly than I did. I remember my first loaf well – even the birds wouldn't eat it. I had followed the two-page recipe to the letter and the cookbook assured me that 'homemade bread is easy'. That was rather hard to swallow (as was my bread). Still, I soldiered on, day after day. After all, practice makes perfect.

There are two kinds of bread in the world: bread that hands have made, and bread that hands have not. In an ideal world, all bread would be hands-have-made – by your hands and my hands, and by the hands of those few professional bakers left in this country who are still doing it properly. I guess there will always be hands-have-not bread, and while it's not that bad, or at least it is surely edible, it seems a shame that bread has become so standard and commonplace, that we don't even consider what a small miracle a risen loaf is.

Mass-produced bread

Some would say that 1961 was a bad year for bread. It was the year the Chorleywood Bread Process came into being. Developed by the Flour Milling and Baking Research Association in Chorleywood, the process revolutionised the baking industry. This high-speed mechanical mixing process allowed the fermentation time to be drastically reduced, and meant that lower-protein British wheats could be used in place of the more expensive North American imports. Various chemical improvers and antifungal agents are necessary ingredients, as are certain hydrogenated or fractionated hard fats. This is high-output, low-labour production, designed to maximise efficiency and profit at the expense of the consumer.

Mass-produced bread is almost undoubtedly worse for you. Apart from the dubious additives and fats it contains, the short fermentation makes the wheat harder to digest. Indeed, some believe the Chorleywood processing method is partly to blame for a sharp increase in gluten intolerance and allergy. It is also probable that

WHY BAKE BREAD? 11

the prolific crossbreeding and modification of modern-day wheat, to produce stronger, tougher, harder-to-digest gluten, has contributed to wheat intolerance.

Somewhere in the region of 98 per cent of bread baked in this country is mass-produced, and most of it comes from around a dozen huge plant bakeries. Supermarkets love to crow about their in-store bakeries, but they are really nothing more than mini versions of these plants. 98 per cent is a lot. That means hands-have-not bread is not just the preserve of the supermarkets; it is the same bread you buy in most local 'bakeries'. I'm talking about the ones that sell white tin loaves with flat tops, apple turnovers and ham rolls with nasty pickle, where there is little hint of baking activity save for the oven-warming of sausage rolls, bacon-and-cheese slices and 'Cornish' pasties. The 'bakeries' whose bread looks the same as everyone else's... Well, nearly everyone else's.

Bread from real bakeries

Real bakeries are special places, where bread is made in small batches by real people's hands and baked on site. You can tell when bread is made by hand. For a start, it will look different from other bread in other shops, because every baker has his own, recognisable style. Shop at one regularly and you may spot changes in the bread from one morning to the next. You may even be able to tell if the baker was in a bad mood, so sensitive is real bread to the hands that make it. Some real bakeries sell their bread to local stores, which is excellent – the more places selling real bread, the better. Real bakeries are a rarity, though. If you are lucky enough to have one near you, then you would be mad not to use it. The bread will cost more... so it should.

Bread made at home

Home is the bakery where handmade bread does not cost more. At home, you can produce a large loaf, made with organic flour, for less than half the price of a similar-sized, mass-produced, non-organic loaf from a local shop. And your homemade bread can be great bread – even if it doesn't quite go to plan the first time.

I still have that first bread recipe I attempted – both pages of it. And now, years later, I realise why my first loaf was such a disaster. The basic method is fine, but to make good bread you need to understand the process. Some professional bakers and cookery writers skirt this all too briefly. As I discovered, being told 'what to do' is simply not enough. There is so much to know, and I really believe that the more you know, the better your bread will be. Two pages? Not even the best baker in the world could teach bread in two pages.

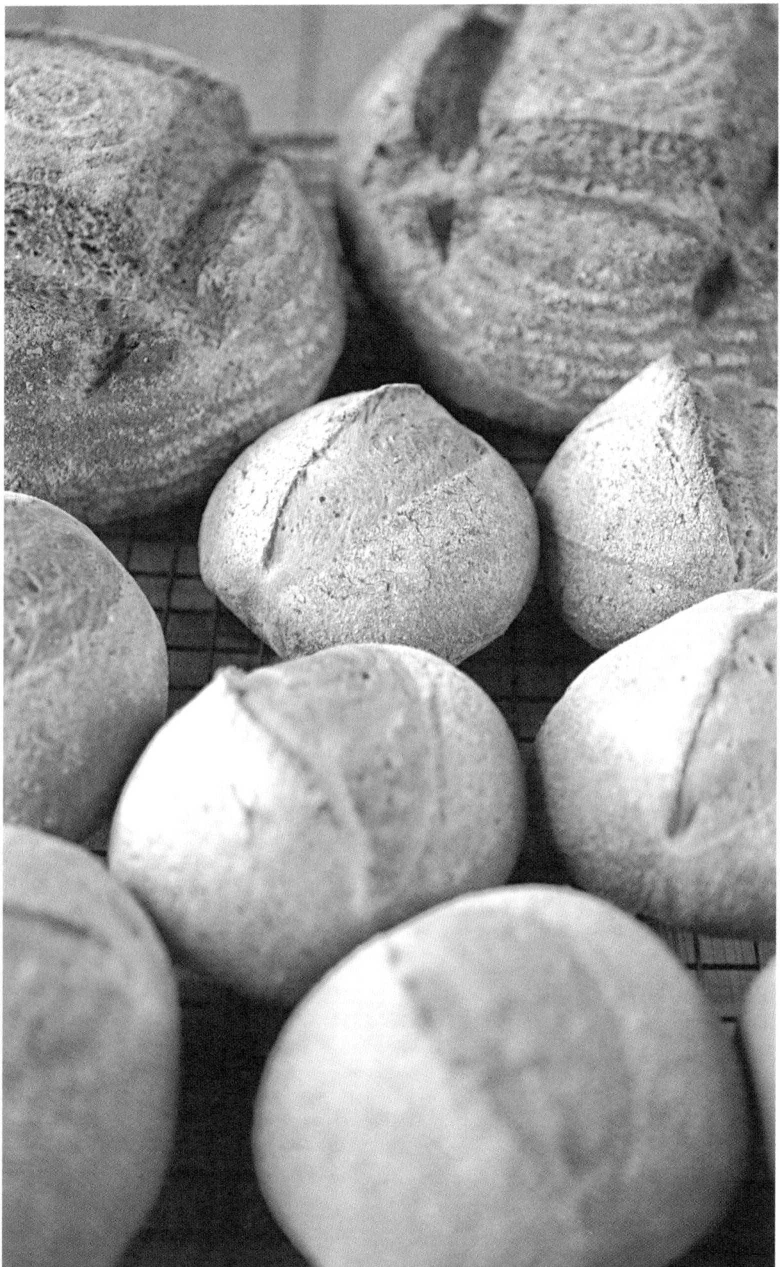

Getting Started

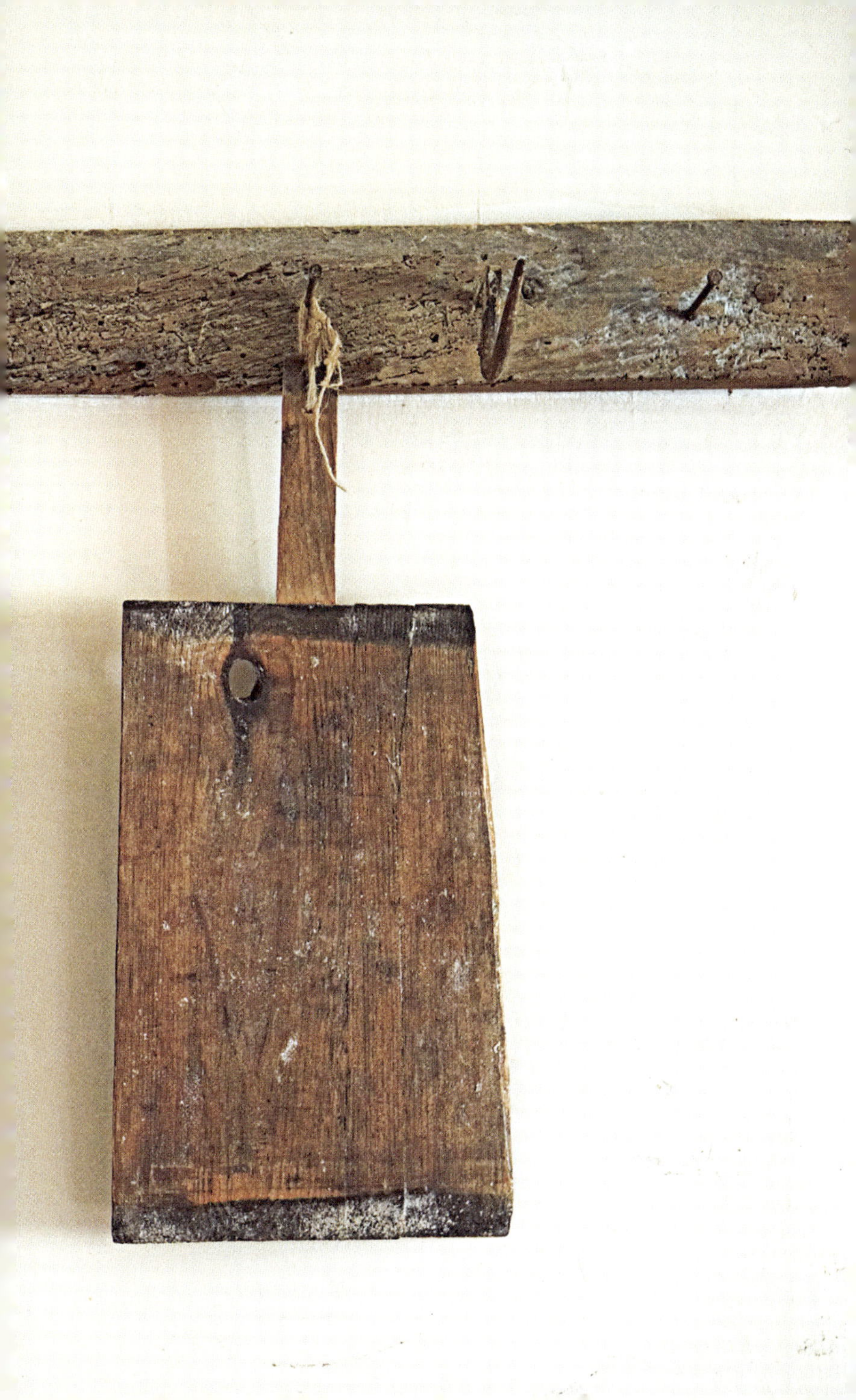

Baking kit

You don't need a vast inventory of special equipment to bake your own bread, but there are a few items that come in very handy, most of which are inexpensive. In addition to those described below, you'll find the following everyday kitchen tools useful: a measuring jug, a rolling pin, a set of pastry cutters, a pastry brush, a palette knife, a bread knife (which I also use as a dough slasher), several sturdy baking trays, a large wire cooling rack, and black dustbin liners (which I use over and over again for covering my doughs). I also have a lidded crock, where my sourdough starter (see p.110) lives.

Linen cloths

Linen draws a tiny amount of moisture from the surface of the dough, drying it just enough to prevent it from sticking. I have never found that dough sticks to a well-floured linen cloth, not even the wettest ciabatta. You can also fold and shape the cloth to make rucks and channels to keep your loaves in shape, and separate. Keep the cloths dry and you shouldn't need to wash them. At some stage of their life, you will want to replace them but I have had mine in regular use for well over a year. Fabric shops are the best place to buy linen; a metre will be more than enough and won't cost you very much. You can use clean tea towels instead, but they may stick; all-linen tea towels would be your best option.

Wooden boards

These are an alternative to cloths, to dust generously with flour and lay your bread on. We have two or three large (1.2 square metre) pieces of cheap, thin plywood at River Cottage, which are excellent for large batch baking. A couple of smaller ones would certainly be useful in your baking kit. They are less versatile than cloths in that you cannot ruck them up, but a little more practical as you can move them around with bread on. A board/cloth combination would be perfect.

Proving baskets

It is nice to own a couple of proving baskets. The best, and most expensive, are generally made of cane or reed, sometimes lined with linen, though you can buy cheaper wicker and plastic ones (see the directory, p.212). They come in different shapes and sizes and are excellent for holding the shape of your loaf as it is proving. Proving baskets are especially useful for wetter doughs, which cannot hold their own weight (large, airy sourdoughs, for example). Lower-gluten breads also benefit from the extra support. Dust the baskets heavily with flour and lay the bread in them, smooth side down.

Baking stone
The best way to bake bread is on a hot stone. Some kitchen shops sell them, but they are invariably too small, too thin and too expensive. Measure your oven, then go to your local hardware store and buy the paving stone that best fits. If you do not have a baking stone, you will need a baking tray – the larger and heavier the better.

Peel
A peel is a sheet of wood or metal with a handle, for sliding bread into the oven. You will need one if you are using a baking stone; either buy one (see the directory, p.212), make one, or use a rimless baking sheet instead. (My peel is simply a thin piece of wood, with a narrow piece nailed on as a handle – see pic on pp.14–15.)

Dough scraper
One of these is useful for handling and cutting the dough, and for scraping work surfaces and bowls clean. Small cheap plastic scrapers are adequate. You may already have something similar in your kitchen that will work; a plastic wallpaper scraper, for example.

Thermometer
A special-purpose thermometer is useful for checking the temperature of oil for deep-frying. A probe cooking thermometer will do the job.

Water spray bottle
I recommend one of these for spraying loaves before they go into the oven. You can buy them cheaply at garden centres and hardware stores.

Weighing scales
It is well worth investing in a set of digital scales. They should measure in increments of 5g or less, and have a capacity of at least 2kg. Alternatively, of course, you can use balance scales.

Large mixing bowl
Earthenware feels just right for making bread, but in truth, plastic and stainless steel bowls are both fine.

Food mixer
Although not essential for bread making, a food mixer fitted with a dough hook can be used for kneading and is particularly helpful for softer, wetter doughs that are difficult to work by hand.

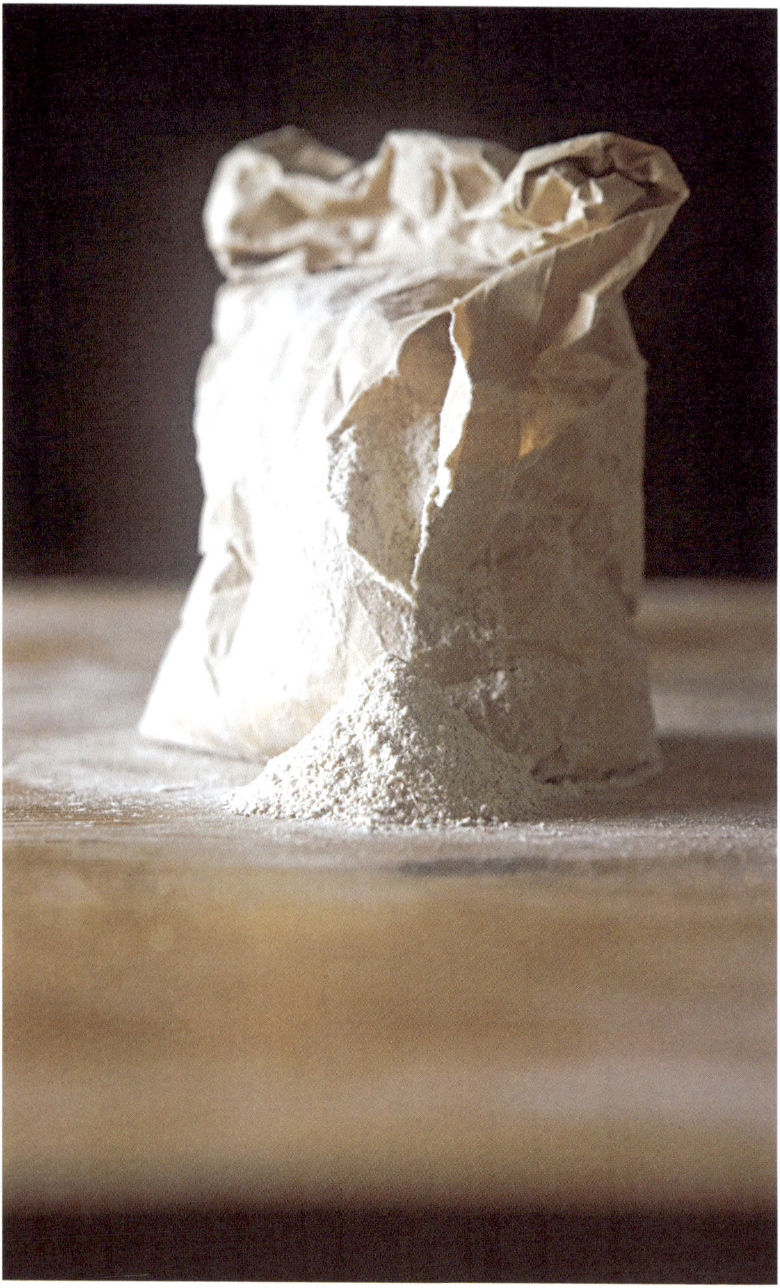

Ingredients

The best bread comprises four simple ingredients: flour, yeast, salt and water. It helps to know something about these – let's start with the most important: flour.

Flour

You must buy good flour – the best you can afford. The price of flour has increased dramatically, but making bread will always be cheaper than buying it, so you can afford the best. Wholefood stores are usually good places to buy flour, but I buy mine locally from my favourite bakeries, Leakers in Bridport and Town Mill in Lyme Regis, who sell the flour they use themselves. Many supermarkets sell good-quality flour too, alongside the cheaper stuff. I don't want pesticides, fungicides, or 'anycides at all' in my bread, and I'm sure you don't either, so I suggest buying organic flour.

Most of the flour on sale in this country is the product of roller milling. This is a large-scale, fully automated process in which the grains pass through a series of grooved rollers, sieves, aspirators and centrifuges, which cut, grind, sift and separate the grains to produce specified grades of flour. For white flour, the bran is removed early on, and only the pale endosperm is ground. Milling whole grains produces wholemeal flour, of course, which may then be sifted to produce a lighter brown flour. An unwelcome side effect of this super-efficient system is that the friction generated by the high-speed rollers can overheat the flour, destroying valuable nutrients. Fortunately, there is still another way.

Traditional stone milling, as you can imagine, is much rougher around the edges. Grain is poured into a hole in the middle of a huge stone disc, which rotates by whatever power is available (electricity/water/wind/donkey) on top of a second, stationary disc. The resulting meal falls away from the sides, and is sieved (or not) and bagged. A preliminary sifting of the wholemeal removes the coarser bits and gives brown flour. Subsequent siftings through finer meshes lighten and whiten the flour, but some bran will stay, so stoneground flour will never be as white as it would be from a roller mill. That is unless it is bleached, of course. Various substances have been used to whiten flour, both stone- and roller-milled, for the last 100 years or so, and the list reads a little scarily. Does anyone fancy a nitrogen peroxide/chlorine/chlorine dioxide/nitrosyl chloride/benzoyl peroxide/azodicarbonamide sandwich? No, I thought not. The function of bleach is purely aesthetic and I don't really approve of such chemical interference – it is vain and unnecessary.

I love using stoneground flour. It seems right that bread, such a basic and traditional staple, is made with basic and traditional methods. Stone milling still has the human touch, and if there is one foodstuff that should never have been sucked into the soulless, automated world of mass production, then surely it is bread. Bread that has been loved and cared for at every stage is better bread, no question.

Wheat flour

Of course, flours are produced from various grains, but in this country wheat flour is by far the most common. A grain of wheat is a seed and is made, basically, of three parts: the bran, which is the outside 'skin' and comprises about 13 per cent of the grain; the germ, which is the wheat plant in embryo (about 2 per cent); and the rest (about 85 per cent) is the endosperm, which supports and feeds the germ in its early stages of growth. The bran is full of flavour and protein; the germ full of vitamins; and the endosperm is packed with carbohydrates (in the form of starches and sugars), and contains proteins, minerals and oil.

All of these end up in your bread, of course, and they all have an effect. The starches and sugars feed the yeast, the proteins bond to form gluten, the minerals strengthen the gluten, and the oil rather gets in the way – wriggling in between newly bonding proteins and splitting them up. It's also the first to turn rancid (which is why it's important to stick to the use-by date on your flour). However, this oil is not all bad. By clinging to the starches, and also by retaining moisture, it helps soften the bread, and keep it soft for longer. Its benefits are such that extra oil (or butter, or lard) is often added to bread dough, though I don't add it straight away. I like to allow the proteins to bond, and become inseparable, first.

I would love to suggest that you only buy flour milled from grain grown in this country for bread making, but for reasons I will explain, I'm not going to. You see, there is wheat and there is wheat. Up to 30,000 different varieties, in fact. Wheats, or *Triticum*, are grasses, grown generally in temperate regions – mainly North America, Europe and the warmer south-western parts of Russia, India, China, Australia and Argentina. Different strains have different properties, the most notable of which is their protein content.

Strong flour When you mix flour with water, certain proteins in the flour (gliadin and glutenin) bond together and form gluten. Gluten is an elastic, extensile substance that forms long chains when it is softened and stretched. The more it is worked, the longer and stretchier it gets (think of Blu-Tack). These elastic chains of gluten form a network, which acts like a membrane, trapping the carbon dioxide produced by fermenting yeast and making thousands of gas pockets inside the dough.

The amount of gluten in the dough depends on the quality of the proteins in the grain. High-quality proteins will produce 'strong' flour with a high percentage of gluten (up to 15 per cent), which is what you want for leavened (yeasted) bread. Such flour is generally sold as 'strong flour' or 'bread flour' (or even 'strong bread flour'), and can be wholemeal, white or brown. Brown flour is sometimes sold as '81 per cent' flour, because a typical first sifting removes about 19 per cent of the total weight.

The problem for food-mile-conscious bread bakers in this country is that the strains of wheat with the best gluten-forming proteins simply will not grow successfully here. They flourish in nitrogen-rich soil and prefer cold winters and hot summers. Our climate is simply too placid, our soil too low in nitrogen. Canada, on the other hand, boasts the perfect conditions. Although it is possible to buy flour milled from 100 per cent Canadian wheat here, imported wheat is more heavily taxed, so the strong bread flours produced in this country are usually blends of British and Canadian wheat. Certainly the bread flour you buy in supermarkets is likely to be a blend of this kind.

However, several British millers are producing small quantities of purely local wheat flour (see the directory, p.212). I have found that bread made with these flours always tastes good, even if it is a little heavier. Indeed, the more I bake, the more I love heavy bread. It feels wholesome, satisfying and *real*. So if someone is growing and milling wheat near you, I would urge you to buy some. That said, when I buy local flour, I always buy wholemeal rather than white, as I find dense white bread much less appealing.

Plain flour 'Soft' flours have a gluten percentage of around 7–9 per cent and are usually sold as 'plain' flour. Their poorer-quality gluten is less extensile, and will struggle to form membranes and trap gas bubbles, so you end up with a weak structure and crumbly texture.

While this feature is not great for loaves of bread, it is perfect for biscuits, cakes and pastry. I sometimes use a combination of plain and strong flour when I am prepared to forgo some of the gluten strength in exchange for a yeast dough that is less resistant and easier to work – when I am making pizzas, for example.

Self-raising flour This is plain flour with raising agents added. It is most commonly used for cakes and sponge puddings, though it also forms the basis of some non-yeasted breads. I rarely have self-raising flour in my storecupboard, so I usually make my own version, by mixing 4g baking powder into every 100g plain flour (i.e. 4 per cent). With all baking, the fresher the flour the better, so I find it more convenient to have fewer open packets of different flours.

Malted grain flour Malting is a process by which whole grains are encouraged to germinate, producing sugars (amongst other things), which are then fixed by drying and browned by roasting. These now sweetly flavoured grains are then added to strong brown flour to produce different blends, which are variously named 'malted grain', 'malted seed', 'cobber', 'malthouse', and even, rather snazzily, 'maltstar'.

'Granary', by the way, is a trademark of Rank Hovis Ltd. It is the name given to a special blend of meal produced by Granary Foods Ltd. Bread can only properly be called Granary if it is made with Hovis Granary flour. You can buy this, and it is very good, but it is not the only malted flour available. Indeed, I am yet to find one that I don't like.

'00' flour This is an Italian grade of flour, usually milled from durum wheat. It is traditionally used for making pasta, but makes good bread too. Try using it to make ciabatta (see p.90) or focaccia (see p.89) in place of the strong white flour.

Other grain flours

While no other grain will make bread as light and well risen as wheat, other grains are used and each has its own character, flavour and history. It is well worth getting yourself acquainted with some of the alternatives, not least because wheat intolerance seems to be on the increase.

Spelt flour An ancestral cousin of modern wheat, spelt is an ancient grain, which has never been modified. The grain we use today is identical to that used by the Romans for their bread.

Spelt is becoming more widely available in this country, as flour/pasta/puffed sugary breakfast cereal, and is recognised as a genuine alternative to wheat. It contains gluten, but the gluten in spelt is more digestible than that in wheat. You can buy white spelt flour, but if the product doesn't claim to be white, assume it is wholemeal.

Traditional wholemeal spelt flour has an orangey tinge and tastes delicious – similar to wheat, and slightly nutty. It is excellent for making bread, but also good for biscuits, cakes and pastry. Spelt grows well in many places, including Britain.

Rye flour Rye thrives in cold climates and poor soil. It is widely cultivated and used across Scandinavia, Russia and Eastern Europe; it grows well in this country, too. Rye proteins form small amounts of weak gluten, producing dense, sometimes cakey, but very tasty bread. It is worth mixing rye with strong white wheat flour for a lighter loaf. I often use rye flour for dusting shaped loaves, and the baskets, boards and cloths on which I leave them to rise. Rye is sometimes sold as 'light' or 'dark', depending on the amount of whole grain left in it.

Kamut flour This yellowish flour is fairly low in gluten and makes decent, but not remarkable bread. It isn't a flour I use, but it is appearing more often in shops and has a tale behind it, which I thought you might find interesting. The story goes that a US airman, shot down over Egypt in the Second World War, discovered a few perfectly preserved grains in an ancient desert tomb. He managed to get himself and the grains to safety, and brought them home, where they were discovered to be an ancient North African wheat-related grain that was thought to be extinct. It was named 'kamut' (now a trademark), after the Egyptian for wheat. You can buy flour milled from the great-great-great-great grandchildren of the airman's grains, which are today grown exclusively in America.

Gluten-free bread flour This is usually made from a blend of rice, potato, tapioca and other flours, and typically contains xantham gum, as a sort of gluten replacement. Gluten-free flours generally come with a recipe on the bag, which you should follow; the method is usually rather different to traditional bread making. Bread made with such flour is, I would say, an acquired taste… one I'm yet to acquire.

GRAIN	FLOUR TYPE	GLUTEN	USES
Wheat	Strong white/wholemeal/brown	High	Bread
	Malted grain	High	Bread
	Plain white/wholemeal/brown	Low	Pastry, pancakes, biscuits. Also blended with strong flour for softer bread doughs (pizzas/flatbreads), soda bread, scones
	Self-raising white/wholemeal/brown	Low	Cakes, soda bread, scones
	'00' pasta flour	High	Pasta, bread
Spelt	Wholemeal/white	Medium high	Bread, biscuits, cakes, pasta
Rye	Dark/light	Low	Bread
Kamut		Medium	Bread
Gluten-free	White/brown	None	Bread

Water

Whether you use hard or soft water will make hardly any difference to your dough. Hard water is a little more alkaline than soft, and yeasts work a little more happily in a slightly acid environment, but it also has a higher mineral content, particularly of calcium and magnesium, which have a tightening and strengthening effect on the gluten. So, between hard and soft water, it's pretty much honours even.

I like the purity of baking with spring water. If you are lucky enough to live close to a natural spring, then you should use it; if you are happy to pay for mineral water, then do so. Otherwise, use tap water – it is perfectly good.

GETTING STARTED 25

Yeast

The term 'yeasts' refers to a group of a hundred or so single-celled organisms, collectively known as *Saccharomyces,* which are a type of fungi. They depend on carbon but, because they do not contain chlorophyll, they cannot obtain carbon from carbon dioxide in the way plants do. Instead, fungi take carbon from carbohydrates. For yeasts, the carbohydrate of choice is sugar, hence their Latin name, literally 'sugar fungus'. One strain of yeast, known as brewer's sugar fungus, is cultivated commercially, though you can – and I hope you will – create and nurture your own culture of wild yeasts for raising sourdough, the most satisfying bread you will ever make (see pp.115–9).

Commercial yeast is cultivated in huge temperature-controlled, aerated vats filled with a solution of minerals and sugars, including molasses, or malted barley, or both, and known as 'wort'. Brewers, by the way, will find this virtually indistinguishable from the wort made in the first stages of beer making. Indeed, this method of yeast cultivation is no more than a controlled and refined version of the old practice of skimming off beer froth, then adding it to dough.

Yeast cells, known as 'seed' yeast, are grown in laboratory conditions from a single healthy cell. The seed yeasts are added to the wort and in this perfect feeding and reproducing environment – yeast heaven – a gluttonous orgy ensues. Yeast cells collect *en masse* on the surface, and are removed, washed, cooled and either pressed into cake form (fresh yeast) or dehydrated and crumbled (dried yeast).

One single yeast cell can be grown into hundreds of tons in a matter of weeks. As there are several billion cells to the gram, this is a reproduction rate of which rabbits could only dream.

> Dried yeast This is readily available, consistent and reliable, and it has a long shelf life. It will become inactive eventually though, so pay attention to the use-by date. The kind of dried yeast you are most likely to buy these days is sold in powdered form, and may be labelled variously as 'fast-action', 'easy-blend', or 'quick'. This is the yeast used throughout this book, which I refer to simply as 'powdered dried yeast'. Traditional dried yeast, which comes in little pellets, requires activating and is used slightly differently. Some yeast packet labels bequeath special bread-making powers upon their contents, claiming they allow you to skip an entire period of rising. Don't be taken in by this. Yeast is yeast, and you can always skip a period of rising, but as you will learn, your bread will be less digestible for it.

> Fresh yeast This is harder to come by than dried yeast. Try asking for fresh yeast at your local health food shop or bakery, where you may find it bagged for sale, in small pieces. And you should only ever buy it in small pieces, as

dried yeast

fresh yeast

its active life is only around 2 weeks from manufacture. Fresh yeast in good condition will be a pale mushroom colour, and firm. If you break it, it will snap cleanly – and the smell should be pleasant. As it stales, it becomes darker, drier and smellier, until it breaks down into a disgusting, rancid putty (but you'll have thrown it away by then). As for freezing, it is generally purported that fresh yeast can be kept in the freezer, at least for short periods, but in my experience it dies more often than it lives, so I would never recommend it.

I enjoy using fresh yeast because I like the feel, and the snap, and the smell. But dried yeast's long shelf life makes it more practical, especially for occasional baking. As for the all-important performance – the ability to make good bread – frankly, I have no preference for fresh over dried. I just can't tell the difference. I nearly always use powdered dried yeast, which can be mixed straight into the dough. It is best to blend fresh, or dried pellet yeast with a little liquid first; if you do not, it is unlikely to fully blend.

For simplicity, all yeasted recipes in this book assume the use of powdered dried yeast. If, however, you prefer to use fresh yeast, simply double the quantity given in the recipe.

How yeast works When you mix yeast with flour and wet it, various things start to happen. In addition to the wheat's own enzymes, which begin to convert starch to sugar, the yeast cells produce several enzymes of their own, which convert the various sugars in the flour into forms the yeast can absorb. This is how yeast feeds. More enzymes inside the yeast cell convert these sugars into carbon dioxide and alcohol (amongst other things), which are excreted. The carbon dioxide forms into bubbles inside the dough, and causes it to rise. This is fermentation (from the Latin *fermo* meaning 'to boil', as the bubbles bear a resemblance to boiling). This enzyme activity helps to make the tough gluten in the flour more digestible. Not surprisingly, bread that ferments for longer is better for you.

After feeding heartily, and passing gas accordingly, the yeast cell's attention turns, inevitably, to reproduction. So it splits in two. Two become four, then eight, sixteen, and so on. Meanwhile, some of the excreted alcohol is converted into acetic acid, which slightly raises the acidity of the dough. Yeasts like that, and their activity increases because of it. All this rumpus noticeably raises the temperature of the dough. Other acids, including lactic and carbonic acid, are produced. And the heady combination of acid and alcohol creates esters, aromatic molecules that contribute to the flavour of the finished bread. The longer fermentation goes on, the more of these reactions take place, and the more reactions, the more flavour. Quite simply, bread that takes longer to rise tastes better.

Dough temperature is a key factor in the rate of yeast activity: between 25°C and 30°C it will be reasonably vigorous. Temperatures higher than this will increase this vigour, resulting in a dough that rises faster, but they will also cause the yeast to produce some undesirable sour flavours. Yeasts will start to feel a little uncomfortable above about 45°C; at around 60°C they will die – which is what happens in the oven, of course. Going the other way, activity will reduce to a steady rate, becoming fairly slow at around 20°C, and will practically stop at perhaps 2°C and below, where it will lie dormant until it either dies from not feeding (after maybe a couple of weeks), is warmed up (when it will pick up where it left off), or is frozen. Although I'm reluctant to advise freezing fresh yeast, I have never had problems freezing yeasted dough, at least for a short time (up to 6 months); it always reactivates on thawing.

While you can control the rate of fermentation by controlling dough temperature, you can also affect it by the amount of yeast you add. Obviously, the less yeast, the slower the rate. This can be literally as little as you like – remember what that single cell can do.

Salt

Although it isn't essential to add salt to bread, I would never consider leaving it out, as unsalted bread tastes so unlovely. Nevertheless, salt has a dark side (ask any slug). When it comes across yeast (and slugs), salt has a propensity to murder. So you must mediate, and you must keep them apart. That said, this only really applies to fresh yeast, or dried yeast that you have rehydrated; dry salt won't react with dry yeast.

Either way, as you mix and the salt is dispersed, so its capacity to harm becomes diluted. Yeast activity is nevertheless inhibited in salted dough, the result being that fermentation is slower than it would otherwise be. Also, salt has a tightening effect on the gluten network, making it stronger and more stable. Gas bubbles are trapped more effectively, and the bread rises higher and more evenly. Salt also helps bread to retain moisture, and salted bread therefore lasts longer.

So salt is a good addition, but which salt is best? There are several methods of harvesting salt from the earth. Rock salt is mined from salt beds, often deep underground. Water also percolates naturally (or is pumped) through to these beds, dissolving the salt and forming a brine, which can be pumped up to the surface and evaporated to form salt.

Sea salt comes from seawater, which is either allowed to evaporate naturally or boiled dry – the quicker method, which results in smaller, harder crystals. The more time-consuming natural drying results in beautiful large crystals, which are sold as flaky sea salt (Maldon is the best known), and are expensive.

Any salt you are likely to buy will contain impurities, although this is not necessarily a bad thing. Unrefined sea salt, for example, will contain traces of

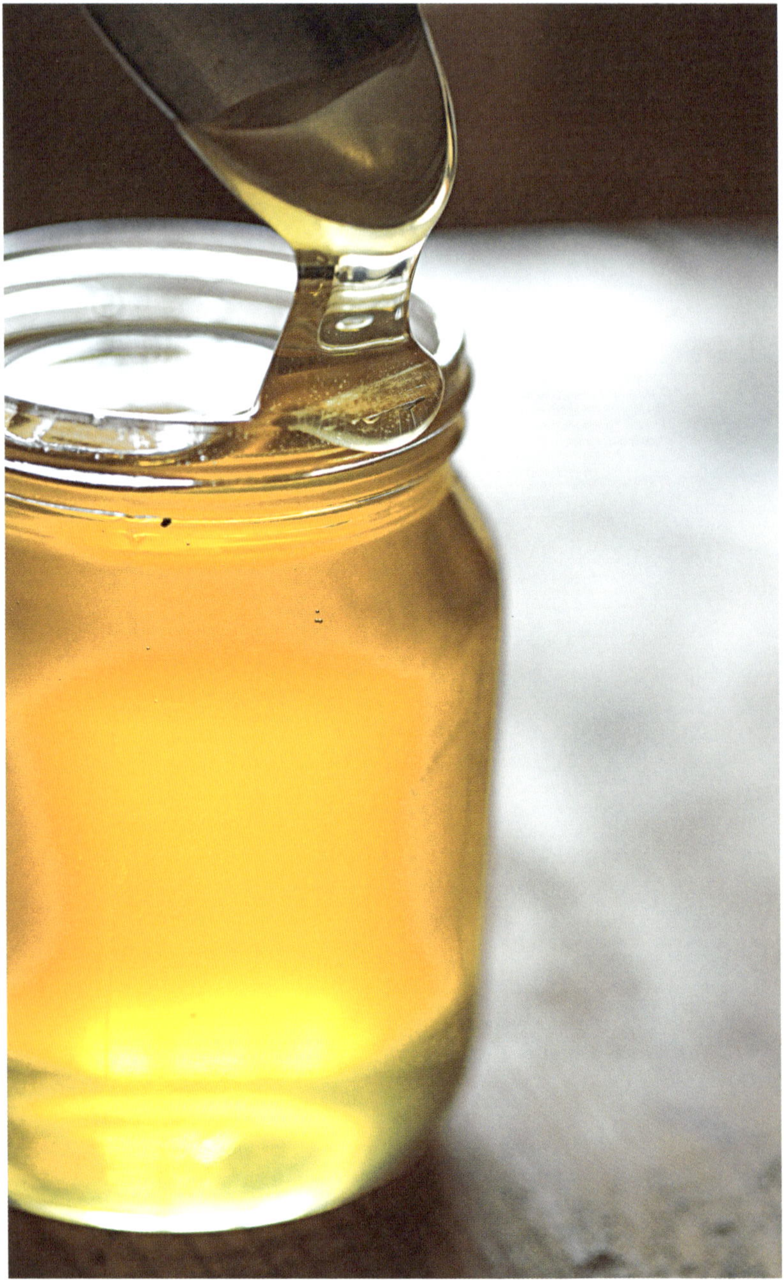

calcium, magnesium and other chlorides and sulphates. The content of salt (sodium chloride) and the concentrations of other minerals mixed with it vary according to where it comes from. This, along with the different methods of harvesting, accounts for the marked variety of natural salts available. French *sel gris* (grey salt), for example, is exactly that – grey, due to its high proportion of other minerals. By contrast, cheap, free-flowing table salt and cooking salt may be technically more 'pure' but will have additives, including anti-caking agents – E504 (magnesium carbonate) and E535 (sodium ferrocyanide).

Some of the impurities found in untreated salt will have an effect on your dough (calcium and magnesium will further tighten the gluten, for example), but I doubt you will notice the difference. My personal, perhaps romantic, preference is for unrefined sea salt, but in all honesty, for baking, I have found standard table salt to be absolutely fine.

Whatever salt you use, it must be ground finely, or it will not mix in properly. You can do this yourself, in a spice mill or a pestle and mortar.

Other ingredients

Now that you have the basics, you can take your bread in any number of directions, with the judicious addition of some choice ingredients. I have offered some suggestions here, though of course you can add what you please. Just don't add things for the sake of it. You could put olives in your bread, but they are better in a bowl. Cheese bread is good, but bread and cheese is better. I have seen bread made with fennel seeds and liquidised mussels. No, seriously. Give me some fennel seed bread, and a bowl of mussels, any day.

> Liquids You do not have to make bread with water. Milk, and even yoghurt, is excellent, and will make bread softer and (in the case of white bread) whiter. Cider and beer can be interesting, though I prefer to water them down a bit. Apple juice is lovely, as long as it is real apple juice.

> Fat As I have said, putting fat in your bread will make it a little softer, and will slightly improve its keeping qualities. Stronger-tasting fats will, of course, add their own hint of flavour, though these effects are not radical. Suffice to say that any animal fats, and any edible oils, can be used.

> Honey Natural and good for you, honey adds a beguiling sweetness to bread.

> Oats Essential in Scottish baking, oats are highly nutritious. I always have medium oatmeal, pinhead oatmeal and rolled oats in the cupboard and I eat them most days, in some form or other.

Cornmeal (or maize meal) In Italy, this is known as polenta and is often cooked as a porridge. It doesn't contain gluten and is therefore unsuitable for making risen loaves. However, cornmeal has a distinctive taste and cornbread (see p.167), which is usually cooked in a cast-iron skillet or frying pan, has a good flavour.

Millet This is a highly nutritional grain, tasting rather like oats. It can be cooked and eaten in a similar way to couscous. A couple of handfuls of millet, flaked or ground, can be added to bread dough for a bit of a health boost.

Barley Low in gluten, barley is unsuitable for making bread on its own, but I like to add barley flakes and barley meal to doughs. I also use them for dusting loaves.

Buckwheat In truth, this is not wheat; it is not even a grain. Surprisingly, perhaps, it is related to rhubarb. In Russia, buckwheat flour is used to make blinis (see p.168); a handful or two in your dough will add flavour and iron to your bread.

Semolina In Italian, this term means 'half-milled'. Semolina is a coarse grade of flour, usually made from durum wheat – the classic wheat for making pasta. I use it in ciabatta (see p.90), and for dusting the outside of English muffins (see p.99).

Seeds There is a simple rule here. If seeds taste pleasant, use them; if they taste strong, use less of them. Buy every seed packet on the shelf and have fun experimenting with them. I especially like sunflower, pumpkin, poppy and fennel; add sesame and linseed to these and you have my favourite six-seed blend.

Dried fruit As with seeds, use these with restraint. You cannot get away from the fact that adding fruit to bread turns it into fruit bread.

Nuts I use hazelnuts a lot, because I love them. To remove their skins, first shake the nuts in a dry frying pan over a medium heat until the skins turn dark and brittle like smouldered paper, then rub them in a clean tea towel and the nuts will shed their skins. Walnuts are worth a mention, too. Make wholemeal bread with walnuts and some honey, and a Stilton sandwich could hardly taste any better. As with seeds, if you like a nut, your bread will, too.

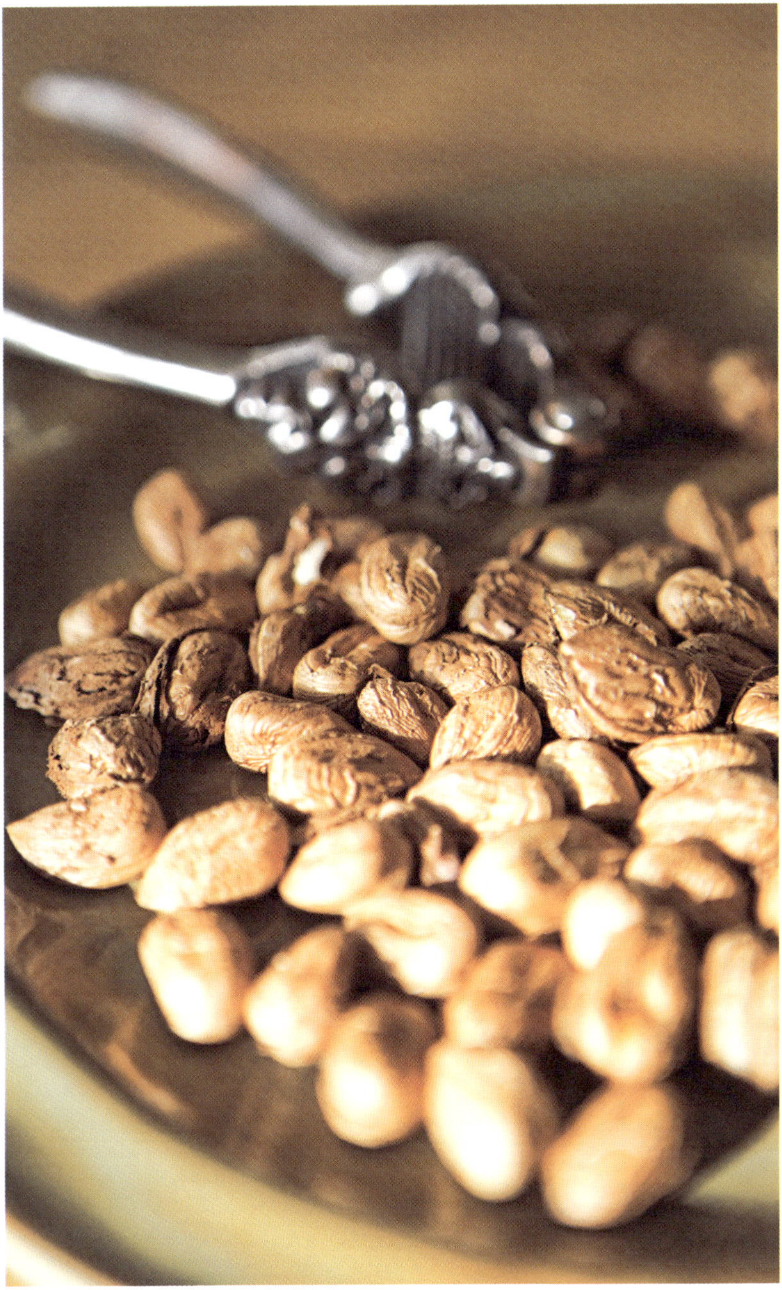

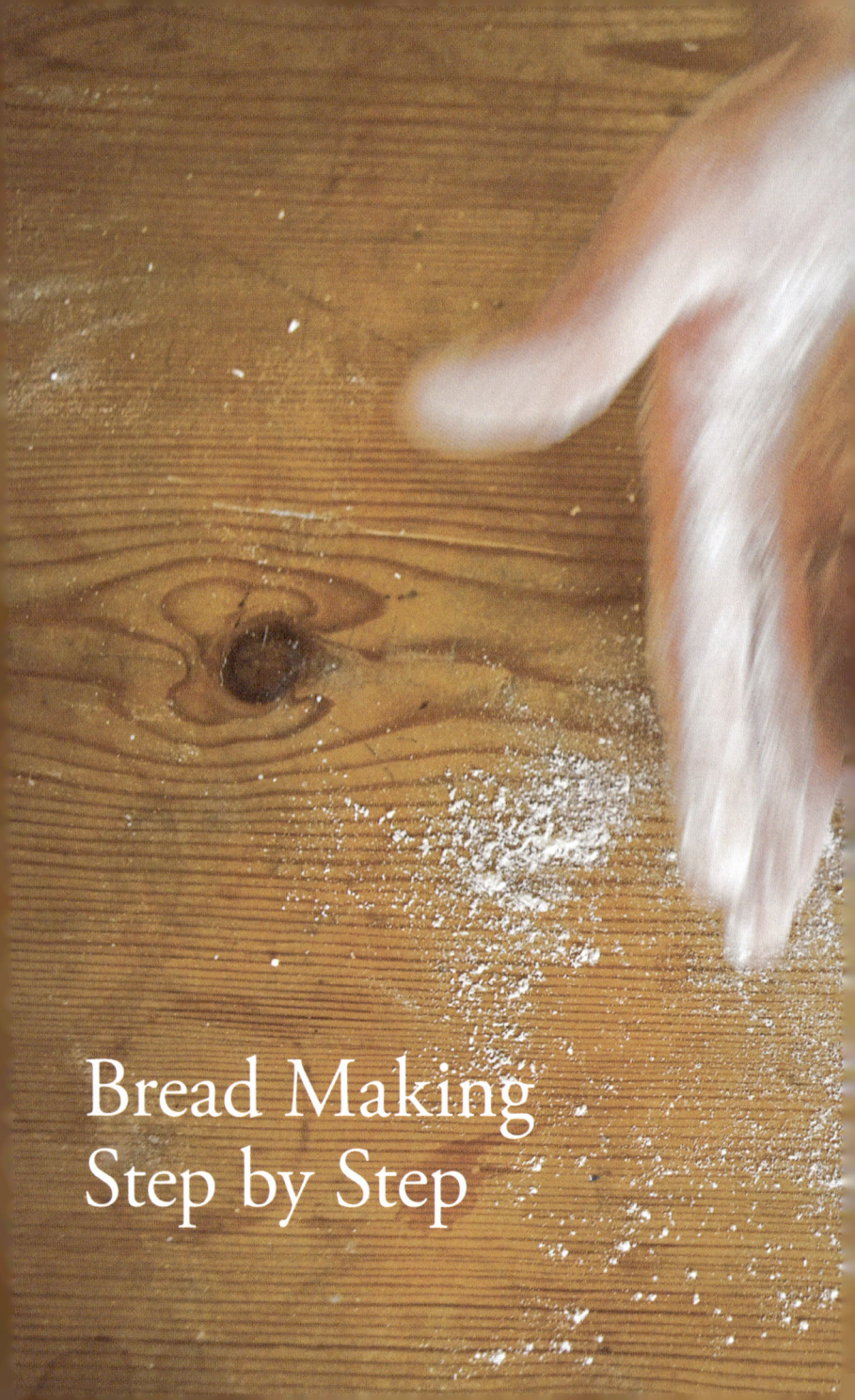

Bread Making
Step by Step

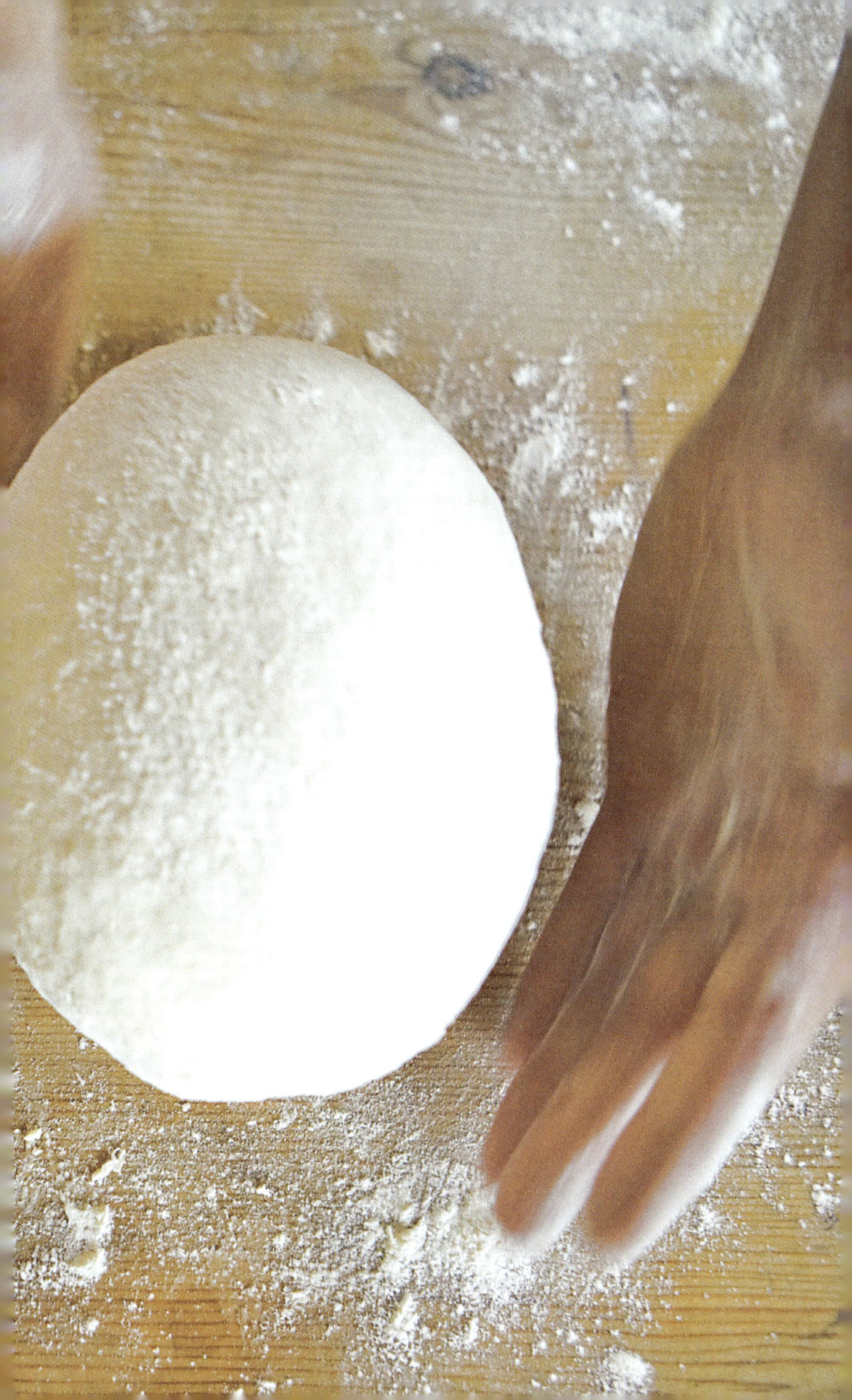

I'm not going to tell you that making really good bread at home is easy. To begin with, it may take you many attempts to make a loaf that you are truly proud of – and even then, the next one might let you down. But if bread making were a piece of cake, it wouldn't feel so amazing when you get it right. And no matter how many loaves you bake in your life, it *always* feels great when you get it right. Bread making is no mystery either, though it helps to know the science – to understand what happens when you make bread, and what affects it.

I have gone into a lot of detail in this section, and I make no apology for that. The more you understand, the better your bread will be. Take your time to absorb as much as you can about each of the bread-making stages before you begin baking. Once you are in the kitchen and the flour starts flying, you will find it easier to follow my own two-page bread recipe (see pp.76–7). It is actually a distillation of the basic method covered here; words highlighted in bold refer back to the headings in this section, for easy reference. I also show you how to adapt the recipe with infinite variations, including a few suggestions of my own, so that you may become master of your own bakery.

Anyone who bakes regularly will know that it is easy to get carried away in pursuit of the perfect loaf. I have often been unhappy with a totally decent batch of bread, for no other reason than that my last batch was better. Seek perfection, by all means, but please, don't be too hard on yourself. Always keep in mind the following wisdom, from the beautiful *Tassajara Bread Book* (see the directory, p.212):

'There are no mistakes. You might do it differently next time, but that's because you did it this way this time. Perfect, even if you say too much this, too little that. It's you and please be yourself.'

Bread making step by step

- Measure the ingredients (p.39)
- Mix the dough (p.42)
- Knead the dough (p.44)
- Shape the dough into a round (p.48)
- Leave to ferment (p.50)
- Deflate the dough (p.50)
- Leave to rise again (p.53)
- Prepare for baking (p.53)
- Divide the dough (p.54)
- Shape the loaves (p.55)
- Coat the outside (p.61)
- Leave to prove (p.63)
- Transfer the loaves for baking (p.63)
- Slash the tops (p.64)
- Bake the bread (p.66)
- Leave to cool (p.68)
- Look after your bread (p.68)

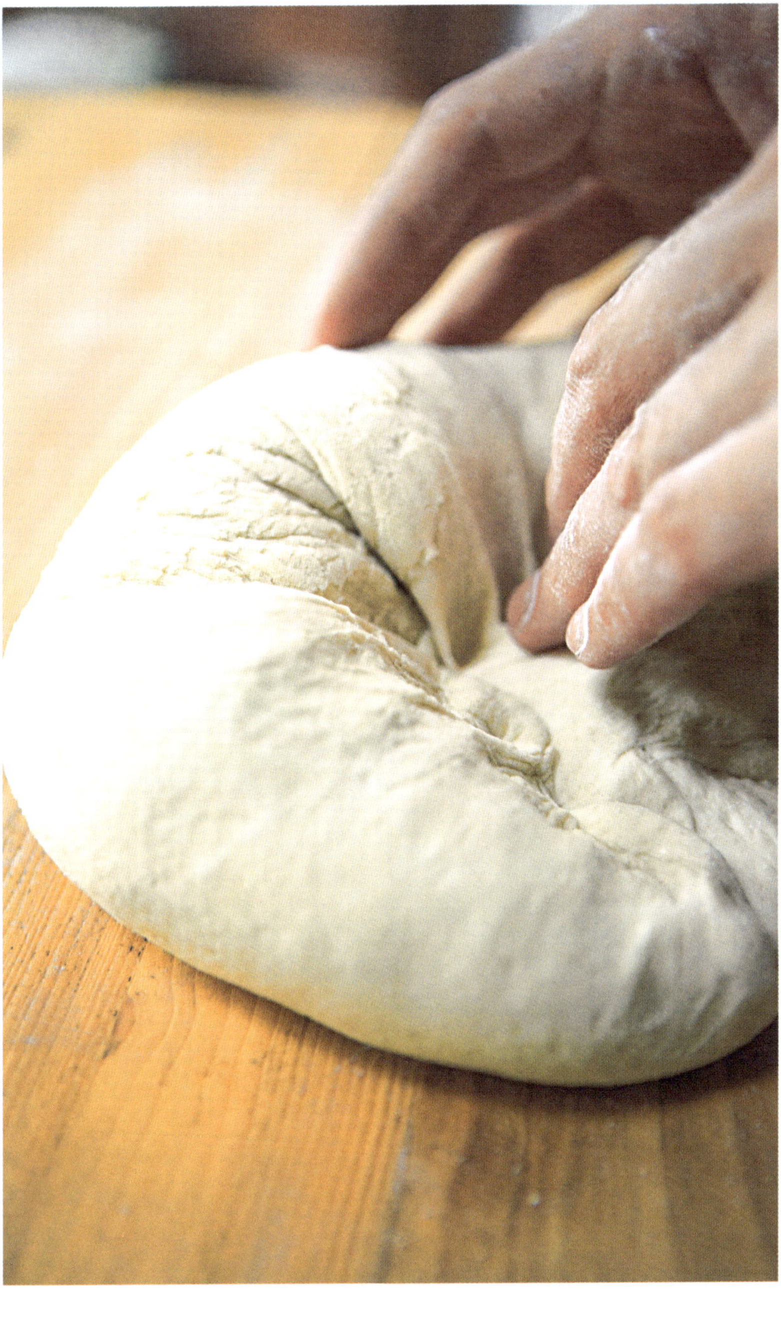

38 BREAD

Measure the ingredients

There is a quick and easy formula for calculating the amount of each ingredient you need when making a batch of bread. Many professional bakers use this method, I use it, and you should learn it. It is known as the baker's percentage, and this is how it works.

First, decide how much flour you want to use. I suggest a kilo: the quantity of dough will be a comfortable size for kneading and will yield two large or three small loaves, or perhaps a dozen rolls – a good batch size for most ovens and most households (eat some, freeze some). Taking the weight of flour as 100 per cent, you measure every other ingredient as a percentage of this.

Water

The percentage of water to flour is sometimes referred to as 'hydration'. As I have indicated, different flours absorb different amounts of water, but a good starting point for a soft, kneadable dough using white flour is 60 parts water to 100 parts flour. This is 60 per cent hydration, or simply 60 per cent. So, for a kilo of dough (1000g) you would use 600g water. You can weigh it, but 1ml water weighs 1g, so 600g=600ml.

You may find that you need more water than this. For example, wholemeal flour, which often absorbs more water than white flour, may take 65 per cent hydration to produce a workable dough. Or you may want to make a wetter dough. For instance, if you are making ciabatta (see p.90), hydration is around 80 per cent. However, you will never want to make a drier dough, so use 60 per cent as your starting point.

Yeast

As a general rule, use 1 per cent for dried yeast, and 2 per cent for fresh. You can use less than this, which makes for a longer, slower fermentation, but you shouldn't really use more otherwise your bread may taste 'yeasty'.

Salt

The standard amount of salt is 2 per cent. There is a little flexibility here, but only a little. I generally use 2½ per cent for sourdough, for example. A loaf containing 3 per cent salt will taste a bit salty for most people. With 1 per cent salt, your bread will be a little bland.

Fat

Though I would not call this a basic ingredient, I usually add fat to bread dough in some form (usually sunflower or olive oil, occasionally melted butter or lard). You could certainly leave it out. But fat will give you bread with a slightly softer crumb, which keeps slightly better. I generally go for a good slug per kilo. I've just measured a good slug – it was a little over a tablespoon, about 20g. That's about 2 per cent, the same as the salt.

So our kilo batch looks like this:

Flour	1000g (100 per cent)
Water	600ml (60 per cent)
Dried yeast	10g (1 per cent), or 20g (2 per cent) if using fresh yeast
Salt	20g (2 per cent)
Fat (optional)	A slug, about 20g (2 per cent)

Before long, you will become so accustomed to these percentages that they become second nature, allowing you to confidently make bread, any time, anywhere. It is best to own a set of electronic scales, which will enable you to accurately measure your ingredients to within a few grams. If you do not, you will have to rough it a little; in which case it will help you to know that 20g fine salt is about 2 level tsp; as is 10g powdered yeast.

In addition to the above, all manner of ingredients can be added in small quantities to dough – to enhance the flavour and/or add interest to the texture.

Extras
Small dry ingredients, such as seeds or grains, are generally added in with the flour, yeast and salt. Nuts and dried fruit are better kneaded in later.

Adding a little old dough or a starter
A common practice in artisan bakery is to keep back a little dough from each batch to incorporate into the next day's baking. Old dough has had time to mature and develop flavour from the yeast activity, so adding a lump (as much as you like) of this a day or two, even a week after you made it, adds depth and character to a new batch. You can do this with any of the mixing methods; add it to your dough just before, or just after, you add the fat. Of course, you will not have any old dough the first time you bake.

If you keep a sourdough starter (see p.110), you can add a ladleful to your yeasted dough with similar results; this is what I do.

BREAD MAKING STEP BY STEP 41

Mix the dough

There are three methods that I use to make a dough. Any of these will work for pretty much any bread; try them all and see which you are most comfortable with.

The one-stage mixing method
This is the simplest method. All the basic ingredients are mixed to a dough and kneaded straight away. At home, I nearly always make bread this way.

Add the flour, water, yeast and salt to your mixing bowl. Using two fingers of one hand, mix until you have formed a very rough, soft dough, adding more water if the dough is dry. Add the fat, if using, and squidge it all together.

The two-stage mixing method
Here, a flour and water dough is made and left to rest, before the yeast and salt are added. This allows the gluten to develop by itself. The effect is remarkable – the dough is easier to work, and it takes less time to knead. It is particularly good for a large amount of dough, which can be hard on your arms; I often use this method at River Cottage, where we generally make 4-kilo batches. The downside is that the yeast and salt don't blend as easily. They will eventually, but the dough will be slower to start fermenting.

Mix the water with the flour in the mixing bowl to form a rough dough, adding more water if you need to. Cover and let it rest for about half an hour, then add the salt, yeast and fat, if using, and squidge it all together.

The sponge method
This method is particularly good for sourdough (see pp.115–125), but will benefit any bread. You start with a yeasted, unsalted batter (the 'sponge'), which is left to ferment and mature for several hours. This wet, salt-free environment allows the yeast to ferment vigorously, and the extra-long fermentation will produce bread with more flavour. I would like to use this method more often, but you need to start it off the night before, which I'm inclined to forget to do. Hopefully, you will be more organised and remember to do so.

Before bedtime, mix half of the measured quantity of flour with all of the water and all of the yeast. Beat the mixture to a thick batter, using a stiff whisk if you wish, though stiff fingers work better. The following morning, add the rest of the flour and the salt. Mix to a rough dough, adding a little more water if it is too dry, then add the fat, if you are using it.

BREAD MAKING STEP BY STEP 43

Knead the dough

First, a note on your work surface: it needs to be flat and smooth. A craggy surface will trap bits of dough; even worse, the dough will pick up whatever is already trapped there. It should also be solid; a flimsy table won't stand up to your vigorous kneading. If you have a wooden work surface, so much the better – wood is generally warmer than formica, granite or stainless steel. What is more important is that you have plenty of room – a good metre width, and maybe an arm's length in depth – for effective kneading. It also makes sense to clear the area a bit. Put the washing up away and move the toaster, as flour and dough tend to get everywhere. And wear an apron.

Tip and scrape your dough out of the bowl on to your work surface. Clean and dry your hands – rub them together with a little flour to get the worst of the dough off, then wash them. By now, your dough is probably well glued to the work surface. Good... you want it to stick. Kneading is all about stretching the gluten; if the dough sticks to the surface, it's doing most of the work of one hand. It is going to stick to your hands as well. This is ok, but the faster you work, the less it will stick. You will get better at this, I promise.

Flour your hands a little. Now, with your left hand if you're right-handed, right hand if you're left-handed, press down on the dough with your fingertips, about a third of the way up (pic 1). With the heel of your other hand, in one smooth, quick motion, press into the dough just above your first hand and push down and away, a full arm's length if you have room (pic 2). Now cup the fingers of this hand and scrape/roll the torn, ripped-up dough back on top of itself (pic 3). Turn the whole dough around roughly 90° (pic 4). Repeat. Repeat. Repeat. Have a look at the dough as you stretch it. You will see long, thin strands developing – this is gluten.

At first, dough will stick all over you. From time to time, stop and clean your hands with more flour. With time, and practice, the whole thing will become one smooth operation. In fact, the 90° rotation will merge seamlessly into the next stretch. With each stretch, the dough will become a little less sticky. After a good 5 minutes, it probably won't be sticking much to anything. The dough will have tightened considerably; it will no longer be breaking into pieces and you will find it more resistant to your stretching. Adapt your kneading action as the dough changes. Start to use shorter and shorter strokes, until you are only stretching it to around double its length. From time to time, spend half a minute or so shaping your dough into a nice tight round, following the method on p.48. Get used to shaping dough into a round; it keeps you in control. If ever your dough is sticky, or slack, or unruly, and getting the better of you, shape it into a round, and you will tame it instantly.

You can knead bread in a machine, of course. Domestic food mixers often have a dough hook attachment, and can just about take a kilo batch of dough. Be warned, though, they get pretty hot with the effort, and mine has a tendency to 'walk'

BREAD MAKING STEP BY STEP   45

1

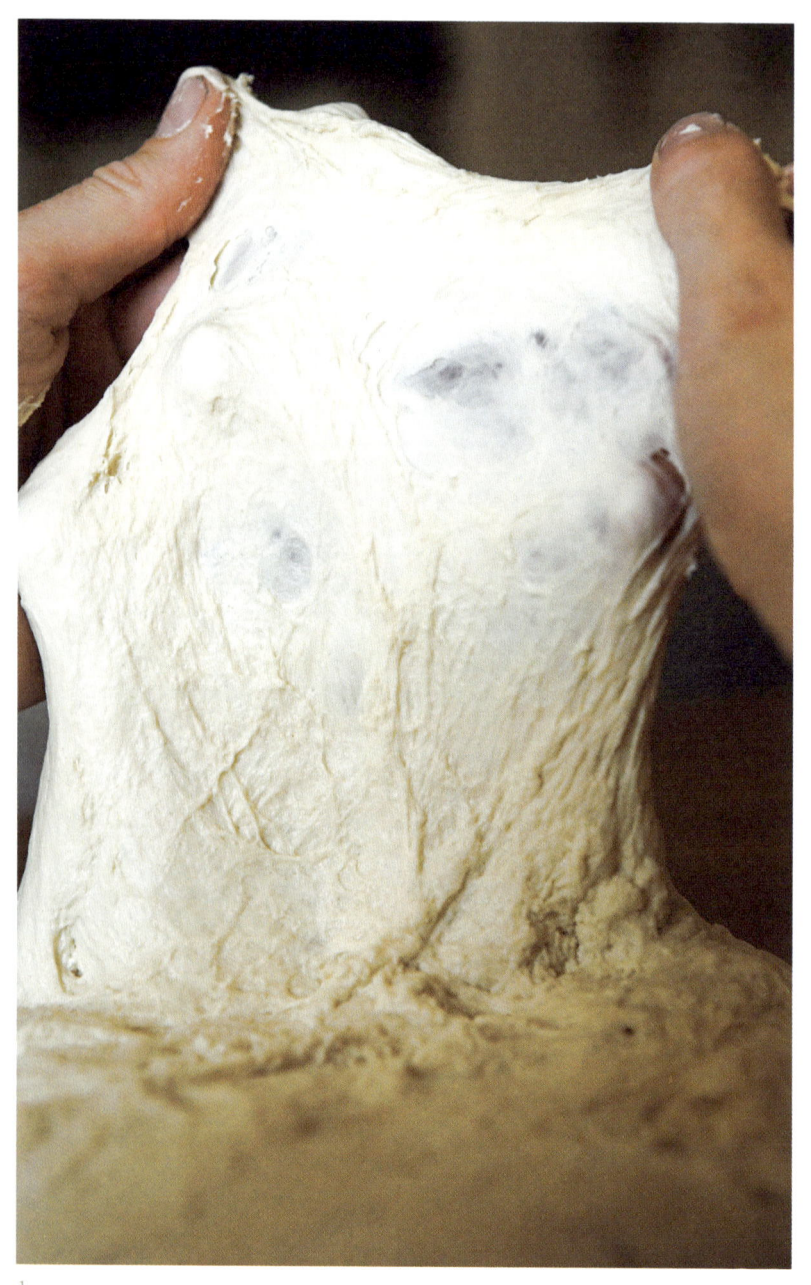

alarmingly across (and once, when I wasn't looking, off) the worktop. I now only use my mixer for softer, wetter, less strenuous doughs, and it is happier for it.

Kneading can take anywhere between 5 and 15 minutes, depending on the flour, your chosen mixing method, your kneading speed, and the size of the dough. Every now and then, try and form a membrane by stretching the dough thinly. Do this every couple of minutes. Each time, you should be able to stretch it thinner than the last. How thinly you can eventually stretch it will depend on the flour you are using. A white dough can usually be stretched quite thinly (pic 1), more so than a wholemeal dough (pic 2). Dough made from a low-gluten flour, such as rye, will snap readily (pic 3), despite your best efforts. When you feel your dough cannot be stretched any thinner, it is ready. As a guide, a dough made from strong wheat flour should stretch thinly enough to let daylight through, at least. Get it as thin as a pair of tights, and either your dough is amazing or your tights are too thick.

A small word of caution: it is possible for dough to be over-kneaded. At some point, the gluten structure will collapse, and the dough will revert to being soft and sticky, a calamitous position from which it will not recover. This is rare when kneading by hand. It is a peril more associated with kneading by machine, in which case vigilance and a slow mixing speed are your best safeguards.

If you are using larger extras, like nuts and fruit, you will need to incorporate them at the end of kneading. Stretch the dough out on the work surface, scatter over the ingredients, then fold, roll and knead briefly, to disperse them.

1   2

Shape the dough into a round

When you are satisfied with your dough, you should shape it into a round. It will then rise evenly, and you can more easily gauge its progress. This also encourages the yeast to work for you during rising. As it ferments, the gas bubbles gently stretch the strands of gluten and this stretching is most effective if the strands are taut to begin with, which they will be, if you do this.

Lay your dough, smoothest side facing down, on the work surface and prod a little with all your fingers to flatten it (pic 1). Now, with one or two fingers and a thumb, lift an edge, fold it into the middle and press down (pic 2). Make about an eighth turn of the dough, pick up the edge at the side of the fold you just made and press into the middle. Repeat, until you get back to where you started (pic 3). Now flip it over (pic 4). You should have a nice, smooth, round dough. Put your hands flat on the work surface, palms up, either side of the dough, one forward, one back (pic 5). Now, in a fluid motion, bring your hands together under the dough, at the same time sliding the forward hand back and the back hand forward (pic 6). This both spins the dough and stretches the upper surface down and under. Repeat this 'spinning' action two or three times. With practice, you can start to cup your hands around the dough; the point of the flat hands is to discipline yourself to use the inside edges of your palms and little fingers to do the stretching work.

BREAD MAKING STEP BY STEP   49

Leave to ferment

First you need to find a container in which your dough can comfortably double in size without billowing over the top. This may well be the mixing bowl you started off with, but give it a quick wipe first and dry with a tea towel.

Now, you can either flour the dough all over, or oil it. If you added oil to the dough, it makes sense to use the same type of oil, but any oil will be fine. Oiling is slightly better than flouring, as it makes an airtight coating, which prevents the dough from drying out. It also enables you to oil the container, which makes it easier to turn the dough out later. (Don't oil the container if you have floured the dough, though; you will just make oily flour lumps.)

Either way, put the dough into the container and cover it. I find the simplest way is to put the container in a bin liner and tuck the opening underneath. This makes a lovely environment for your dough – a little humidity from the fermentation process, and a little extra warmth from the bag (black absorbs and radiates heat). Covering the bowl with cling film would be nearly as good, though a little more wasteful, as you can't reuse it.

Now you need to leave your dough to rise in a warmish place. A pleasantly heated kitchen is ideal, but a slightly cold room is still fine – the dough will just take longer to rise. An airing cupboard, with the boiler going, is likely to be too warm. On top of the Aga is too warm. For a really slow overnight rise, you could put the covered dough in the fridge, but you will rarely want to (unless you are making brioche, see p.95).

During this period of rising, we want the gluten to be stretched by the activity of the yeast to the limit of its elasticity, at which point the dough will have roughly doubled in size. Beyond this, the dough noticeably loses its structure and elasticity; it will start to look flaccid and a bit holey. This is not a disaster, but the dough will be a little weaker for it.

Deflate the dough

Once the dough has risen sufficiently, uncover and tip it out on to your lightly floured work surface (pic 1). Gently press into the dough with your fingertips and squash it all over (pic 2), until it is roughly the size you started with. A common term for this is 'knocking back', which suggests punching and battering – a level of domestic violence not conducive to a happy relationship with your bread. You have spent a long time loving it… Don't ruin it all now.

1

2

BREAD MAKING STEP BY STEP   51

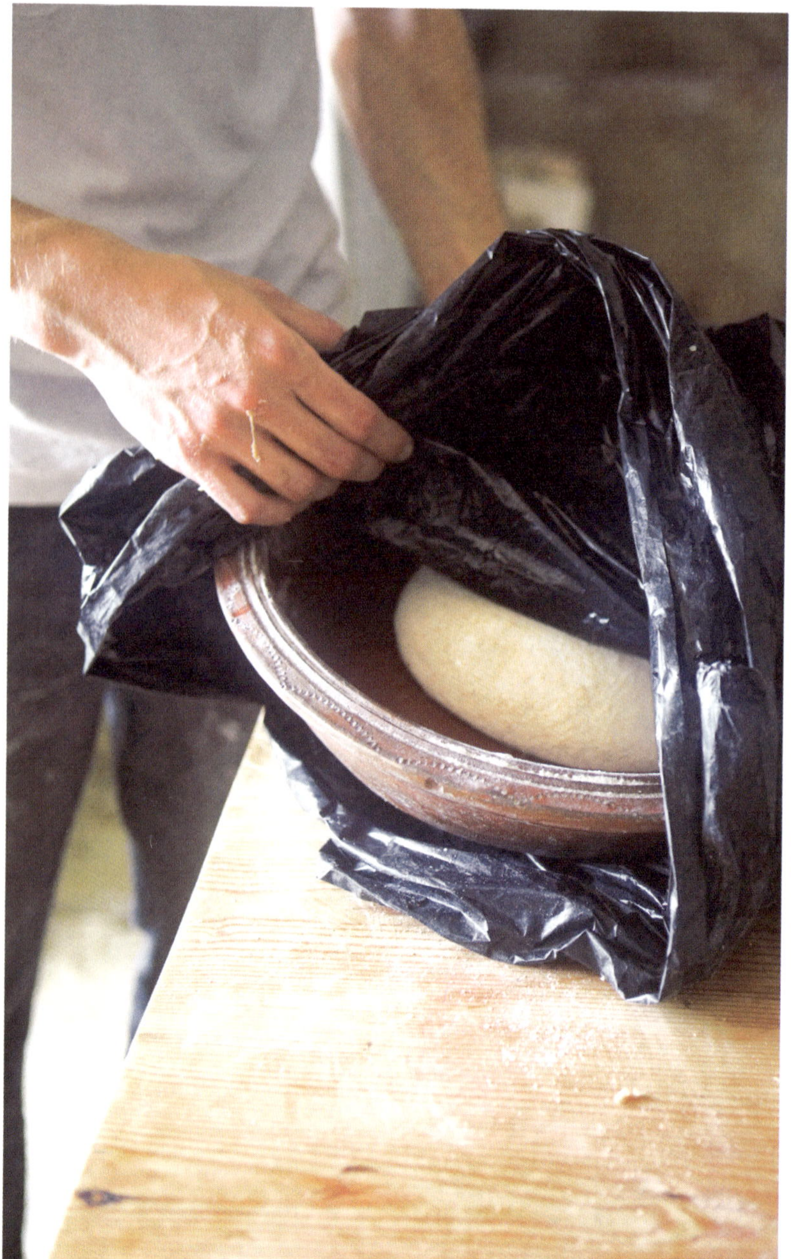

Leave to rise again (optional)

You can now leave your dough to rise a second time, following the same spinning and shaping process as before, in order to further mature and improve it. You can even repeat the rising and deflating process three, four, maybe five times. Each time you'll notice the dough becoming more satiny and pillowy. You cannot do this indefinitely, though. Eventually there will be no sugars left for the yeast to feed on, and you need it to have enough oomph for the final prove (see p.63) before baking.

Prepare for baking

Before you shape your loaves, which you are about to do, it is worth getting ready to bake them. Timing becomes fairly critical later and you don't want to get caught out, with a cold oven, for example. So, turn the oven on now – to maximum.

With the odd exception, for the first 5–10 minutes of baking you want two things in your oven (besides the bread). The first is as much heat as you can get. With enough heat, your bread will rise dramatically in the oven. Known as 'oven spring', this rising is caused by the heat-induced expansion of the gas bubbles in the dough; this expansion will continue until the crust hardens enough to suppress it. I think 260°C is the upper limit, but most domestic ovens don't get that high, so my advice is simply to turn up the dial as far as it will go.

If you have a baking stone (see p.17), it should be in the oven from the start, on the middle shelf or thereabouts (remember your bread needs plenty of headroom). If not, find your largest, heaviest baking tray and use it in the same way. You will be baking your bread directly on this, somewhat replicating the old, traditional brick-floored bakers' ovens. (You can replicate these even better by building one of your own, see Building a clay oven, pp.192–209.) If using a baking tray, you can remove it from the oven to load the bread, but this is not practical with a heavy stone. You will need to leave it in the oven and use a 'peel' (see p.17) to slip the bread on to it.

The second thing you want is steam. If the air in your oven is humid, the crust will take longer to dry so it stays soft for longer, and the bread can rise higher and more evenly. To mimic a professional baker's steam-injected oven, I heat a heavy roasting tin in the bottom of the oven, then pour in boiling water from the kettle as I put the bread in. This gives a nice whack of steam straight away, as well as some slow-release steam for a few minutes afterwards. I also use a spray bottle, the kind you get in a garden centre, to wet the bread just before it goes in. This goes some way towards making up for the lack of sophisticated technology in a domestic oven.

With your oven set up, you should clear space around it. You'll need to work fast so move anything you might crash into. You will also need a sharp serrated knife, for slashing the loaves, if you so wish, and an oven glove if you are using a baking tray. Have these within grabbing distance of the oven, along with your spray bottle if you have one. Put some water in the kettle, ready to boil. With everything in place, and your oven gently warming your kitchen, you are ready to shape your bread.

Divide the dough

First, divide your dough as precisely as you can. Make your loaves or rolls the same size and shape, and they'll cook in the same time. If you started with a kilo batch of flour, the weight of dough will be a little over 1.6kg (1kg flour and 600g water, plus a little salt, yeast, etc). Halve this and you'll make two 800g loaves. I never make loaves much larger than this. My preference is for loaves of 500–600g, so I usually divide my batch into three. If you want rolls, weigh them at 120g and you'll get a baker's dozen. Keep some dough back for your next baking session, if you wish.

Thus divided, your loaves-to-be must be shaped into rounds (see p.48), lightly floured and left to rest, on the worktop, covered with plastic. This intermediate shaping stage is key to getting an even, uniform finish to your loaf. About 10–15 minutes' rest is ideal, just to relax the gluten, in preparation for the final shaping.

Shape the loaves

You can make any shape of loaf you like, but I tend to stick to just four shapes: a round, a tapered baton, a baguette-type stick and a sort of stubby cylinder, which is my favourite. I rarely bake bread in a loaf tin, because I much prefer the appearance of a naturally formed loaf; also I don't much like the texture of the pale lower crust of a tin loaf. But for those of you who would like to use a loaf tin, I will show you how to shape the dough for it.

However you want to shape your bread, I will make the assumption that your dough is already formed into loose rounds and lightly floured.

A baguette-type stick

I usually make four of these long, thin loaves from a kilo batch, so they weigh about 400g each. With the dough smooth side down on your work surface, prod it flat, then roll it up towards you fairly tightly. Now working with both hands flat, roll and stretch the dough like a Plasticine snake, as thin and long as you like, remembering, of course, that it still has to fit in your oven. You can leave the ends rounded, but I like to taper them into a tight point, in which case do as for a tapered baton (see p.56), but press a little harder.

A tapered baton

With your dough smooth side down, prod all over with your fingertips to flatten it (pic 1). Fold the top edge down to the middle (pic 2) and press along the seam. Fold the two top corners in towards the middle, at a 45° angle (pic 3) and press down along the edges. Roll it up tightly, starting from the top (pic 4), and press all along the seam to seal (pic 5). Now, with your hands cupped over the dough, roll it back and forth, using increasing pressure on the outsides of your hands to taper the ends (pic 6).

A stubby cylinder

There is rather more to shaping this loaf than may be apparent from its appearance. Of the various loaves described, this shaping is the most complicated procedure and it takes a little more practice to perfect. The result is a really tightly moulded loaf that holds its shape brilliantly and rises dramatically in the oven. It is the loaf I bake more often than not, partly because it delivers just the right proportion of lovely, crisp crust and soft, chewy interior.

To shape a stubby cylinder, lay the dough smooth side down and prod it flat with your fingertips. Roll it up tightly towards you, using the fleshy part of your thumbs to really tuck it in (pic 1). With the seam upwards, press all along the seam with your fingertips (pic 2). Now flatten and stretch the dough sideways to about twice its width (pic 3). Fold one end in by a third and fold the other over it (pic 4). Flatten with your fingertips to a rough square (pic 5), then roll up tightly (pic 6). Seal the seam by pressing with your fingertips, then roll gently to get an even shape (pic 7).

1

2

3

4

5

6

7

A tin loaf

With your dough smooth side down, prod it fairly flat with your fingertips until it is as wide as your tin is long. Now roll up the dough towards you as tightly as you can, then press along the seam with your fingers and lay seam side down. Smooth and stretch the ends down and tuck them underneath. Lift up the dough and drop it into the loaf tin.

Rolls

Weigh or slice off pieces of dough between 100g and 150g, according to how large you want your rolls to be, but do try to keep them roughly the same size. Choose any shape you like – I favour a round or a tapered baton. To shape rounds, simply follow the technique for shaping a batch of dough (see pp.48–9); for tapered batons, shape as for a large loaf (see p.56).

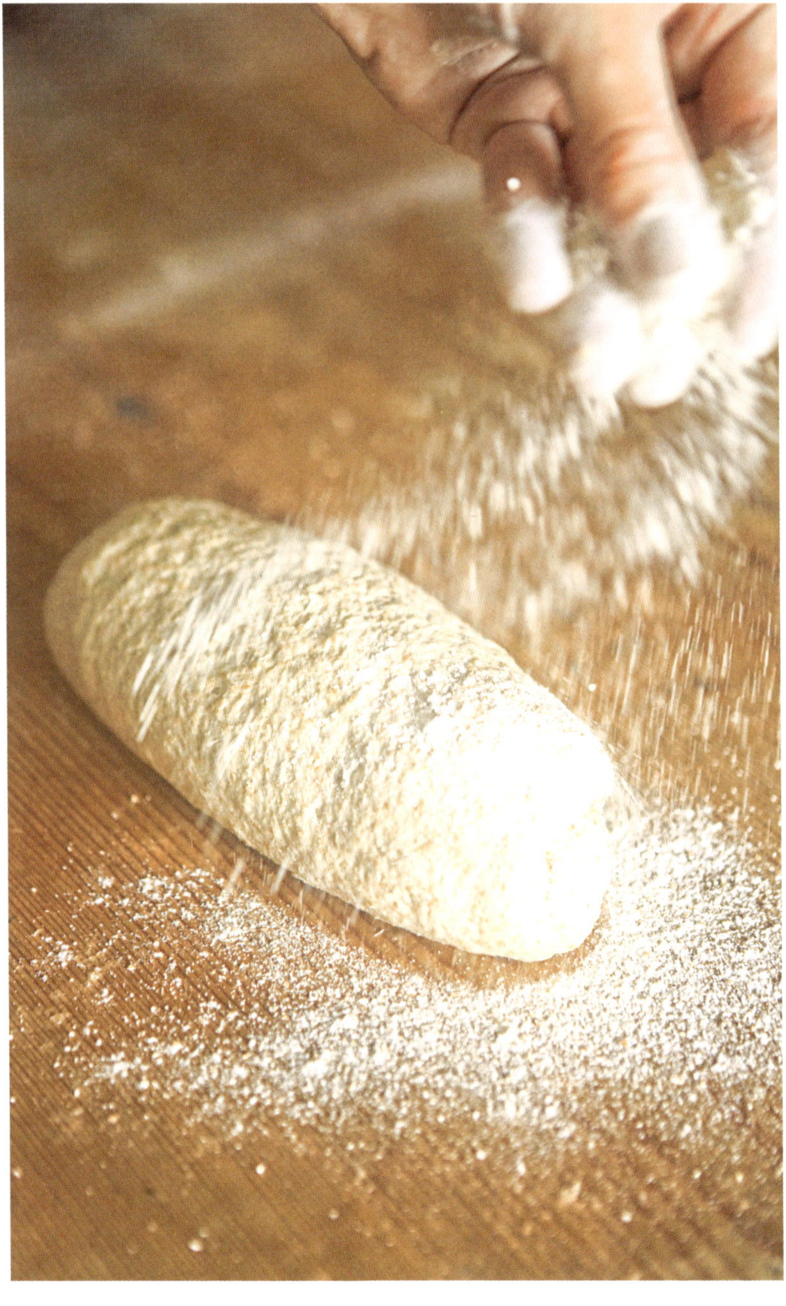

Coat the outside

You can leave your loaves naked, but they will be much more grateful – and feel much more beautiful – if you give them a lovely coat to wear. Select a flour, or choose grains and seeds.

Flour

You can use the same flour that you made your bread with, but I usually use rye flour. It gives a pleasing greyish, matt surface to the finished loaf that contrasts beautifully with the golden brown of the opened-out slashes. Coarse-milled flours – wholegrain rather than white – give a better finish, in my view. Drop a fistful of flour on top of the shaped loaf and roll it about to coat it all over and under.

Grains and seeds

Roll your bread thoroughly in a bowl of milk or water, then in a bowl of one or more of the following: rolled oats, oatmeal, barley, rye or millet flakes, bran, cracked wheat, linseed or other mild-tasting seeds, such as poppy, sesame, pumpkin or sunflower seeds. You could also include a small amount of stronger-flavoured seeds like cumin, caraway, coriander and fennel in your mix. Coat the loaves generously – they should be totally covered. Pat all over to help everything stick.

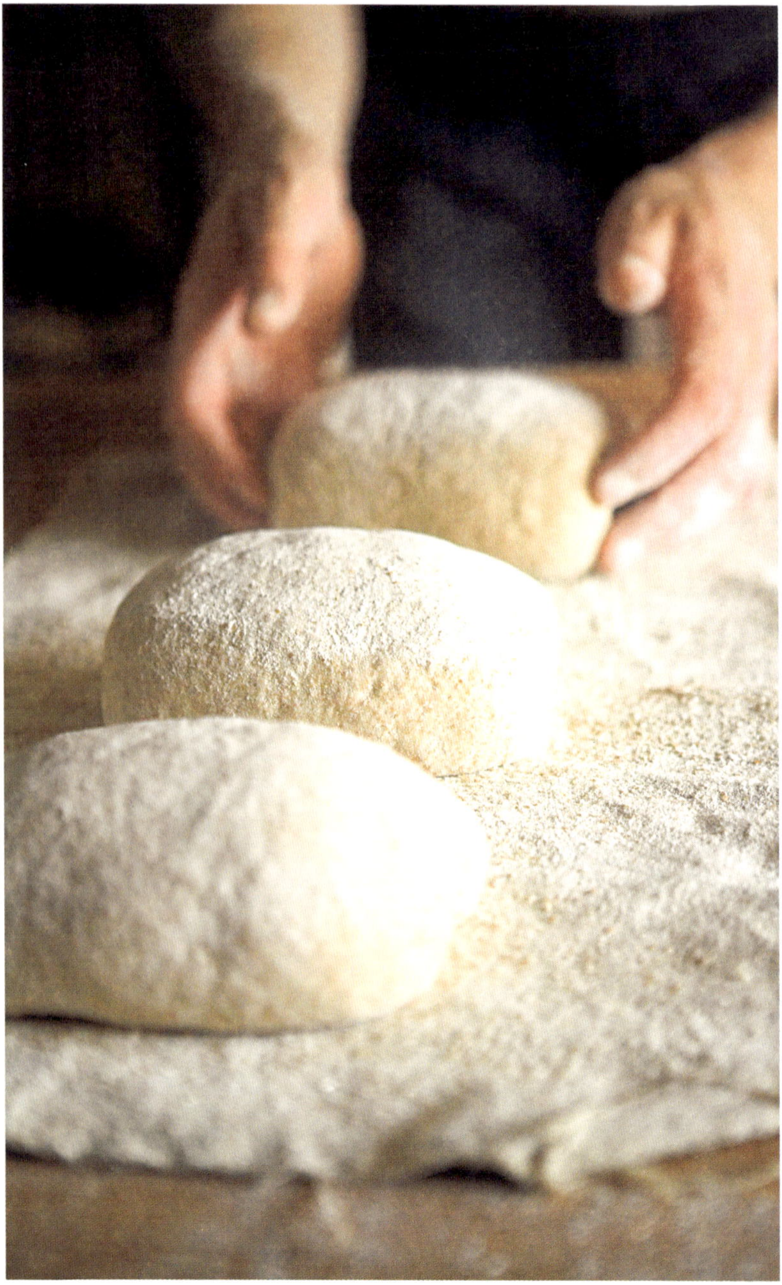

Leave to prove

Proving is the final rising of your shaped loaf before baking (the fact that your dough rises a final time 'proves' that it is still active). If you are not baking in a loaf tin, you will need to sit it in a basket, or on a cloth or board (see p.16). Whichever you use, dust it generously with flour – I usually use rye, for reasons given earlier, but any will do. Loaves in proving baskets should always be smooth side down. With linen cloths or wooden boards, I suggest proving loaves the right way up, as they will keep their shape better this way. If you are using cloths, you can ruck them up a little to give some support to the sides of the loaves. This is particularly effective with baguettes. Always cover your dough with plastic bags.

Giving precise times for proving is not helpful but, again, you want the dough to roughly double in size; this could take as little as 20 minutes, or as long as 2 hours, depending on the vigour with which the dough is fermenting.

Keep an eye on the dough as it proves. When it's looking significantly bigger, give it a gentle squeeze at the sides. Do this every so often and you will feel it getting lighter and airier. If, after such a gentle squeeze, the dough springs airily back to its original shape, and if it has almost (but not quite) doubled in size, it is about right. It is hard to describe the perfect moment in words. The best I can say is that a really well-shaped, tightly moulded, perfectly risen loaf has a certain look and feel about it, as if it is just bursting to be baked.

If the bread is over-proved, the gluten will lose its structure, the dough will start to look a little saggy, and the finished crumb will end up coarse, and too 'holey'. Under-proved bread will be a little dense and heavy – and also prone to the dreaded 'flying crust' syndrome, whereby the top crust deceitfully balloons away from the rest of the dough in the oven.

You should err on the side of under- rather than over-proving, though; it will rise some more in the oven.

Transfer the loaves for baking

If you are using a baking tray, get it out of the oven, shut the door quickly and set the hot tray close to your bread. If you are using a baking stone, lay the peel on the work surface.

If you've proved your bread in baskets, use one hand to gently support the bread as you tip it out on to the tray or peel; it will now be the right way up. If you have used cloths or boards, the loaves are already the right way up. To pick one up, roll it towards you so you can get your hands on the underside, then roll it back on to your hands, and lift it.

If you are using a baking tray, leave as much space as you can between the loaves. If you are using a peel, then you will need to work one loaf (or a few rolls) at a time. Flour the peel if your bread is in any way sticky, then lay one loaf (or a few rolls) along the leading edge.

Slash the tops

Making cuts in a loaf helps it to expand in the oven. Proved bread already has a slightly dry crust from contact with the air, which inhibits rising, and slashing through this crust exposes the soft, stretchy dough inside. I nearly always slash my bread, but there are a couple of exceptions. I usually leave round rolls just as they are – they stay rounder that way. And low-gluten breads, such as rye, rise very little in the oven, so the slashes are, in effect, redundant – they would open only a little, which looks ugly. Low-gluten breads have a beauty all their own. During proving, because of the low surface tension, the dough crackles all over as it expands, like a shattered windscreen.

Many bakers use an old-fashioned razor blade for slashing. I prefer a sharp, long-bladed, serrated knife – a bread knife, in fact. Don't just pile in. Imagine a line on the dough then cut along it, using your spare hand just to hold the loaf in place. Use long strokes and be controlled, but confident. It is crucial that you don't press down when you cut – you will squash the dough, and press out precious gas. Work swiftly, but don't rush – you will end up snagging and stretching the dough. Slash up to 1cm (half an inch) deep, using two or three strokes on each cut if you need to. Make your slashes evenly deep, and evenly spaced.

Your slashes should be simple. Beautiful though they can be, they are not made purely for decoration – they have a job to do, which is to help the bread expand. And they will do their job that much better if you let the gluten help, too. Let me explain how.

When you shaped the loaves tightly, you put tension on the gluten; now you can use this tension to pull the slashes open. Round loaves have equal tension all around, pulling outwards and downwards, so a cut in any direction will open well. All the longer-shaped loaves (see pp.55–8) have lateral tension. They have been rolled up, like a carpet, or a coiled spring. The more you cut across (perpendicular to) this tense gluten, the more the cuts will open. So a lengthways cut opens most, crossways cuts open least. Experiment with the different options and decide which you like the look of best. Scoring the loaf on the diagonal is a good compromise.

Slashing is a very good test of the quality of your dough. If it is well kneaded and perfectly risen, the cuts will open out, even as you make them.

BREAD MAKING STEP BY STEP 65

Bake the bread

Once you've slashed your loaf (or not), spray it all over with water, if you want to (see p.53). Now either put the baking tray in the oven or slip the dough from the peel on to the baking stone. To do this, lay the front edge of the peel in position, resting on the stone, then pull it away, like a tablecloth party trick.

As soon as all the loaves are in, pour a good slosh of boiling water from the kettle into the roasting tray (keep your face back), and shut the door. Do all this as fast as you possibly can, to keep the precious heat in.

Now, for a few minutes at least, you must leave the door shut, to keep the heat in; this is the time for 'oven spring', the final rise before the crust hardens. After 10 minutes, have a look. Shuffle the bread about if it is colouring unevenly and lower the temperature to:

200°C/Gas Mark 6	if the crust is still very pale
180°C/Gas Mark 4	if the crust is noticeably browning
170°C/Gas Mark 3	if the crust seems to be browning quickly

These temperatures apply to fan-assisted ovens. If you are using a conventional non-fan-assisted gas or electric oven, you will need to have your oven approximately 15°C/1 Gas Mark hotter. Continue baking, adjusting the temperature as you see fit. The total baking time will depend on your particular oven and the size of your loaves. If during baking the crust appears to be fully browned, cover it loosely with foil to prevent over-browning.

Use the following timings as a guide, but rely on your own judgement. These represent total baking time in the oven:

12 rolls	10–20 minutes
3 small loaves	30–40 minutes
2 large loaves	40–50 minutes

When your bread is fully baked, it will feel lighter than when it went in. This is because it will have lost about 20 per cent of its weight through evaporation. The crust should feel firm (though less so on rolls), and it should sound hollow when tapped on the base. This is no definitive test, though – a loaf will also sound hollow when it could really do with another 10 minutes' baking. So, if in doubt, bake for a bit longer. If your bread is a little over-baked, all it will have is a slightly over-thick crust... and there is nothing wrong with that.

BREAD MAKING STEP BY STEP 67

Leave to cool

If you have a cooling rack, put your bread on it. If not, a propped-up oven shelf would do fine. Now leave it alone to cool. Your bread is full of steam, and is in fact still cooking. You must let it finish, in its own time. If you cut hot bread, it will be steamy, heavy and doughy. Hot rolls are about the only exception to the leave-it-alone rule, but only if you pull them apart. Don't squash or cut them.

Look after your bread

Having lovingly produced your handmade bread, it makes sense to treat it properly, whether you are serving it straight away or storing it.

Slicing

Telling you the best way to slice bread may seem totally unnecessary, but I've seen too many people squashing, ripping and hacking at once-beautiful loaves. You should use a sharp serrated knife and avoid pressing down as you cut. Use a rhythmic sawing action and the weight of the blade will be enough. Brace the sides of the loaf with your other hand, close to where you are cutting, so it holds its shape.

Storing

The advice is anywhere but the fridge. According to Harold McGee, the food science guru, bread stored in the refrigerator stales as much in one day as bread held at 30°C does in 6 days. So, store your bread at room temperature, wrapped in paper, or in a bread bin, or both. Plastic and foil keep too much moisture in and make the crust soft. Uncovered loaves let too much moisture out. Bread freezes successfully, but it must be well wrapped – in plastic, this time. After defrosting, your bread will probably benefit from refreshing.

Refreshing

Day-old bread can be returned (almost) to its former glory with a short stint in the oven. Staling is the re-hardening of starch granules that had been softened in the oven. By reheating the bread – to 60°C or above – the starch softens again. You can do this again and again, but each time the crust will dry out a little more and become thicker and harder. You will not be able to refresh bread after more than a couple of days' staling, though. It will have lost too much moisture. But all is not lost – you just need some ideas for Using leftover bread (see pp.174–191).

To refresh bread, I suggest a moderate oven, preheated to about 170°C/Gas Mark 3: allow 5–10 minutes for rolls; 15–20 minutes for loaves.

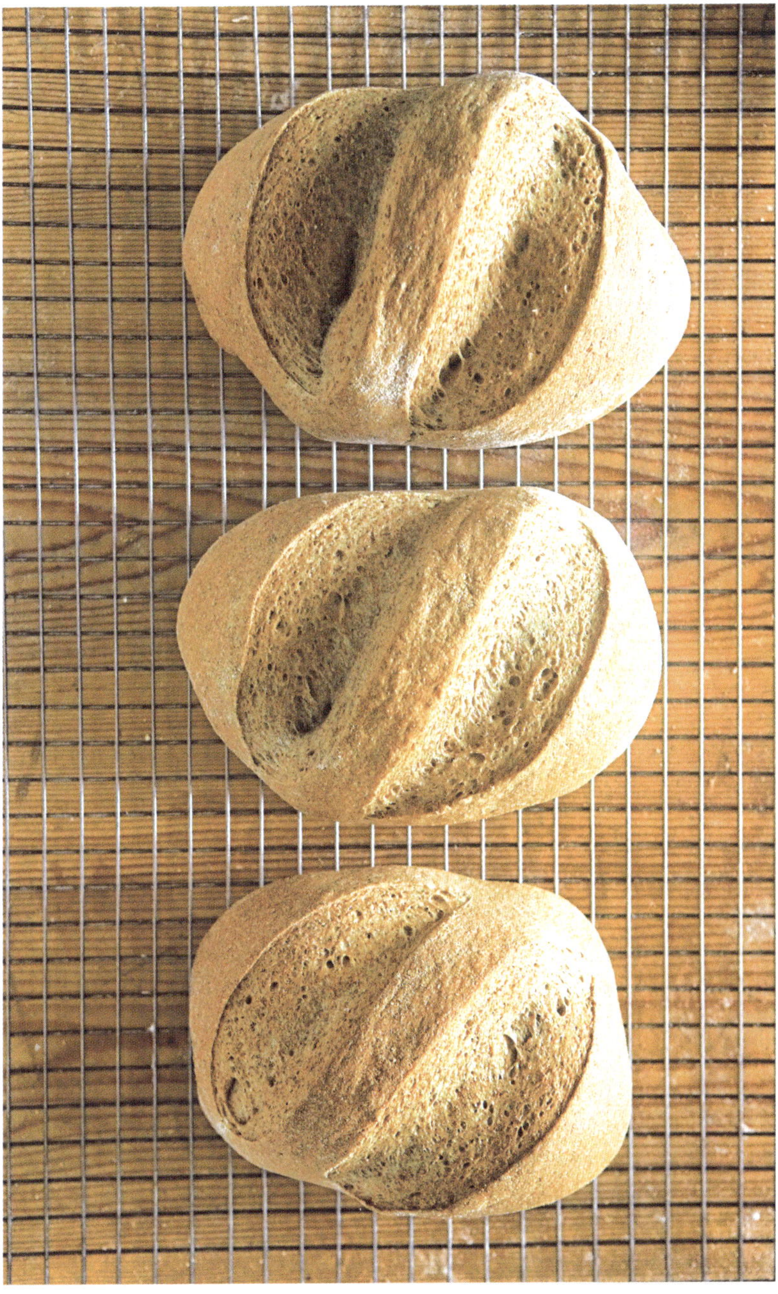

Troubleshooting

Problem	Possible reasons
Heavy bread, with a dense, 'cakey' texture	Low-gluten flour Under-kneaded
Heavy bread with a solid, rubbery texture	Under-proved
Solid, rubbery bread with large air holes at the top ('flying crust')	Under-proved
Flat, 'tired' shape	Low-gluten flour Under-kneaded Initial oven temperature too low Loaf not shaped tightly enough Dough not supported enough during proving
Well risen, but uneven shape	Over-proved Loaf not shaped tightly enough Dough not supported enough during proving
Slashes don't open out fully	Low-gluten flour Under-kneaded Initial oven temperature too low Loaf not shaped tightly enough Dough not supported during proving Slashes too deep Slashes cut too 'crossways' instead of 'lengthways' (except round loaves)
Soft crust	Under-baked Oven too cool
Hard, thick crust	Over-baked
Doughy texture	Under-baked Sliced while still hot
Coarse, dry, 'holey' texture	Over-proved

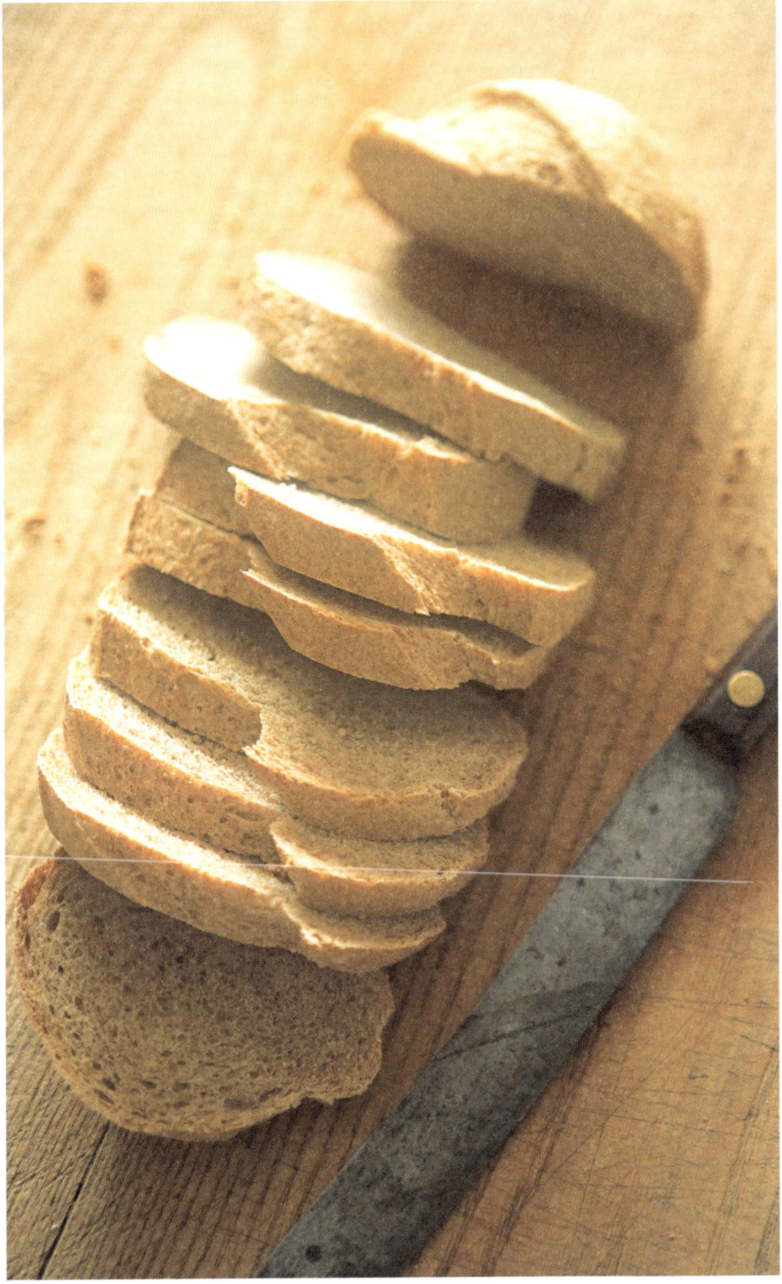

The Basic Bread Recipe

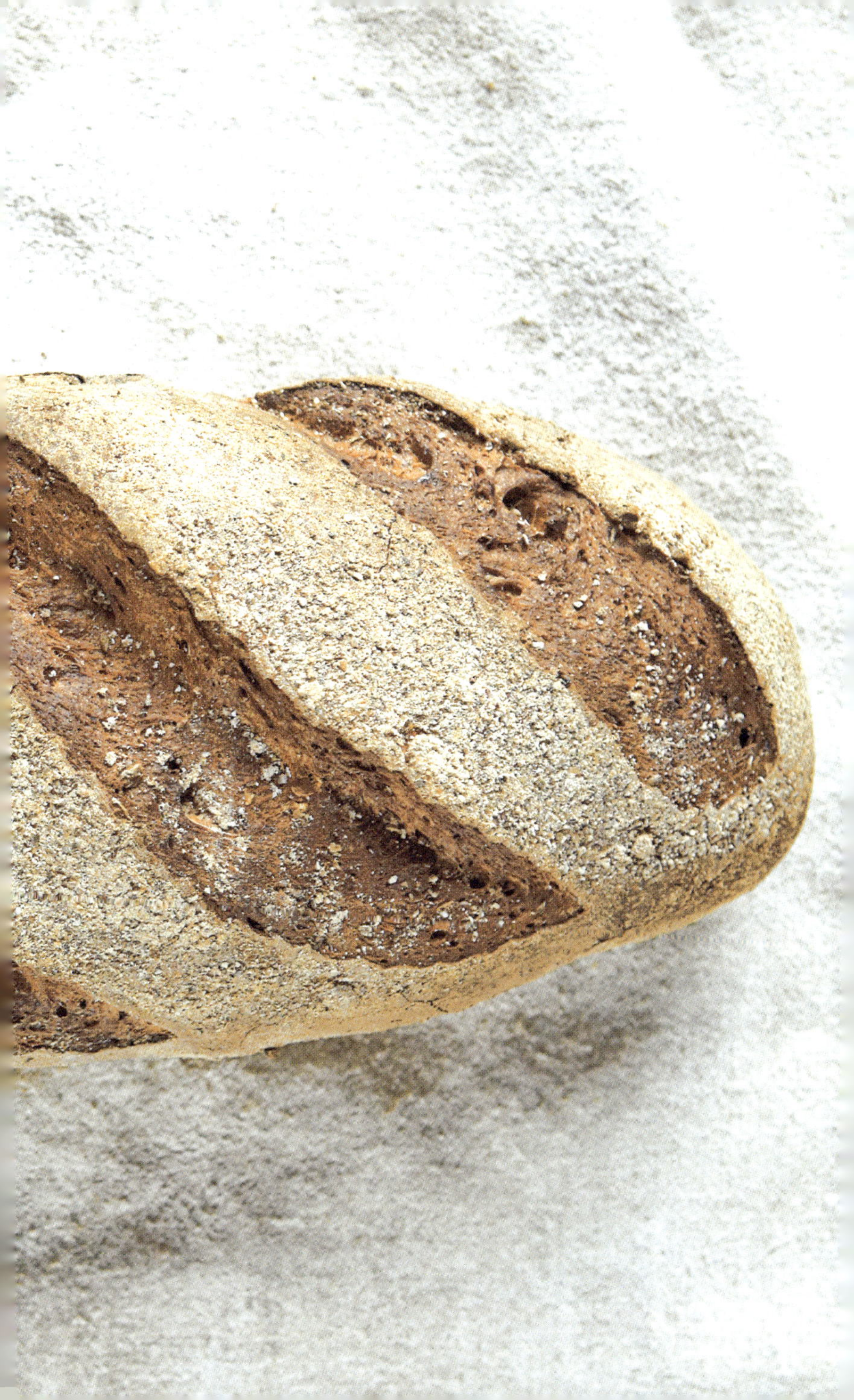

This basic bread recipe is the most important recipe in the

book. As you will gather, it is a condensed version of the previous section: Bread making step by step (pp.34–71). It is the recipe that I hope you will use the most to begin with, as it is your route to making good, everyday bread. The more you make it, the more you will get used to the feel of the dough in your hands, and the changes it goes through during the various stages of bread making. You will start to recognise how one day's baking differs from another. And hopefully, with the help of the previous section, you will start to understand why. Get good at this recipe and you will be much better at all of the others in the book.

In time, I hope it will become the recipe you will use the least. I expect that you will soon memorise the 'baker's percentage' – the ratio of one ingredient to another – so that you no longer need to look it up. I hope the method will become so familiar that you can fit it into your daily life without even thinking about it. And I'd like to think that, before long, you will never need to look at these pages again.

Once you are comfortable with the basic principles of flour-water-yeast-salt, and the effects of different liquids, and once you understand the boundless fun you can have with the addition of a few grains, seeds and spices, I hope you will discover your own favourites. By all means go wild with your experiments (after all, you don't know until you try), but please remember one thing: bread is beautiful all by itself. As Robert Browning wrote:

'If thou tastest a crust of bread, thou tastest all the stars and all the heavens.'

So there you go... now you know what stars taste like.

Ingredients for bread making

My basic bread recipe is infinitely adaptable. Simply choose one or more options from the ingredients listed below (or add your own), and slot them into the ingredients list (overleaf), in place of the *italics*.

Essential	Choices
Flour	Strong white, strong brown, strong wholemeal, '00', malted grain, wholemeal spelt, white spelt, rye, kamut
Yeast	Powdered dried yeast
Salt	Fine sea salt
Liquid (warm)	Water, milk, yoghurt, apple juice, cider, beer; 1 tbsp honey can be added to any of these
Optional	
Fat	Oils, such as sunflower, vegetable, corn, rapeseed, hempseed, olive, groundnut or any other nut oils; or melted hard fats, such as butter or lard
Old dough/starter	A piece of old dough (see p.40), or a ladleful of sourdough starter (see p.110)
Extras	Flakes, meal or flour of oats, barley, rye, millet, buckwheat, maize, chickpea or rice, or semolina; seeds, such as pumpkin, sunflower, linseed, poppy, sesame, fennel, caraway, cumin, coriander or alfalfa; bashed nuts, such as hazelnuts, walnuts or any other nuts; dried fruit, such as raisins, dried apricots or chopped dates
Coating	Rye or any other flour; anything on the extras list except nuts and dried fruit; plus about 200ml milk or water, if coating with anything other than flour (to help it stick)

The basic bread recipe

This is my simplified bread recipe, which can be adapted to create a host of different breads (see chart on p.75). You will find more detail on the essential stages (highlighted in bold below) in the previous chapter. To begin, you need to measure the ingredients.

Makes 2 large or 3 small loaves, or 12 rolls

Essential
**1kg *flour*
10g powdered dried yeast
20g fine salt
600ml *liquid* (warm)**

Optional
**2 handfuls of *extras*
A piece of old dough, or a ladleful
 of sourdough starter
About 1 tbsp (a good slug) of *fat*
2 handfuls of *coating*
About 200ml milk or water (if coating
 with anything other than flour)**

First, mix the dough. This is the one-stage method; you can adapt it for other methods. Combine the *flour*, yeast and salt in a large mixing bowl. Add smaller *extras* if you are using them (save nuts and dried fruit for after kneading). Add the *liquid*, and with one hand, mix to a rough dough. Add a piece of old dough or the starter if you are using one. Add the *fat* if you are including and mix it all together. Adjust the consistency if you need to, with a little more flour or water (or your chosen liquid), to make a soft, easily kneadable, sticky dough. Turn the dough out on to a work surface and clean your hands.

Knead the dough until it is as smooth and satiny as you can make it – as a rough guide, this will take about 10 minutes. If you are using larger *extras*, like nuts and fruit, stretch the dough out on the work surface, scatter over the ingredients, then fold, roll and knead briefly, to disperse them.

Shape the dough into a round once you have finished kneading. Then oil or flour the surface and put the dough into the wiped-out mixing bowl. Put the bowl in a bin liner and leave to ferment and rise until doubled in size. This could be anywhere between 45 minutes and 1½ hours – or longer still, if the dough is cold.

Deflate the dough by tipping it on to the work surface and pressing all over with your fingertips. Then form it into a round. If you like, leave to rise again up to four times. This will improve the texture and flavour.

Now, prepare for baking. Switch the oven to 250°C/Gas Mark 10 or its highest setting, put your baking stone or baking tray in position and remove any unwanted shelves. Put the roasting tin in the bottom if you are using it for steam (in which case, put the kettle on). Get your water spray bottle ready if you have one, your serrated knife if using, an oven cloth, and your 'peel' if you are using a baking stone. Clear the area around the oven.

Divide the dough into as many pieces as you wish (I suggest two large or three small loaves, or a dozen rolls). Shape these into rounds and leave them to rest, covered, for 10–15 minutes.

Shape the loaves as you wish, and coat the outside with your chosen *coating*. Transfer the loaves to well-floured wooden boards, linen cloths, tea towels or proving baskets and lay a plastic bag over the whole batch, to stop it drying out. Leave to prove, checking often by giving gentle squeezes, until the loaves have almost doubled in size.

Transfer the loaves for baking to the hot tray (removed from the oven), or one at a time to the 'peel'. Slash the tops, if you wish, with the serrated knife, and before you bake the bread, spray it all over with water if you can. Bring the boiling kettle to the oven, if you are using it. Put the tray in the oven, or slide each loaf on to the stone, pour some boiling water into the roasting tin, if using, and close the door as quickly as you can.

Turn the heat down after about 10 minutes to: 200°C/Gas Mark 6 if the crust still looks very pale; 180°C/Gas Mark 4 if the crust is noticeably browning; 170°C/Gas Mark 3 if the crust seems to be browning quickly. Bake until the loaves are well browned and crusty, and feel hollow when you tap them: in total, 10–20 minutes for rolls; 30–40 minutes for small loaves; 40–50 minutes for large loaves. If in doubt, bake for a few minutes longer.

Leave to cool on a wire rack, or anything similar that allows air underneath. Bread for tearing can be served warm, but bread for slicing must be cooled completely.

Look after your bread and enjoy it. After all, you have put a lot of work into it... and don't waste a crumb.

P.S. Remember that timing in the recipe relates to fan-assisted ovens. If using a conventional electric or gas oven (without a fan), increase the temperature by 15°C (1 Gas Mark). Use an oven thermometer to check the accuracy of your oven.

Variations
on the basic bread recipe

There is no end to the possibilities, of course, but to get you going, here are a few combinations of my own. You might make one, or all, or none of them… though I'd like to insist that you make my favourite malted and seeded loaf (see p.80).

Malted grain bread

There is something special about malted flour. I don't know what it is, but like candlelight or a soft-focus lens, it is flattering – the Don Juan of home baking. As Elizabeth David wrote in her excellent *English Bread and Yeast Cookery*, 'Homemade granary bread is very good-tempered, exceptionally easy to mix and bake. It has so much to recommend it, especially to beginners in bread-making.' I couldn't agree more.

Makes 2 large or 3 small loaves, or 12 rolls
1kg malted grain flour
10g powdered dried yeast
20g fine salt
600ml warm water
About 1 tbsp melted butter
A piece of old dough, or a ladleful of sourdough starter (optional)
No extras
2 handfuls of rye flour, for coating

Follow the basic bread recipe method (see pp.76–7).

White bread

With full-flavoured brown and wholemeal breads, you can get away with a loaf that is firm or dense – in fact, it can be a bonus. However, if white bread isn't soft, light and crusty, it is pretty disappointing. It is far harder to make good white bread than any other kind of bread, so don't feel downhearted if it takes you a while to get it right. Adding milk, or better still yoghurt, makes a softer, richer crumb.

Makes 2 large or 3 small loaves, or 12 rolls
1kg strong white flour
10g powdered dried yeast
20g fine salt
600ml warm water (or half water, half milk or yoghurt)
About 1 tbsp sunflower oil
A piece of old dough, or a ladleful of sourdough starter (optional)
No extras
2 handfuls of strong white flour, for coating

Follow the basic bread recipe method (see pp.76–7).

Spelt bread

Due to its comparatively low gluten content, spelt bread is often considered to be rather dense and heavy. That's because it often is, but it shouldn't be. Spelt dough just needs to be treated properly. I reckon there are two secrets: a little more kneading than normal – an extra 5 minutes or so; and proving in baskets to hold the loaves up (or make small loaves if you do not have any baskets). It is very satisfying to make bread from the same grain the Romans baked with.

Makes 2 large or 3 small loaves, or 12 rolls
1kg wholemeal spelt flour
10g powdered dried yeast
20g fine salt
600ml warm water
About 1 tbsp sunflower oil
A piece of old dough, or a ladleful of sourdough starter (optional)
No extras
2 handfuls of spelt flour, for coating

Follow the basic bread recipe method (see pp.76–7).

Oaty wholemeal

This bread is coated in three grades of oatmeal for a really interesting texture and a beautiful look. I have been making it a lot recently, with a variety of wheat called 'Einstein' which I buy from a local grower. The pale oats contrast strikingly with the wonderful chestnut-coloured crust. It is a perfect example of how bread should taste.

Makes 2 large or 3 small loaves, or 12 rolls
1kg strong wholemeal flour
10g powdered dried yeast
20g fine salt
600ml warm water
About 1 tbsp sunflower oil
A piece of old dough, or a ladleful of sourdough starter (optional)
No extras
2 handfuls of mixed pinhead oatmeal, medium oatmeal and oat flakes, plus about 200ml milk, for coating

Follow the basic bread recipe method (see pp.76–7).

Malted and seeded loaf

I can't stop making this at the moment. Everyone at River Cottage is going mad for it. The recipe is inspired by a five-seeded malted grain flour made by Bacheldre Watermill (see the directory, p.212). I have added a sixth seed – poppy, because I love it. Go a little easier on the fennel, as they are the most strongly flavoured of the seeds.

Makes 2 large or 3 small loaves, or 12 rolls
1kg malted grain flour
10g powdered dried yeast
20g fine salt
600ml warm water
About 1 tbsp sunflower oil
A piece of old dough, or a ladleful of sourdough starter (optional)
2 handfuls of extras: a mix of sunflower, pumpkin, linseed, sesame, poppy and a few fennel seeds
2 extra handfuls of the above seed mix, plus about 200ml milk or water, for coating

Follow the basic bread recipe method (see pp.76–7).

Breakfast rolls

You could get up before the birds to make rolls in time for everyone else's breakfast, or you could bake them ahead and freeze them in batches. Simply grab a batch out of the freezer, give them about 15 minutes in a moderate oven, rub a bit of flour in your hair and pretend you've been up half the night. Much better... and it should get you out of the washing up.

Makes 12 rolls
1kg strong brown flour
10g powdered dried yeast
20g fine salt
600ml warm milk
About 1 tbsp melted butter
A piece of old dough, or a ladleful of sourdough starter (optional)
No extras
2 handfuls of white (or brown) flour, for coating

Follow the basic bread recipe method (see pp.76–7).

Festival bread

As a celebration of the inaugural River Cottage Festival, we thought we'd have a bit of fun. So, from a choice of five or six different flours and a couple of dozen other ingredients, around sixty guests, my co-host Steven and I came up with this unlikely recipe – through nominating, voting and a little cajoling. The alfalfa seeds got in on novelty rather than merit. Steven was the only voice in favour of poppy seeds, so we put one in… to keep him happy.

Makes 2 large or 3 small loaves, or 12 rolls
1kg wholemeal spelt flour
10g powdered dried yeast
20g fine salt
300ml warm water
300ml warm cider
1 tbsp honey
1 tbsp rapeseed oil
A piece of old dough, or a ladleful of sourdough starter (optional)
2 handfuls of extras: a mix of barley flakes, oat flakes, golden raisins, chopped dried apricots, bashed hazelnuts, alfalfa seeds and a poppy seed
2 handfuls of spelt flour, for coating

Follow the basic bread recipe method (see pp.76–7).

Monastery bread

If you prefer bread that is soft, airy and light as a feather, skip this one. If, however, you are of wholesome and earthy ilk, make it. But be warned: this one hurts. The dough is solid and uncooperative when it comes to kneading. You will notice the ample quantity of extras in the form of rolled oats; this bread is all about oats. I like it sliced thinly, with butter or cheese, or honey… and a flagon of mead. Sitting in the refectory, after vespers, might be just the place to enjoy it.

Makes 2 large or 3 small loaves, or 12 rolls
1kg strong brown flour
10g powdered dried yeast
20g fine salt
600ml warm water
1 tbsp honey
About 1 tbsp melted butter
A piece of old dough, or a ladleful of sourdough starter (optional)
6 handfuls of extras: rolled oats
2 handfuls of rye flour, for coating

Follow the basic bread recipe method (see pp.76–7).

Hazel maizel bread

This bread is sweet and delicious. The maize meal gives a pleasing, slightly cakey texture, along with an alluring undertone of sunshine. The honey, nuts and apple juice make it a natural accompaniment to cheese. As you are shaping the bread, you will find bits escape everywhere. This is the nature of nuts in bread – and this is why you should only add them after kneading.

Makes 2 large or 3 small loaves, or 12 rolls
800g strong wholemeal flour
200g maize meal
10g powdered dried yeast
20g fine salt
300ml warm water
300ml warm apple juice
1 tbsp honey
About 1 tbsp melted butter
A piece of old dough, or a ladleful of sourdough starter (optional)
2 handfuls of extras: bashed hazelnuts
2 handfuls of wholemeal flour, for coating

Follow the basic bread recipe method (see pp.76–7).

Empty-the-shelf bread

Peasants of old would often bulk out their bread with whatever they could lay their hands on: oats, millet, bone meal, even sawdust. I felt a little peasanty recently as I was clearing out my kitchen cupboards and found myself with various near-empty packets of flour, meal and seeds that needed using up. Feel free to adapt this recipe to use whatever you have around… within reason, of course. Empty-the-cereal-box bread would be interesting; empty-the-Hoover-bag bread… perhaps rather less so.

Makes 2 large or 3 small loaves, or 12 rolls
1kg strong wholemeal flour, or a mixture of bag-ends
10g powdered dried yeast
20g fine salt
600ml warm water
About 1 tbsp fat (whatever needs using up)
A piece of old dough, or a ladleful of sourdough starter (optional)
2 handfuls of extras: a mix of any or all of wheatgerm, bran, oats or oatmeal, millet flakes, barley flakes, seeds (sunflower/poppy/pumpkin/linseed/sesame)
2 extra handfuls of these extras, plus about 200ml water, for coating

Follow the basic bread recipe method (see pp.76–7).

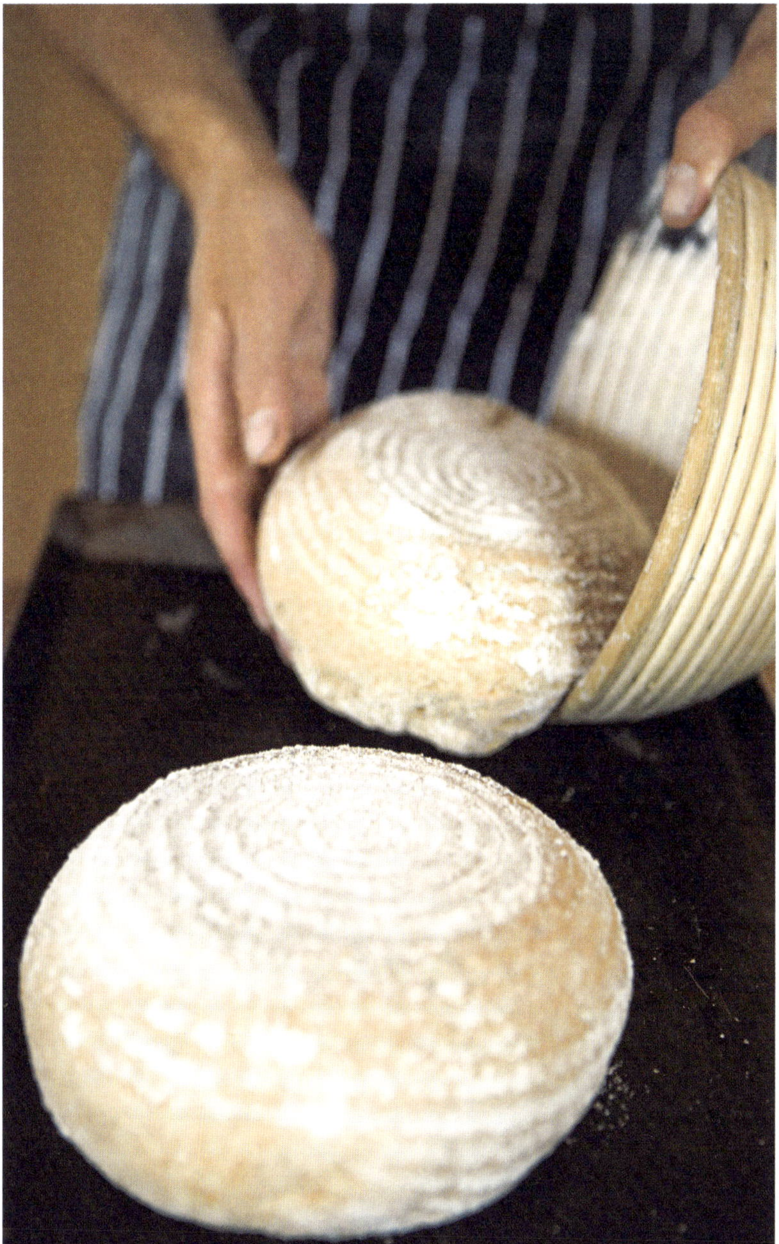

Beyond the Basic Loaf

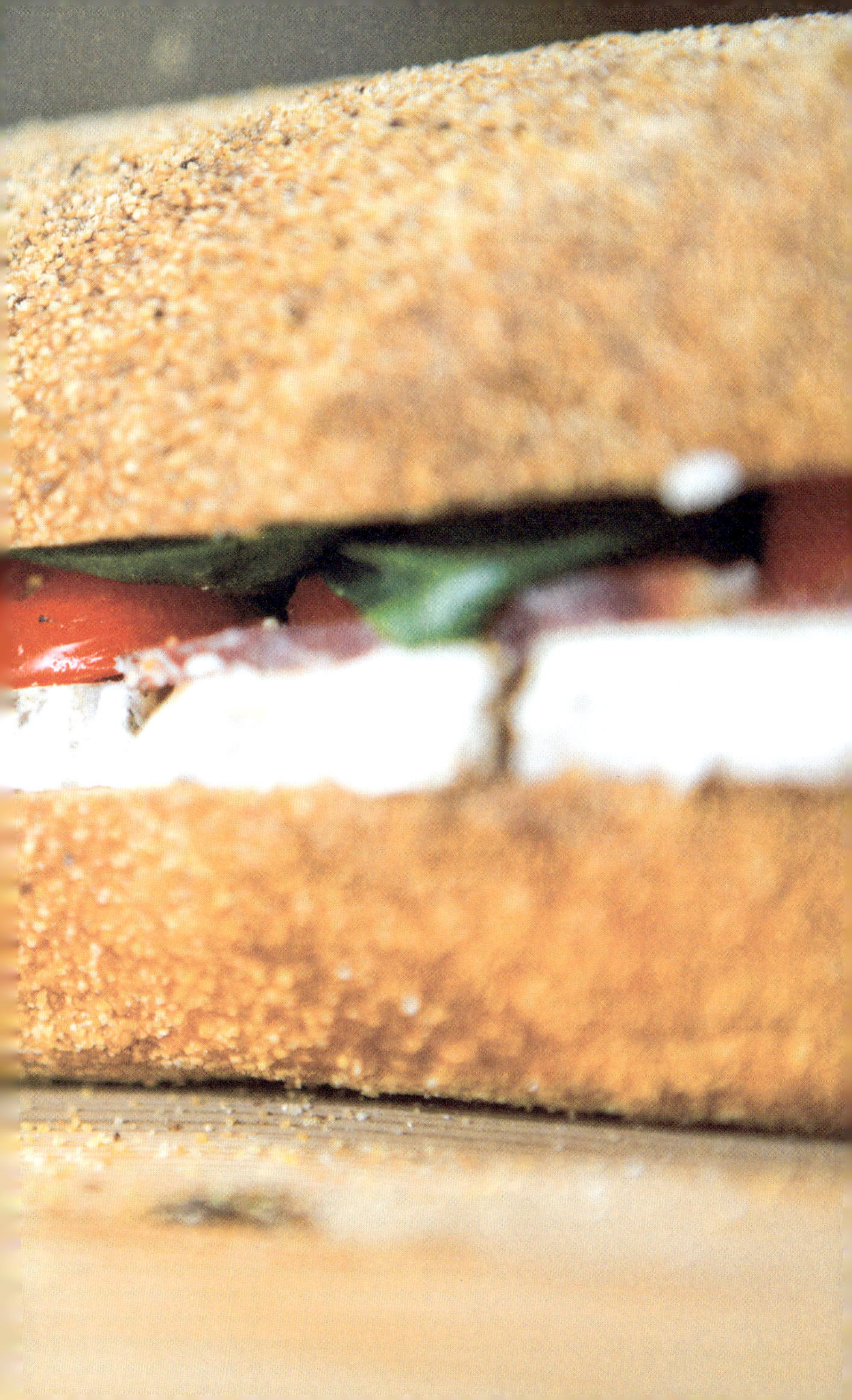

If you skipped

Bread making step by step (pp.34–71), you really need to go back and un-skip it. You will be much better at all of the breads in this section if you do. Some are more difficult than others.

Ciabatta, for example, is tricky, to say the least. I suggest you don't attempt it until you are a reasonably proficient baker, or it will make you feel disheartened. The dough you make it with is wet… impossibly wet. It has to be this way, to create the big air holes and the classic irregular, slightly saggy shape, supposedly mimicking the carpet-slipper that gives it its name.

Focaccia, on the other hand, is quite forgiving – perfect for less experienced bakers. Because it is shallow, and supported by a rimmed tray, the strength and structure of the dough is not so critical; it can be under-kneaded or over-proved, and you will still end up with bread you can be proud of.

I also want to introduce you to the delights of traditional English muffins, real bagels and proper pizza… this chapter is all about expanding your repertoire of bread doughs. Dive in and have fun. Choose from the following:

Beyond the basic loaf

- Focaccia (p.89)
- Ciabatta (p.90)
- Breadsticks (p.92)
- Brioche (p.95)
- Bagels (p.96)
- English muffins (p.99)
- Vetkoek (p.100)
- Flatbread (p.103)
- Pizza (p.104)
- Barbecue breads (p.107)

Reminder: Oven timings in the recipes relate to fan-assisted ovens. If using a conventional electric or gas oven (without a fan), increase the temperature by 15°C (1 Gas Mark). Use an oven thermometer to check the accuracy of your oven.

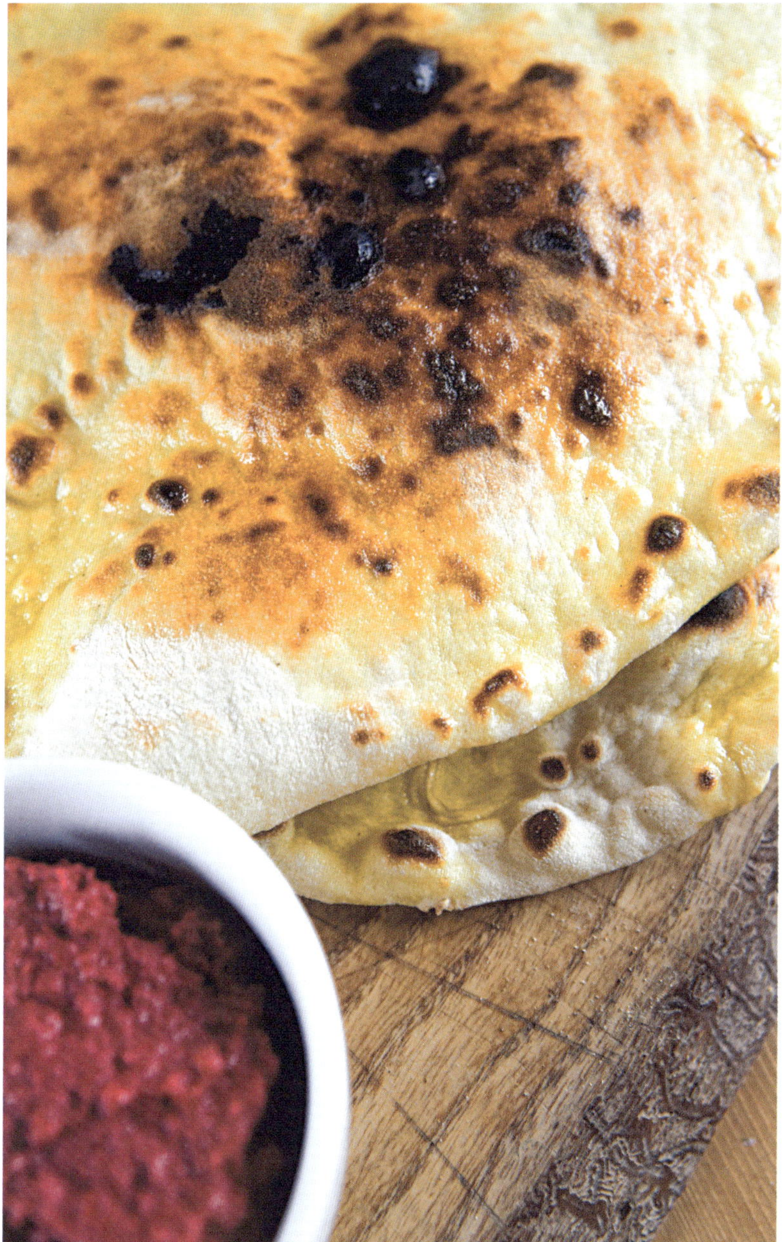

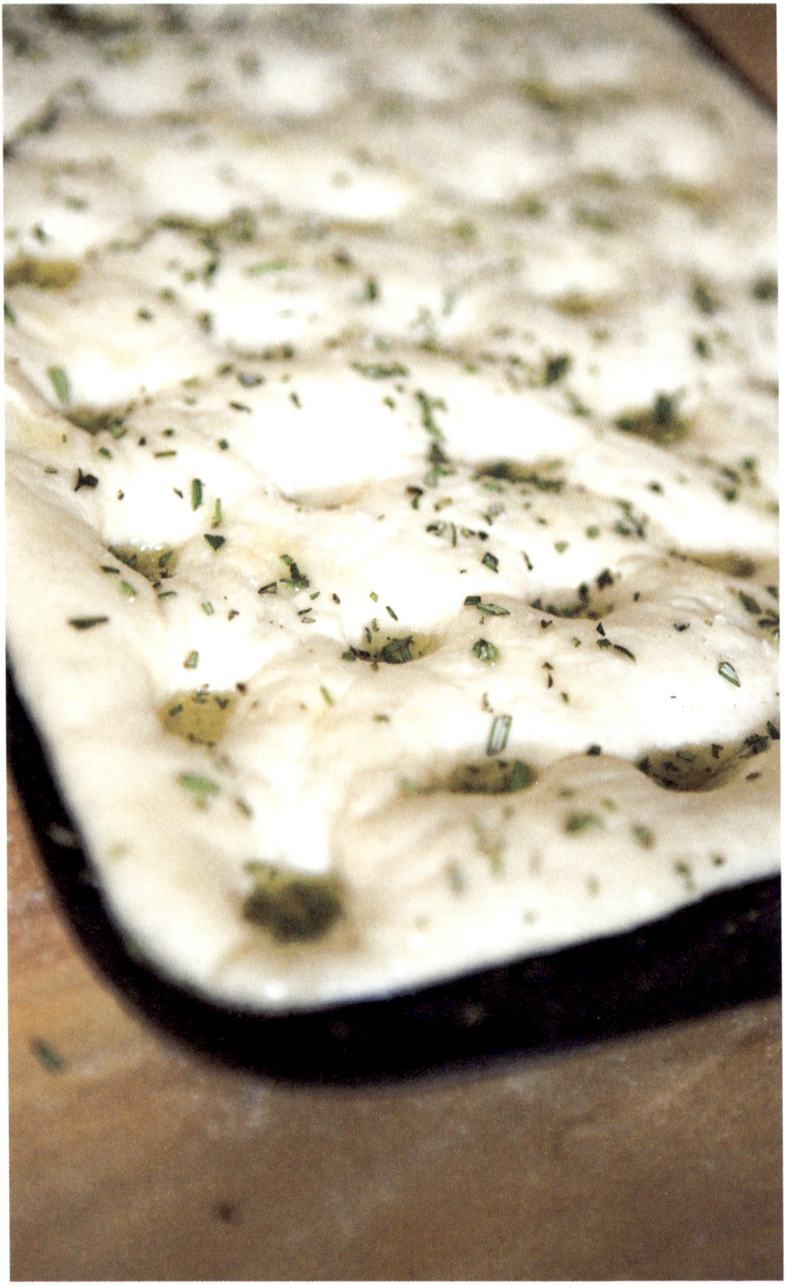

Focaccia

Focaccia is excellent sharing bread for serving with supper, and is really easy to make. You can certainly miss out the rosemary, and you don't have to sprinkle the top with salt, though it is authentic. You could expand this recipe and experiment as I have often done, mixing various herbs and other flavourings into the actual dough, though I think you'd have to ask an Italian if you can still call it focaccia. You could use a food mixer to knead this soft dough.

Makes 1 focaccia
500g strong white bread flour
5g powdered dried yeast
10g fine salt
325ml warm water
About 1 tbsp olive oil, plus extra for coating

To finish
A generous drizzle of olive oil
A sprinkle of flaky sea salt
A couple of rosemary sprigs, leaves stripped and finely chopped

To knead by hand: mix the flour, yeast, salt and water in a bowl to form a sticky dough. Add the oil, mix it in, then turn the dough out on to a clean work surface. Knead until smooth and silky, about 10 minutes.

Or, to use a food mixer: fit the dough hook and add the flour, yeast, salt and water to the mixer bowl. Mix on low speed until evenly combined, then add the oil and leave to knead for about 10 minutes, until smooth and silky.

Shape the dough into a round (see p.48) and coat with a little extra oil. Leave to rise in a clean bowl, covered with a plastic bag. When it has doubled in size, tip it on to the work surface and press into a rough rectangle. Place in a lightly oiled shallow baking tray, measuring about 26 x 36cm. Press the dough in with your fingers, right into the corners. Now leave to rise, covered, for about half an hour.

Preheat your oven to 250°C/Gas Mark 10, or as high as it will go. When the bread looks puffed up and airy, use your fingertips to poke deep holes across the whole surface, almost to the bottom. Drizzle the top generously (but not swimmingly) with olive oil and sprinkle with salt and rosemary. Bake for about 10 minutes, then turn the oven down to about 200°C/Gas Mark 6 and bake for a further 10 minutes.

Focaccia is best eaten warm, but not hot; leave to cool on a wire rack for about 10 minutes before serving, or leave to cool completely.

Ciabatta

This bread is pretty special. I love the flavour from the olive oil, the really big air holes and the roughness of the semolina-coated crust. I highly recommend a baking stone in your oven for this bread. It cannot hold its own weight and the instant fierce heat from beneath gives an essential lift. If you use a baking stone, you will of course need a peel, or a rimless baking sheet, for sliding the bread on to it. You will notice the salt content is slightly higher than usual; this takes into account the large amount of extra semolina flour you will need to use later, for shaping and coating. A food mixer would be useful for kneading this very wet dough.

Makes 6 small loaves

750g '00' flour or strong white bread flour
250g fine semolina, plus up to 500g for dusting
10g powdered dried yeast
25g fine salt
800ml warm water
A generous tbsp extra virgin olive oil, plus extra for drizzling

To knead by hand: mix the flour, semolina, yeast, salt and water together in a very large bowl, then add the oil. You won't be kneading this in the conventional manner. Instead, form your strongest hand into an 'eagle-claw' and beat the mix for about 5 minutes, until smooth.

Or, to use a food mixer: fit the dough hook and add the flour, semolina, yeast, salt and water to the mixer bowl. Mix on low speed until evenly combined, then add the oil and mix for about 5 minutes.

Put the bowl in a bin liner and leave to ferment. Every half an hour for the next 3 hours, do the following: uncover the bowl, slug in some olive oil, smooth it all over, and underneath, then make an attempt to fold the whole thing in two in one direction, then in three in the other (a bit like folding a blanket). The first time this will not really work, but this repeated action over the next 3 hours gives real structure to the gluten, and the dough will become more cohesive and elastic.

Now, prepare yourself. Have ready some linen cloth and dust this, the work surface, the dough and your hands generously with semolina. Make a big pile of semolina to one side, so it's easy to grab. Now tip the dough out on to the work surface. Dust with more semolina. Divide the dough into six, using a dough cutter, a fish slice, or a knife. Use quick chopping motions, dusting as you go. Everything is sticking to everything, I know. Add more semolina.

Now, one piece at a time, fold the edges in to make a rough rectangle. Flatten the rectangle, roll up lengthways, press along the seam to seal, coat in semolina and lay on the cloth. Stretch it out as you do this, so it is roughly four times as long as it is wide.

Cover your bread with plastic and leave to rise until doubled in size. Meanwhile, preheat your oven, with your baking stone (or tray) inside, to 250°C/Gas Mark 10, or as high as it will go.

You will probably see big, satisfying blisters all over the loaves – these are your big air pockets. When you are ready to bake, flip the loaves, one at a time, on to your dusted peel (or straight on to the hot tray), give them a little stretch lengthways, and slide into the oven. Do all this as fast as you can, to minimise heat loss. Bake at maximum heat for 10 minutes, then at 200°C/Gas Mark 6 for about another 15 minutes. Remove from the oven, drizzle with olive oil, then leave to cool on a wire rack, where everyone can see them.

P.S. To make a real Italian-style panino from one of your freshly baked ciabatta, split it lengthways and layer with a few slices of good air-dried salami, pieces of soft, ripe goat's cheese, 1 sliced fat tomato and lots of basil leaves. A little sea salt on the tomatoes would be good, but check the saltiness of the cheese. Add a grinding of black pepper. Close the sandwich and squash down with both hands. Rub the top and bottom with olive oil. Heat a ridged griddle pan and toast your panino, pressing it down often. When nicely charred on the bottom, turn it over and press down again, using a fish slice now, as the top will be hot. After 10 minutes or so, the cheese will have melted and your panino should be nicely stuck together and ready to eat.

Breadsticks

Breadsticks are brilliant. You can make lots in no time at all. They come out long and rough and misshapen, not remotely resembling anything you can buy. Make these if you have friends coming round for drinks. You may not want to bake all of the dough – freeze any you don't need now, in batches, and use within 6 months. This is another soft dough, so a food mixer would be useful for kneading.

Makes about 30

250g strong white flour, plus extra for dusting
250g plain white flour
5g powdered dried yeast
10g fine salt
325ml warm water
A drizzle of sunflower or olive oil, plus extra for coating

To finish
Olive (or other) oil, for brushing
A sprinkling of any of the following:
  Flaky sea salt
  Black pepper
  Poppy seeds
  Smoked paprika
  Chopped rosemary leaves
  Finely grated Parmesan

To knead by hand: mix the flours, yeast, salt and water in a bowl to form a sticky dough. Add the oil, mix it in, then turn the dough out on to a clean work surface. Knead until smooth and silky.

Or, to use a food mixer: fit the dough hook and add the flours, yeast, salt and water to the mixer bowl. Mix on low speed until combined, then add the oil and leave to knead for about 10 minutes, until smooth and silky.

Shape the dough into a round (see p.48), coat with a little extra oil and place in a clean bowl. Leave to rise, covered with a plastic bag, until doubled in size.

Turn the dough out on to the work surface, and using plenty of flour, roll out to between 5mm and 1cm thick. (You may have to do this in batches – it depends how much room you have.) Dust the top evenly with more flour, then flip the whole thing over and dust the other side.

Now cut into strips, about 1cm wide and as long as you like (pic 1). If you want to flavour the breadsticks, brush the tops with oil and sprinkle lightly with your chosen flavouring(s) (pic 2). Now oil your baking trays and lay the bread strips out on them, curling some if you like (pic 3). Leave to prove for about half an hour, then bake at 200°C/Gas Mark 6 for about 20 minutes until golden and just dried out through to the middle. Cool on a wire rack. Stand in a jug or pot (pic 4) to serve.

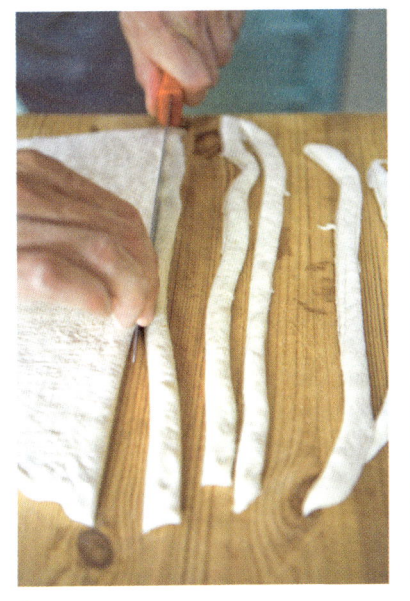

1

2

3

4

BEYOND THE BASIC LOAF 93

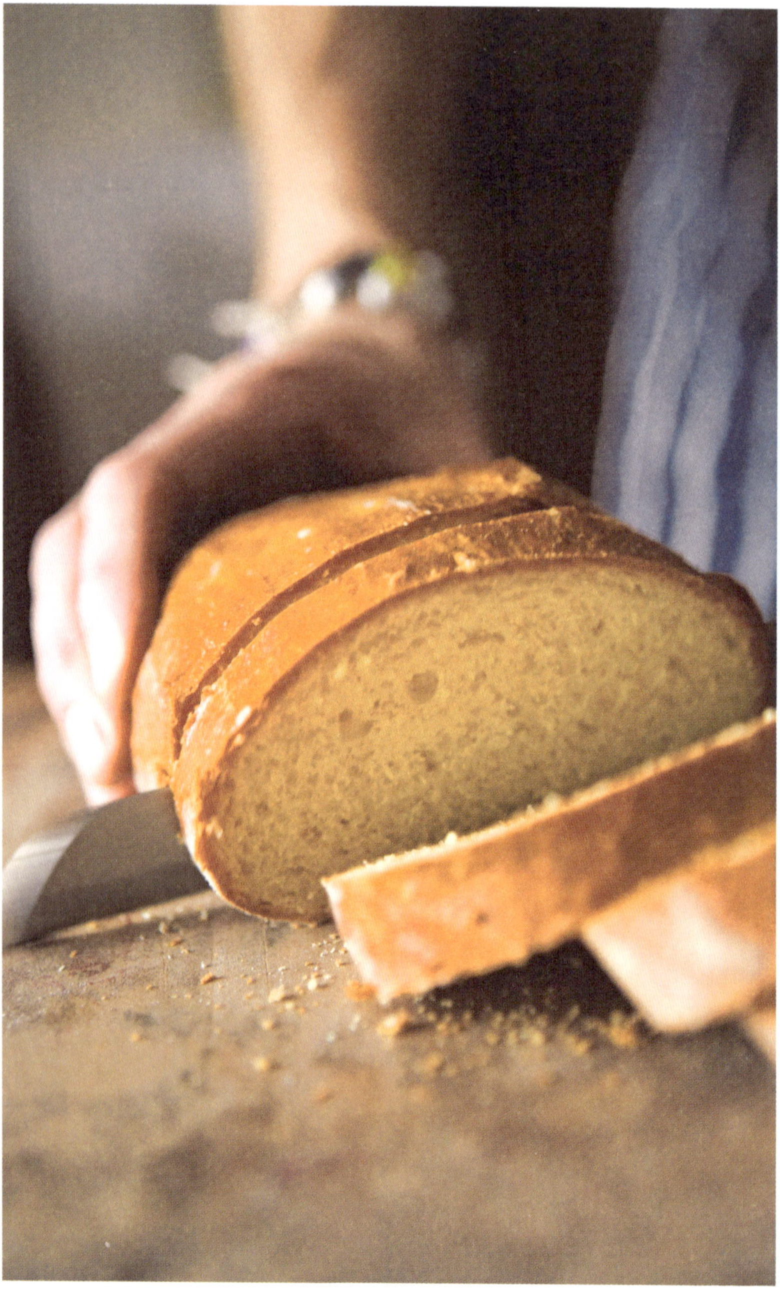

Brioche

This classic French bread is rich and slightly sweet, with a soft, golden crust and a yellow, buttery, cakey crumb. It is widely eaten in France – with coffee for breakfast, as a roll with dinner, or as a base for any number of desserts. At River Cottage, we like to toast brioche and serve it with a smooth chicken liver pâté, and a little fruit jelly.

Contrary to popular belief, as bread goes, brioche is pretty straightforward. The dough is very soft to handle though, so kneading in a food mixer is easier. You can make and bake brioche all in one day, but it benefits from sitting overnight in the fridge – the very soft dough stiffens as it chills, making it easier to shape.

Makes 2 small loaves
400g strong white bread flour, plus extra for dusting
5g powdered dried yeast
10g fine salt
90ml warm milk
2 tbsp caster sugar
100g butter, softened
4 medium free-range eggs, beaten

To glaze
1 medium free-range egg
2 tbsp milk

To knead by hand: mix all the ingredients in a large bowl, and bring it all together to form a dough. Knead for about 10 minutes, until smooth and shiny.

Or, to use a food mixer: fit the dough hook and add all the dough ingredients to the mixer bowl. Mix on low speed until combined, and leave to knead for about 10 minutes, until smooth and shiny.

Shape the dough into a round (see p.48), place in a bowl and cover tightly. Leave in the fridge overnight.

The next day, divide the dough in two and form into the shape of your choice (see pp.55–59). Lightly flour the loaves, lay them on a wooden board or linen cloth and cover with a plastic bag. Leave them somewhere nice and warm to prove until almost doubled in size; this could take 3 or 4 hours, as the dough is cold.

Preheat the oven to 200°C/Gas Mark 6. For the glaze, beat the egg and milk together. Transfer the risen loaves to a baking tray and brush all over with the glaze. Bake for about 10 minutes, then lower the oven setting to 180°C/Gas Mark 4 and bake for a further 30 minutes or until golden brown. Cool on a wire rack.

Bagels

Until recently, most of the bagels I had eaten seemed bland, somewhat dry and rather boring. That was until I came across a bagel recipe in an old Jewish cookbook and was enlightened. Good bagels, like the ones you are about to make, are slightly sweet and curiously chewy, with a soft, shiny, tasty crust. You poach them for a couple of minutes in water before you bake them – the oddest thing you are ever likely to do to a piece of dough.

Makes 12
500g strong white bread flour
5g powdered dried yeast
10g fine salt
250ml warm water
20g caster sugar
50ml vegetable oil, plus extra for coating

To finish
1 medium free-range egg, beaten
Poppy or sesame seeds (optional)

In a large bowl, mix together all the ingredients to make a dough. Knead on a clean surface until smooth and elastic. Shape into a round (see p.48), coat with a little extra oil and place in a clean bowl. Leave to rise, covered with a plastic bag.

When the dough has doubled in size, deflate it and divide into 12 pieces. One at a time, roll into a sausage shape, about 15cm long. Wet the ends and press them together to make a ring. Leave to prove, covered, on a lightly oiled plastic board or metal baking sheet (not floured cloths or boards).

Preheat the oven to 200°C/Gas Mark 6. Lightly oil a couple of baking sheets and in a wide pan bring around a 10cm depth of water to the boil.

When the bagels have roughly doubled in size, they are ready for poaching. You will need to do this in batches. Turn the pan of water down to a simmer, then slip as many bagels as will fit comfortably into the water (allow room for them to puff up). Cook for a minute on each side, then remove and drain on a clean tea towel (not kitchen paper as it will stick).

When they are all poached, lay the bagels on the baking sheets, gently sticking any that uncurled in the water back together again. Brush all over with beaten egg, then sprinkle with seeds if you like. Bake for 15 minutes, until the bagels are a uniform, glossy golden brown. Cool on a wire rack.

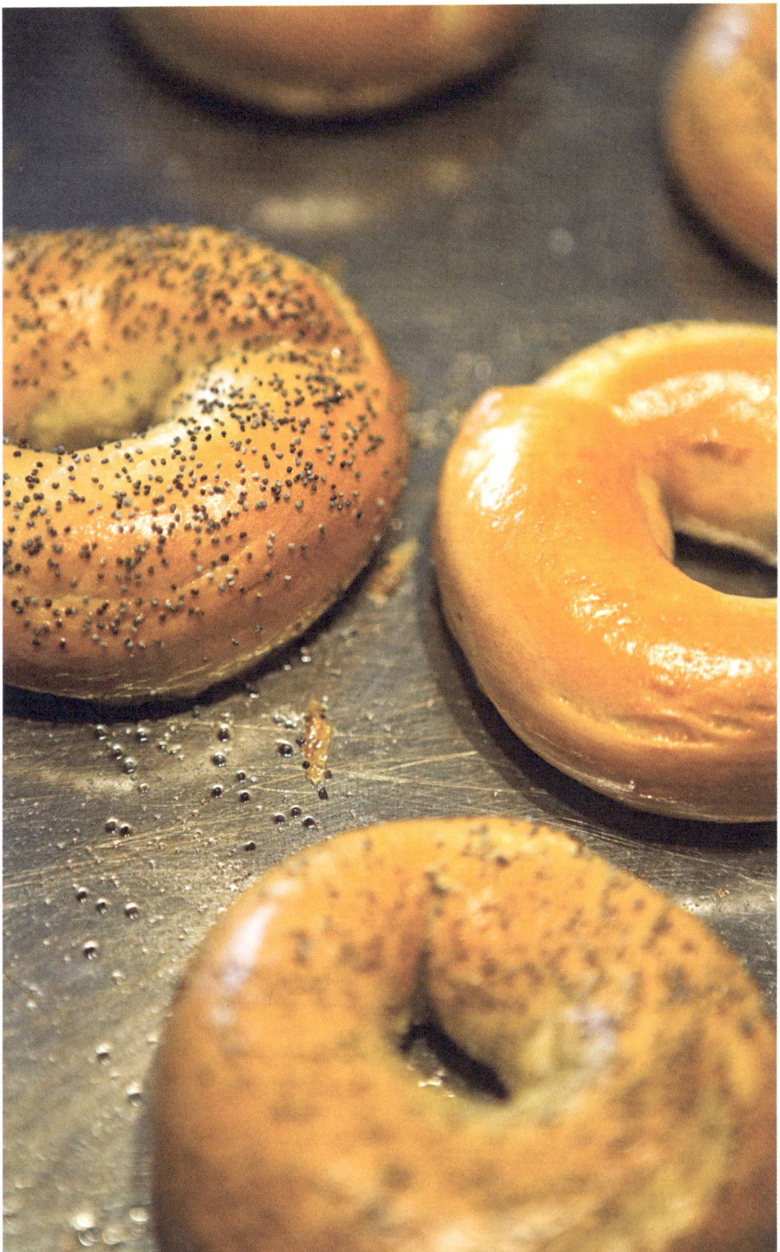

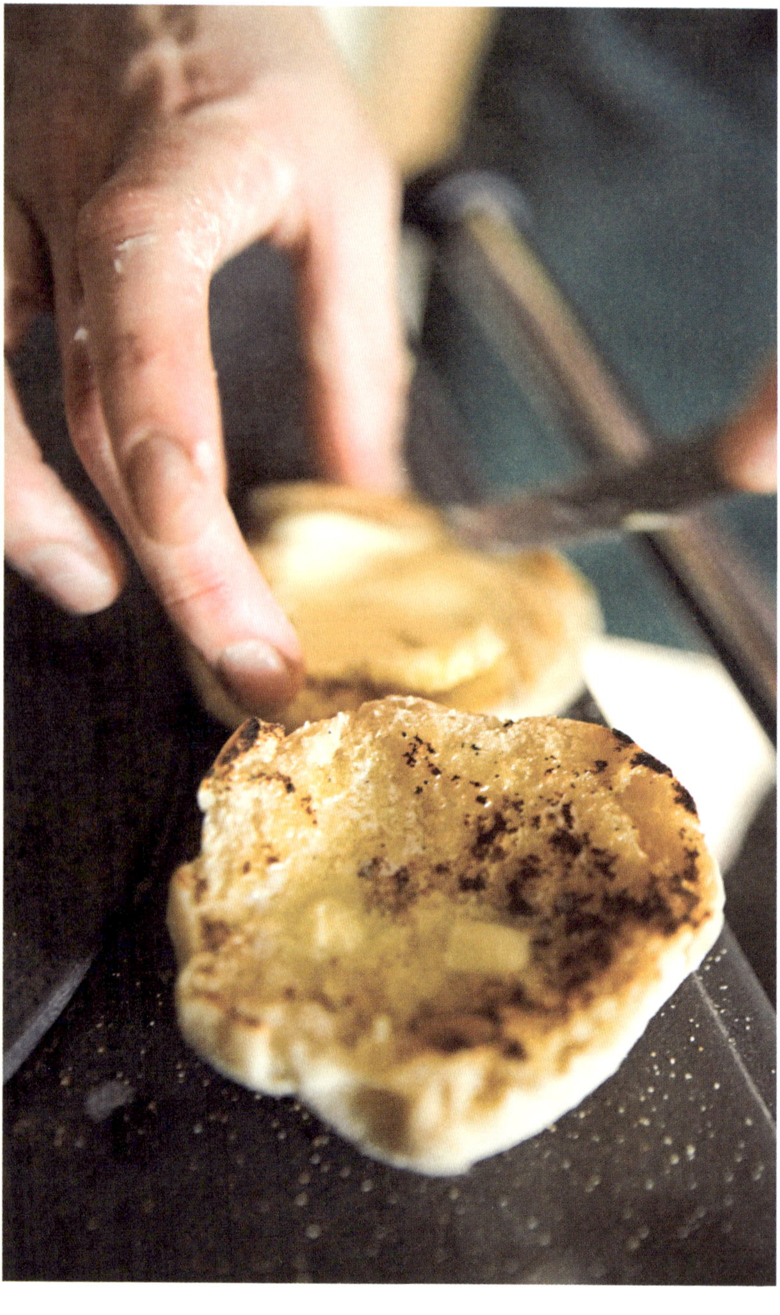

English muffins

A muffin – split, toasted and buttered – is my very favourite bread to have with eggs for breakfast. If you own an Aga, then lucky you – muffins were made for cooking straight on the top. If not, you will need a couple of heavy-based frying pans (each large enough to hold 4 or 5 muffins). This dough is soft, so you might prefer to use a food mixer to knead it.

Makes 9

500g strong white bread flour, plus extra for dusting
5g powdered dried yeast
10g fine salt
325ml warm water

A drizzle of sunflower oil, plus extra for coating
A handful of semolina flour, for coating

To knead by hand: mix the flour, yeast, salt and water in a bowl to form a sticky dough. Add the oil, mix it in, then turn the dough out on to a clean work surface. Knead until smooth and silky.

Or, to use a food mixer: fit the dough hook and add the flour, yeast, salt and water to the mixer bowl. Mix on low speed until combined, then add the oil and leave to knead for about 10 minutes, until smooth and silky.

Shape the dough into a round (see p.48), coat with a little extra oil and place in a clean bowl. Leave to rise, covered with a plastic bag, until doubled in size.

Tip the dough out on to the work surface and press all over to deflate. Divide into 9 pieces, shape each into a round and flatten to about 1–2cm. Dust them all over with semolina flour; this gives a lovely texture to the crust. Leave to prove on a linen cloth or wooden board, covered with a plastic bag, until doubled in size.

Heat a couple of large heavy-based frying pans over a medium heat. Lay the muffins in the pans and cook for a minute or so, then turn them over gently. Cook slowly for a further 10 minutes, turning every now and then. You may need to adjust the heat if they seem to be colouring too fast, or not fast enough. Alternatively, if you are using an Aga, cook the muffins directly on the warm plate for up to 15 minutes, giving them a quick blast on the hot side at the end, if you think they need it. Leave to cool on a wire rack.

Vetkoek

Vetkoek, pronounced 'fet cook', is an Afrikaans word, meaning 'fat cake'. I once knew a guy called Andre, a South African taxidermist, who lived in a tiny caravan. He made me four things: a badger tooth necklace, boiled rabbit, coffee so strong you could chew it... and *vetkoek*. The *vetkoek* were excellent.

Makes 12

500g strong white bread flour, plus extra for dusting
5g powdered dried yeast
10g fine salt
300ml warm water
At least 1 litre sunflower or vegetable oil, for deep-frying

In a bowl, mix together the flour, yeast, salt and water. Turn out on to a clean work surface and knead until smooth and silky. Shape into a round (see p.48), coat with a little extra flour and place in a clean bowl. Leave to rise, covered with a plastic bag, until doubled in size.

Divide the risen dough into 12 pieces, shape into rough rounds and dust lightly with flour. Cover these and leave them for about 10 minutes, to rise a little.

Heat a 5–8cm depth of oil in a deep, heavy-based pan to 170°C. If you do not have a frying thermometer, check the oil temperature by dropping in a cube of bread; it should turn golden in less than a minute. Deep-fry the *vetkoek*, a few at a time, for 3–4 minutes each side. Let them cool a little before eating.

BEYOND THE BASIC LOAF 101

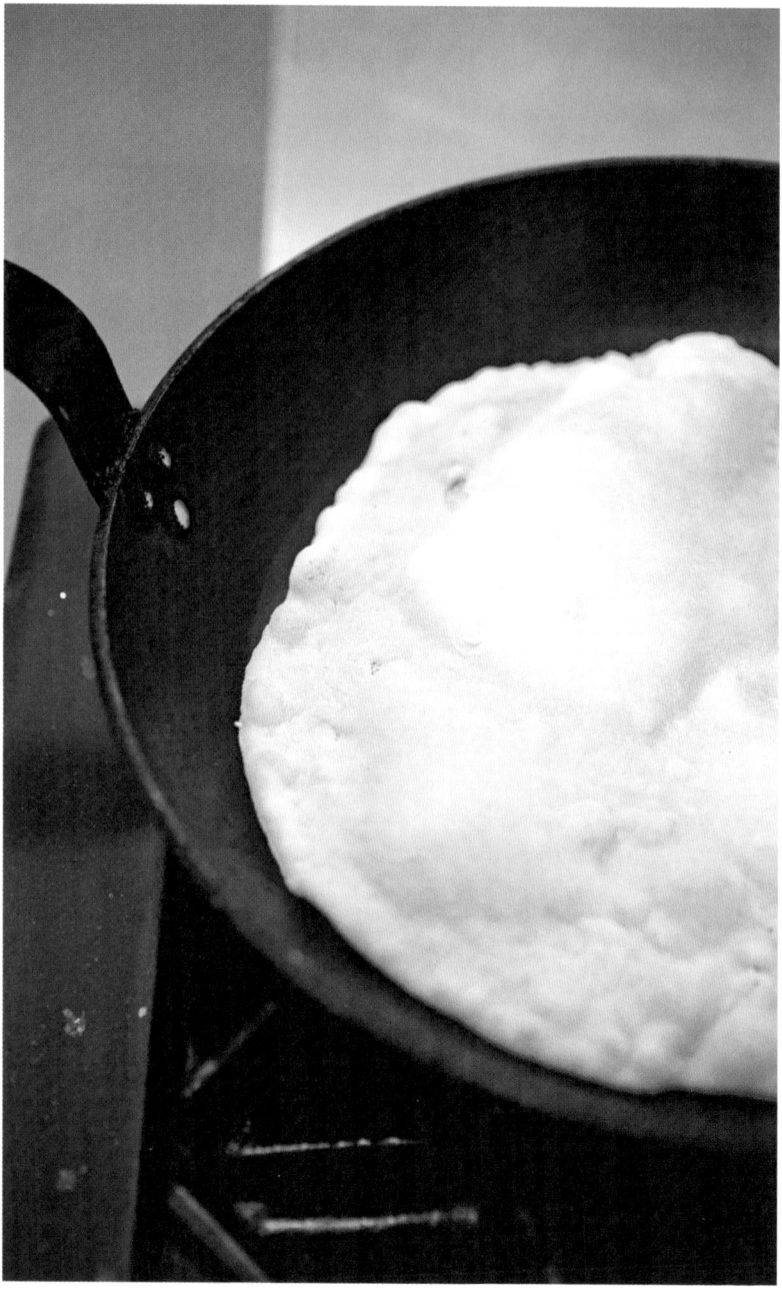

Flatbread

In restaurants in southwest Turkey, fantastic bread is served – steaming hot and cooked to order. It's a bit like pitta, but lighter, softer, and as long as your table. You can make similar bread at home, though you may struggle to make it the size of your table. The dough is soft, so use a food mixer to knead it, if you can.

Makes about 12

500g plain white flour, plus extra for dusting
500g strong white bread flour
10g powdered dried yeast
20g fine salt
325ml warm water
325ml natural yoghurt, warmed
2 tbsp good olive oil, plus extra for coating

To knead by hand: mix the flours, yeast, salt, water and yoghurt in a bowl to form a sticky dough. Add the oil, mix it in, then turn the dough out on to a clean work surface. Knead until smooth and silky.

Or, to use a food mixer: fit the dough hook and add the flours, yeast, salt, water and yoghurt to the mixer bowl. Mix on low speed until combined, then add the oil and leave to knead for about 10 minutes, until smooth and silky.

Shape the dough into a round (see p.48), then place in a clean bowl. Leave to rise, covered with a plastic bag, until doubled in size. Deflate the dough, then if you have time, leave to rise a second, third, even a fourth time (this improves the dough but is by no means essential).

Tear off pieces the size of small lemons (or smaller, or larger, if you like). One at a time, shape into a round, then using plenty of flour, roll out to a 3–4mm thickness and leave to rest for 5 minutes or so; this improves the finished bread dramatically.

Meanwhile, heat a large, heavy-based frying pan over the highest heat and set the grill to maximum. When the pan is super-hot, lay the first bread in it. After a minute, or possibly less, the bread should be puffy and starting to char on the bottom. Slide the pan under the hot grill, a good 15cm from the heat, and watch your creation balloon magnificently.

Remove the bread when it starts to char on the top, slip a lick of olive oil over, and feed your awestruck friends. They will need something to dip the bread into, such as taramasalata (see p.179), and/or beetroot houmous (see p.178). Repeat and repeat, to use all the dough.

Pizza

The best way to bake pizza is in a fiercely hot (400°C+) brick-floored, wood-fired oven. Cooked this way, your pizza will be charred, blistered and ready in as little as 1½ minutes. It will also taste sensational. If you do not have a wood-fired oven or home-built clay oven (see pp.192–209), the next best way is on a baking stone in a domestic oven. The base won't char as much and it will take longer, but it will still be amazing. You'll need a peel, or rimless baking sheet, to slide the pizza on to the stone. If you do not own a baking stone, you can lay pizzas on baking trays. They will cook more slowly and won't blister, but they'll still taste good. Make either the roast tomato sauce or garlicky olive oil, and choose as many toppings as you wish.

Makes at least 8 small pizzas
250g strong white bread flour
250g plain white flour
5g powdered dried yeast
10g salt
325ml warm water
About 1 tbsp olive oil
A handful of coarse flour (rye, semolina or polenta), for dusting

For the roast tomato sauce (optional)
500g tomatoes
2 large garlic cloves, peeled and sliced
2 tbsp olive oil
Salt and black pepper

For the garlicky olive oil (optional)
6 large garlic cloves, peeled and grated
6 tbsp extra virgin olive oil

Toppings to add before baking
A small bowl of: grated Parmesan; grated Cheddar; sliced buffalo mozzarella

A ramekin of: good salami; chopped dry-cured bacon; air-dried ham; anchovy fillets; thinly sliced cooked artichoke hearts; wild mushrooms fried gently in olive oil with garlic and thyme.

A sprinkling of: capers; finely chopped rosemary leaves; black pepper; thinly sliced mild red chilli

Toppings to add after baking
A scattering of: basil leaves; rocket leaves; chopped parsley; wild garlic flowers

To make the dough by hand: mix the flours, yeast, salt and water in a bowl to form a sticky dough. Add the oil, mix it in, then turn the dough out on to a clean work surface. Knead until smooth and silky.

Or, to use a food mixer: fit the dough hook and add the flours, yeast, salt and water to the mixer bowl. Mix on low speed, then add the oil and leave to knead for about 10 minutes, until smooth and silky.

(continued overleaf)

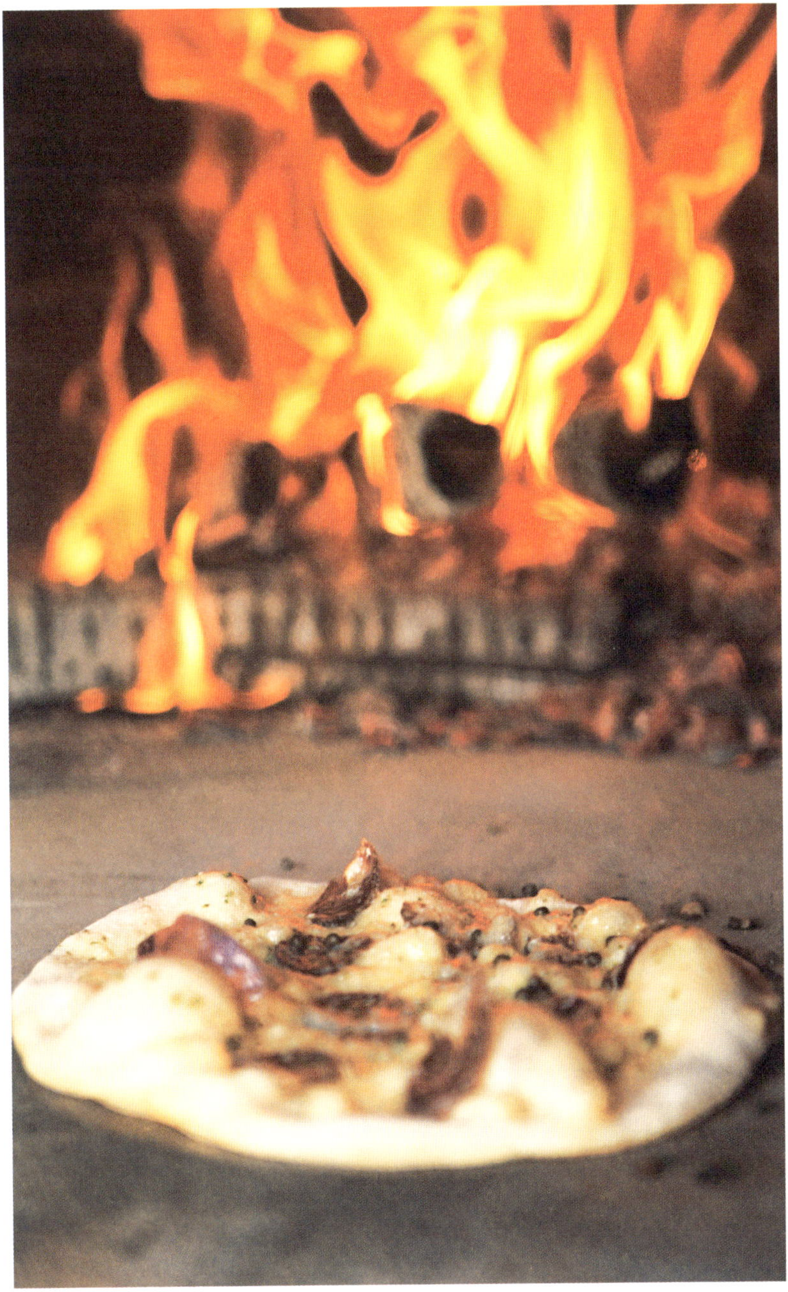

Shape the dough into a round (see p.48), then leave to rise in a clean bowl, covered with a plastic bag, until doubled in size.

To prepare the roast tomato sauce, if using, preheat the oven to 180°C/Gas Mark 4. Halve the tomatoes and lay them, cut side up, in a roasting tin. Mix the garlic with the oil, pour over the tomatoes and shake the tin a little, to distribute the oil. Season with salt and pepper. Roast for 30–45 minutes, until the tomatoes are soft and slightly charred. Rub through a sieve into a bowl.

Or, for the garlicky olive oil, simply mix the garlic with the oil.

Have your toppings laid out in little bowls, or in piles, so everyone can make their own selection.

If using a domestic oven, preheat your oven, with your baking stone (or tray) inside, to 250°C/Gas Mark 10, or as high as it will go. (Alternatively, have your clay oven raging hot and rake the embers out.)

To shape and bake the pizzas

If using a wood-fired oven or a baking stone in a domestic oven, take a lime-sized piece of your risen dough and roll it out until about 5mm thick, keeping it as round as you can. Dust the peel or rimless baking sheet with coarse flour, and lay the dough on it. If you are using a baking tray: either roll out a lime-sized piece as above, or you could take a larger piece, and press it into the tray, to fit.

Think thin and delicate with your toppings, including the cheese, as befits thin, delicate bases. Overloaded pizzas will be hard to handle and will quite probably tear; they will also come out soggy. Try to use only three or four toppings on each pizza. The following combinations work well:

- Garlicky oil, artichokes, Parmesan and basil
- Garlicky oil, anchovy, capers and Parmesan
- Roast tomato sauce, mozzarella, black pepper and basil (Margherita)
- Garlicky oil, chilli, mozzarella and rocket
- Garlicky oil and rosemary
- Roast tomato sauce, salami, Parmesan and parsley
- Fried wild mushrooms with their oil, Parmesan and parsley (my favourite)

Apply the toppings to be added before baking, then either slip the pizza briskly but carefully on to the baking stone (or brick floor), or transfer the baking tray to the top shelf of the oven. Bake until the cheese is melted and bubbling: this should take about 1½ minutes in a wood-fired oven; more like 7–9 minutes in a domestic oven. Remove from the oven and scatter over any leaves or other raw toppings you may be using. Cut your pizza up and dig in… while somebody else bakes the next one.

Barbecue breads

Like the *vetkoek (*on p.100), this is not so much a recipe as a different way of cooking bread dough. If you want to make your dough outdoors, and have no suitable surface for kneading, you could employ my (no longer) secret 'soggy tea towel' technique (described below).

Makes at least 8

500g strong white bread flour (or other bread flour of your choice), plus extra for dusting
5g powdered dried yeast
10g fine salt
300ml warm water
A drizzle of sunflower or other oil

In a bowl, mix together the flour, yeast, salt and water. Drizzle in a little oil and squidge the dough together. Turn out on to a clean work surface and knead until smooth and silky. Alternatively, to use the 'soggy tea towel' technique: wring the dough between your hands, as if you were wringing a tea towel. Fold it in half every few wrings as it gets too thin, and keep wringing until the dough becomes smooth and springy.

Shape the dough into a round (see p.48), coat with a little extra flour and place in a clean bowl. Leave to rise, covered with a plastic bag, until doubled in size.

You can be very flexible about proving. Make the dough in the morning if you like, then keep deflating it through the day until it's time to eat. At this point, tear off pieces of dough and pull and squash them into roughish rounds, as thin as you can get them by hand.

Leave to rise for about 10 minutes, or until you have space on the barbecue, then slap them on. How long they will take to cook depends on how thick they are, and how hot the barbecue is, but around 7–10 minutes should be about right – tear one open and check it is cooked in the middle. Let cool slightly before eating.

Bread Made with Wild Yeast

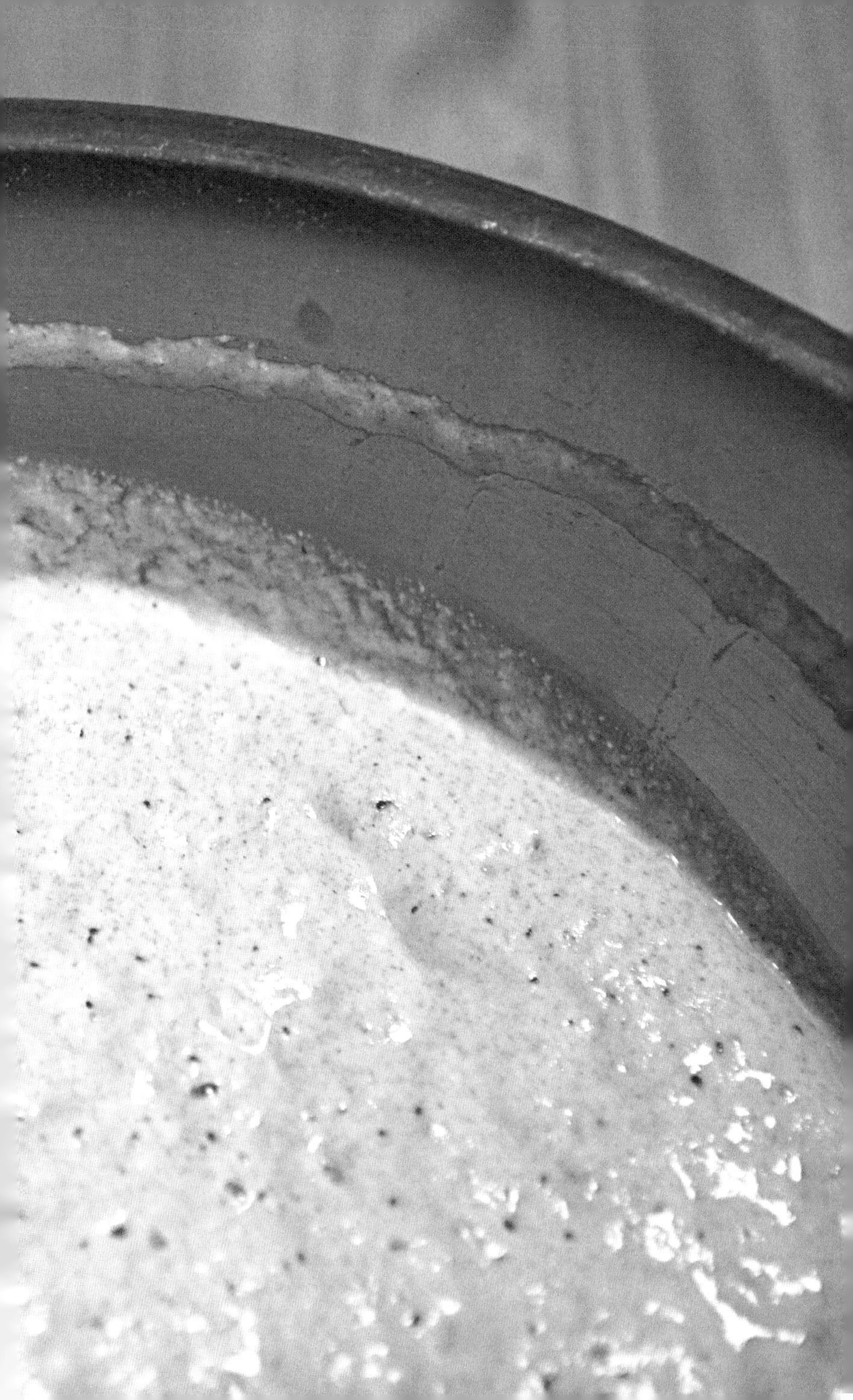

You don't have to buy yeast from the shop to make your bread.

You can get your own, from the wild. What's more, you don't need any special equipment, local knowledge or expert tuition. There are dormant yeast spores all around you – in the air, in your fruit bowl, and in that lovely bag of organic flour in your cupboard. As wild foraging goes, it's a bit of a doddle – you don't even need to leave the house, unless, of course, you need to buy that bag of flour. You just need to create an environment in which the yeast spores will become active.

Sourdough starter

A starter (also known as a *poolish*, or *levain*) is a fermenting dough or batter, all or part of which is used to raise a batch of bread. The term sourdough broadly applies to bread raised with wild yeasts. Defining characteristics of such breads are a slower fermentation and a distinctly sour (but by no means unpleasant) flavour. Both are the result of high acidity caused by the presence of certain bacteria, among them lactic acid bacteria (the same bacteria used to make yoghurt), which colonise the starter along with the yeasts. Making a starter is easy. We know that yeasts need sugar, warmth and moisture to reproduce. All you need to do is provide these. Here's the recipe, if you can call it that.

For the first stage
A cupful of flour (about 150g)
A cupful of warm water (about 250ml)

For the first 'feeding'
A cupful of flour (about 150g)
About 100ml warm water (about 250ml)

For each subsequent feeding
A cupful of flour (about 150g)
A cupful of cold water (about 250ml)

The first stage

You really need a plastic or earthenware container with a lid to make your starter in. It should be big enough to allow plenty of room for frothing – at least four times the volume of your initial batter (because you will add more later). You can use any type of flour you like; I have made excellent starters from rye, spelt and wheat. I recommend that you use wholemeal rather than white flour though; it will ferment sooner – and more vigorously.

1: the first signs of fermentation

2: vigorous fermentation

BREAD MADE WITH WILD YEAST 111

There is no need to be precise about the quantities of flour and water. For the first stage, just use roughly equal volumes of each to make a thick batter and whisk it well – this incorporates more air, and therefore more yeast spores. If you have a food mixer, then 10 minutes at high speed would be ideal. Put the batter into the container, put the lid on and leave it somewhere fairly warm – a warm kitchen is fine; an airing cupboard would do, but don't put it too close to the boiler.

The first feeding

At some point, your starter will begin to ferment. This depends on many factors, such as the flour used, how much you whisked it, which yeasts and bacteria happen to be around, and how warm it is. To give you some idea, a white wheat starter I made at home took two full days to puff a couple of little air bubbles to the surface; a wholemeal spelt starter I made at work was frothing rapidly after only a few hours. So, check every 12 hours or so, and when you see the first signs of fermentation (p.111, pic 1), give your starter its first 'feeding' by whisking in another 150g or so of flour and another 250ml warm water. Replace the lid and leave it again.

Check your starter again after another day (though in reality you will be so fascinated by now that you won't be able to keep away from it). Don't worry if all this takes longer than you expected – it will get there in the end. And when it does, I should warn you about the smell. You will either love it, or hate it. It might be sickly sweet or sickly sour, smelling of vinegar, or rotten apples, or brandy, or gone-off milk, perhaps. Breathe in deeply; I want you to remember this smell.

Subsequent feedings

Now tip out half of the starter (into a plastic bag or an old milk carton) and discard it. Replace this with another 150g flour, and 250ml cold water this time, and leave it another day, at a fairly cool room temperature now. In fact, find it a permanent home – it may be with you for life, after all. Hereafter, you are into a feeding programme, and you need to find one that suits you.

I suggest for the first week at least, while your sourdough starter is getting established, you feed it daily, discarding half and replacing it. Keep smelling it and you'll become aware of the aroma changing, becoming less harsh and more complex as it matures. You will also notice different smells at different stages of fermentation. Without sounding too cosy, you should develop a living relationship with your starter. It is very much like keeping a pet. You will get to know when it needs feeding, when it is most active, when it is tired and sluggish, and (sorry about this) when it could do with a good beating (I whip mine up in the food mixer every couple of weeks – the oxygen does the yeast a lot of good). About a week into your routine of daily feeding, when fermentation is vigorous (p.111, pic 2) and regular, and the smells have become recognisable and established, you are ready to use your starter.

If you are likely to bake regularly, as we do at River Cottage, keep your starter as it is – as a thick batter, at room temperature, feeding it daily. But if you will only be using it every couple of weeks or less, you may as well slow the fermentation; then you'll need to feed it less. To do so, you can either make it colder or drier, or both:

- Keep your starter in the fridge and it can go a week without being fed.
- Alternatively, add enough flour to make a stiff dough and you could happily feed it every three or four days. To feed a dough, discard half (or better still, bake with it), make a new flour and water dough the same volume as the discarded part, and knead it into the remaining starter. A dough that is fed like this will still be pretty active. Many bakers keep starters permanently in the form of a dough (when it is more usually known as a *levain*), and bake with them daily.
- Or do both: keep it as a dough in the fridge and you only need to feed it every couple of weeks.

What is important, though, is that your starter is really active when it comes to baking, so at least a couple of days ahead, remove it from the fridge and/or bring it back to a thick batter by adding water, then feed it daily until you bake.

Nurtured this way, your starter will live for ever. However, you may get to a stage where you have no room in your life to look after it but you don't want to throw your starter away. It is worth freezing it for the future – well sealed and labelled clearly.

Currently at River Cottage, we have two starters: a wheat one, an offshoot of my own 3-year-old starter; and an older rye starter, given to us by Clive Mellum from Shipton Mill. Clive's batter has been continuously fermenting for 12 years. But at 12, it is still young. Aidan Chapman, an outstanding baker at the Town Mill bakery, tells me his rye starter was first made 30 years ago in Russia. It is the tradition in many communities to hand down starters from one generation to the next. How satisfying it must be to bake with them – a little piece of ancestry in every loaf.

Making bread with your starter

Sourdough baking is different from conventional bread baking only in that the process takes longer. You should familiarise yourself with the detailed section: Bread making step by step (pp.34–71), as the following recipes refer back to it.

Bread made with wild yeast

- Sourdough (p.115)
- My sourdough (p.117)
- Sour rye bread (p.120)
- Spelt sourdough (p.122)
- Pumpernickel (p.124)

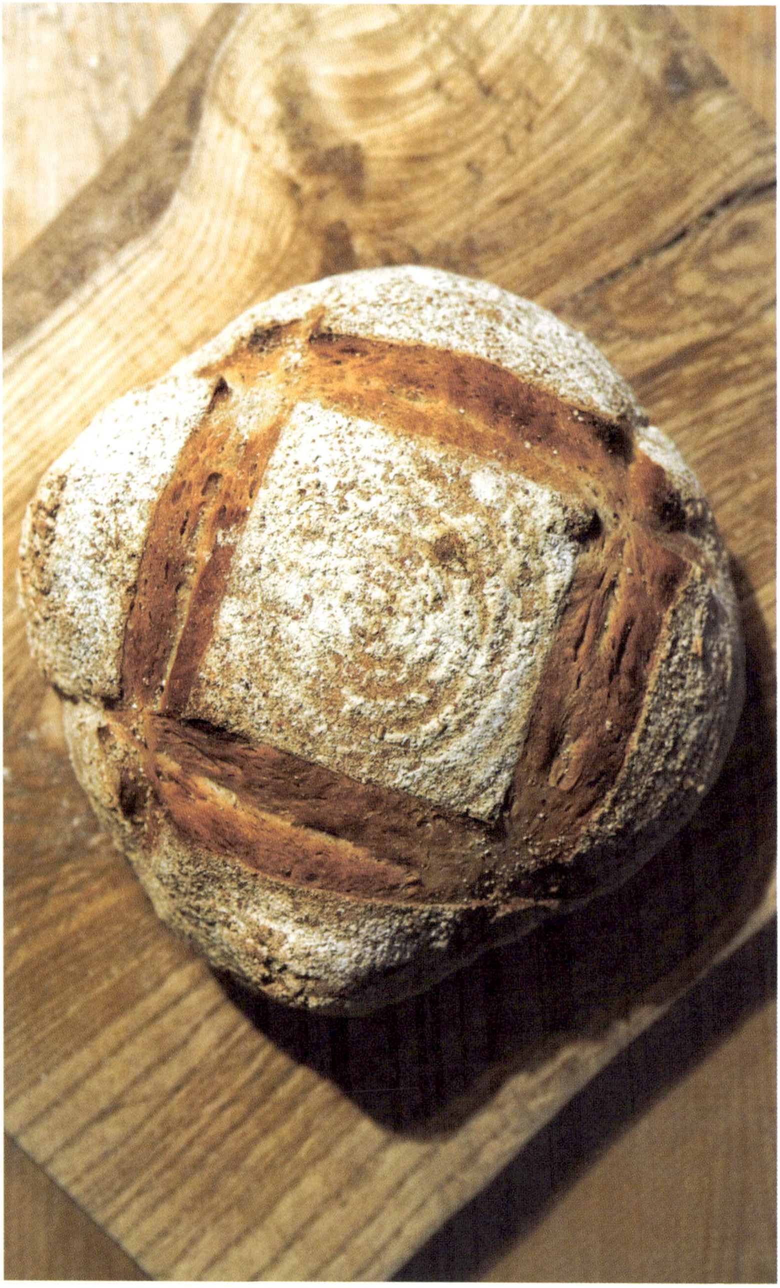

Sourdough

This is a simple wholemeal sourdough, which you can adapt infinitely, in the same way as the basic bread recipe (see pp.72–7). I have also given you the River Cottage variation (see p.116).

Makes 2–3 loaves

For the sponge
500g strong wholemeal wheat flour
600ml warm water
A ladleful of very active sourdough starter (see p.110)

For the dough
600g strong wholemeal wheat flour, plus extra for dusting
25g salt

Before you go to bed, make the sponge: mix all the ingredients together by hand in a large bowl or plastic container. Beat for a while, squeezing the lumps of flour out as you come across them. Put the container in a plastic bag and leave it somewhere fairly warm until the morning.

The next day, mix in the flour and salt, and squash it all together, adding more flour or water as necessary, to make a soft, easily kneadable, sticky dough. Turn it out on to a clean work surface and knead for about 10 minutes, until smooth and springy.

Form the dough into a tight round (see p.48), flour it all over and place in a clean bowl. Cover with a plastic bag and leave to rise. After an hour, tip it out on to your work surface (it may not have risen much at this point). Form it into a tight round again, return to the bowl, cover and leave to rise for another hour. Repeat this process once, or even twice more – you will notice the dough becoming increasingly airy.

After the final rising period, tip the dough out on to the work surface and deflate it by pressing all over with your hands. Divide into two or three, and shape into loaves (see pp.55–9). Coat with flour, then transfer the loaves to well-floured wooden boards, linen cloths, tea towels or proving baskets. Lay a plastic bag over the whole batch, to stop it drying out, and leave to prove until almost doubled in size; this could be anywhere from 1–4 hours, depending on the temperature of the dough and the vigour of your sourdough starter.

When the loaves are almost ready, switch the oven to 250°C/Gas Mark 10 or its highest setting, put a baking stone or a heavy baking tray inside, and place a roasting tin on the bottom shelf. Put the kettle on. Have a water spray bottle, a serrated knife and an oven cloth ready, as well as a peel or rimless baking sheet, if you are using a baking stone. Clear the area around the oven. *(continued overleaf)*

When the loaves are ready, either transfer them to the hot tray (removed from the oven), or one at a time to the peel. Slash the tops with the serrated knife and spray the bread all over with water. Put the tray into the oven, or slide each loaf on to the baking stone, pour some boiling water into the roasting tin and close the door as quickly as you can.

Turn the heat down after about 10 minutes to 200°C/Gas Mark 6 if the crust is still very pale; 180°C/Gas Mark 4 if the crust is noticeably browning; or 170°C/Gas Mark 3 if the crust seems to be browning quickly. Bake until the loaves are well browned and crusty, and feel hollow when you tap them: in total allow 30–40 minutes for small loaves; 40–50 minutes for large loaves. If in doubt, bake for a few minutes longer. Leave to cool on a wire rack.

Variation

To make River Cottage sourdough, use strong white rather than wholemeal flour. For the sponge, use a 50:50 mix of wheat and rye flour (250g each). Add a good slug of sunflower oil after you have formed the dough.

My sourdough

Deliciously chewy and tangy, with enormous air holes and a fine savoury crust, this is one of my favourite breads. The large holes are due to a wetter than usual dough, so you will find it a little trickier than usual to handle. The shaped loaves will be rather saggy and would certainly benefit from the support of a rucked-up linen cloth or, better still, proving baskets. In any case, this sourdough will rise dramatically in the oven and will always end up looking glorious, if occasionally perhaps a little misshapen.

Makes 2–3 loaves

For the sponge
650ml warm water
500g strong white bread flour
A ladleful of sourdough starter (see p.110)

For the dough
600g strong white bread flour, plus extra for dusting
25g salt

To finish
A handful of rye flour

Before you go to bed, make the sponge. Mix the water, flour and starter together in a bowl. Cover and leave in a fairly warm place overnight.

The next morning, to knead the dough by hand: mix the flour and salt into the sponge. Bring it together and squidge in the oil if using. The dough should be soft and sticky – just kneadable, but rather wetter than a normal dough. You will need some extra flour – for your hands, the dough and the worktop. It will be quite messy to begin with. Every now and then, clean your hands and scrape the worktop. Use more flour when you need to, but be sparing with it – you don't want to make the dough stiff, or you won't get the big air holes.

Or, to use a food mixer: fit the dough hook and add the sponge, flour and salt. Mix on low speed until combined, then add the oil and knead for about 10 minutes.

When your dough is smooth and satiny, shape it into a nice tight round (see p.48) and place in a bowl. Cover and leave somewhere warm for about an hour.

Now lightly flour the dough, tip it out on to the work surface and press it out flat with your fingertips. Shape into a round again, put it back in its bowl, cover and leave in a warm place for another hour. Do this twice more. You will see and feel the dough becoming smoother, shinier and more airy.

(continued overleaf)

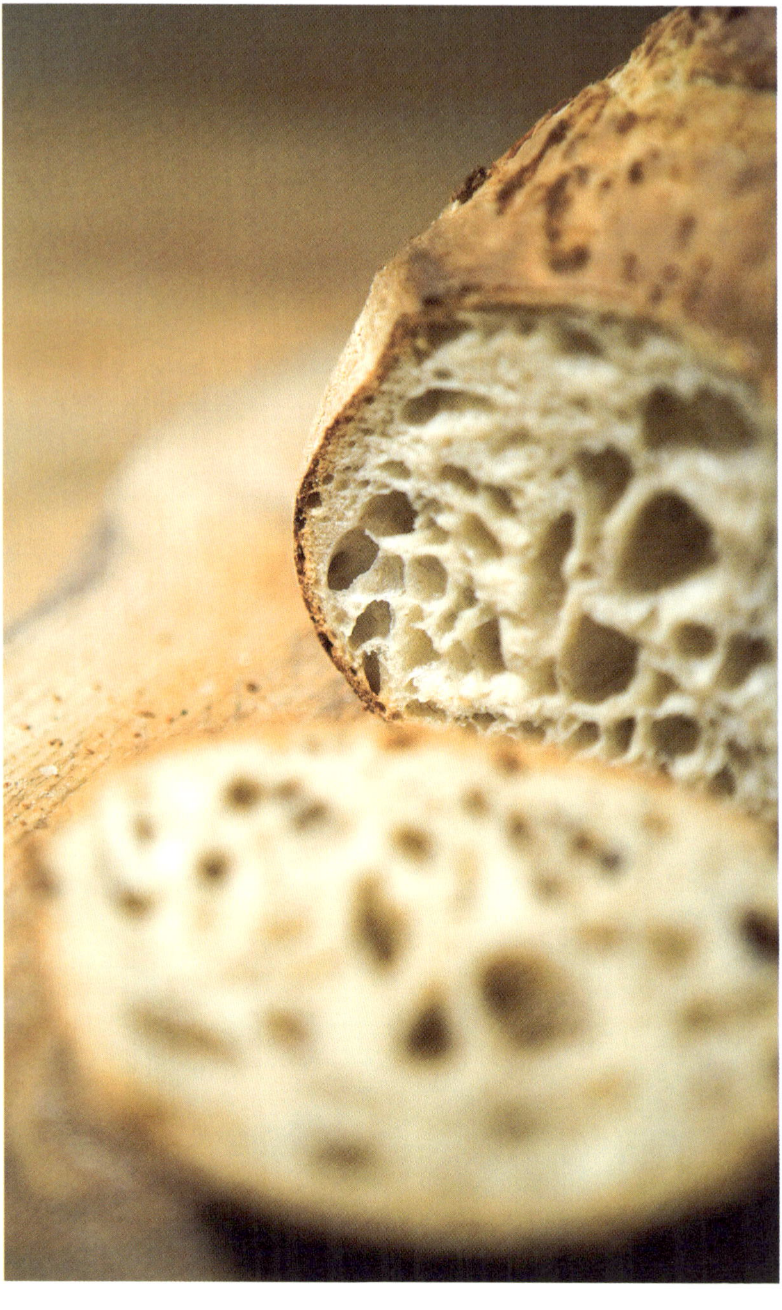

After these 4 hours of rising and deflating, the dough will feel soft and puffy, like an angel's pillow. Sink your hands in and deflate it once more. Divide into two or three and shape into loaves (see pp.55–9). Coat with the rye flour and transfer to well-floured wooden boards, linen cloths, tea towels or proving baskets.

Lay a plastic bag over the whole batch, to stop it drying out, and leave to prove for 2–3 hours or until doubled in size; you will probably notice big air holes developing near the surface. Unlike with other breads, you should err on the side of over-proving; the loaves may end up a little misshapen, but the air holes will be bigger.

When the loaves are almost ready, switch the oven to 250°C/Gas Mark 10 or its highest setting, put a baking stone or a heavy baking tray inside, and place a roasting tin on the bottom shelf. Put the kettle on. Have a water spray bottle, a serrated knife and an oven cloth ready, as well as a peel or rimless baking sheet, if you are using a baking stone. Clear the area around the oven.

When the loaves are ready, either transfer them to the hot tray (removed from the oven), or one at a time to the peel. Slash the tops with the serrated knife. Spray the bread all over with water. Put the tray into the oven, or slide each loaf on to the baking stone, pour some boiling water into the roasting tin and close the door as quickly as you can.

Turn the heat down after about 10 minutes to 200°C/Gas Mark 6 if the crust is still very pale; 180°C/Gas Mark 4 if the crust is noticeably browning; or 170°C/Gas Mark 3 if the crust seems to be browning quickly. Bake until the loaves are well browned and crusty, and feel hollow when you tap them: in total allow 30–40 minutes for small loaves; 40–50 minutes for large loaves. If in doubt, bake for a few minutes longer. Leave to cool on a wire rack.

Sour rye bread

Rye makes dense, heavy bread, as it has very few gluten-forming proteins. It is very tasty, though, and well worth making. You could replace some of the flour (perhaps 250g) with strong white bread flour to lighten it if you like, but I love the full flavour of pure rye and as long as it is sliced thinly, its texture is a pleasure, not a chore. Kneading it is somewhat less satisfying than with high-gluten doughs, in that it doesn't become stretchy, or resilient, or silky. In fact, it doesn't seem to change much at all. This means less work for you, though; 5 minutes should be quite enough. I also suggest shaping the loaves straight away, giving them a single, long rise. Rye bread doesn't seem to benefit from the usual longer process of rising and deflating, which mainly serves to develop the structure of high-gluten breads.

Makes 2–3 loaves

1.1kg dark rye flour, plus extra for dusting
25g salt
600ml warm water
A ladleful of sourdough starter (see p.110)
A good slug of sunflower oil (optional)

Combine the rye flour, salt, water and starter in a large bowl and mix to a dough, adding more flour or water if needed, to make a soft, easily kneadable dough. Mix in the oil, if using. Turn the dough out on to a clean worktop and knead for about 5 minutes; you'll probably need extra flour as it will be quite sticky. Divide the dough into two or three, shape into loaves (see pp.55–9) and dust well with flour.

Leave to rise somewhere fairly warm, covered, ideally in well-floured proving baskets. You can use linen cloths or wooden boards, but as it is so low in gluten, unsupported rye bread tends to spread outwards rather than upwards, giving you flat loaves. Loaf tins would give higher, though less attractive loaves. Your dough needs to double in size, which can take anywhere from 1–4 hours, depending on the temperature of the dough and vigour of your starter. When almost ready, place your baking stone or tray in the oven and preheat the oven to 250°C/Gas Mark 10, or as hot as it will go.

When ready to bake, turn your loaves, one at a time, on to a peel and slide them on to the baking stone in the oven or remove the tray, turn the loaves on to it and return to the oven. There is no need to slash rye bread. It will hardly rise, so slashes would barely open up anyway, and it is likely to crack attractively in the oven, especially if it has been well floured. Bake at the high temperature for about 10 minutes, then lower the heat to 180°C/Gas Mark 4 and bake for a further 20–30 minutes. Cool on a wire rack.

BREAD MADE WITH WILD YEAST 121

Spelt sourdough

Enriched with hemp seeds, this sourdough is deeply flavoured, savoury and nutty. As with any bread made with spelt, a little extra kneading and some proving baskets to hold the shape of the loaves work wonders. I love to eat this bread with hearty winter soups.

Makes 2–3 loaves

For the sponge
500g spelt flour
600ml warm water
A ladleful of sourdough starter
  (see p.110)

For the dough
50g hemp seeds
600g spelt flour, plus extra for dusting
25g salt
A good slug of hemp oil

Before you go to bed, beat all the sponge ingredients together in a large bowl, cover and leave somewhere fairly warm overnight.

In the morning, toast the hemp seeds in a dry frying pan over a medium heat, tossing them often, for about 2 minutes until they smell strong and nutty. Grind them, using a pestle and mortar if you have one; otherwise use a spice grinder or small blender. I like to leave them quite coarse, for a bit of texture. Add the seeds to the sponge with the flour and salt, mix to a dough, then incorporate the oil. Use more water or flour as necessary to give a kneadable dough.

Turn the dough out on to a clean work surface and knead for about 10 minutes, until smooth and springy. Form the dough into a tight round (see p.48), flour it all over and place in a clean bowl. Cover with a plastic bag and leave to rise. After an hour, tip it out on to your work surface (it may not have risen much at this point). Form it into a tight round again, return to the bowl, cover and leave to rise for another hour. Repeat this process once, or even twice more – you will notice the dough becoming increasingly airy.

After the final rising period, tip the dough out and deflate it by pressing all over with your hands. Divide into two or three, and shape into loaves (see pp.55–9). Coat with flour, then transfer to well-floured wooden boards, linen cloths, tea towels or proving baskets. Lay a plastic bag over the whole batch, to stop it drying out, and leave to prove until almost doubled in size; this could be anywhere from 1–4 hours, depending on the temperature of the dough and the vigour of your starter.

When the loaves are almost ready, switch the oven to 250°C/Gas Mark 10 or its highest setting, put a baking stone or a heavy baking tray inside, and place a roasting tin on the bottom shelf. Put the kettle on. Have a water spray bottle, a serrated knife and an oven cloth ready, as well as a peel or rimless baking sheet, if you are using a baking stone. Clear the area around the oven.

When the loaves are ready, either transfer them to the hot tray (removed from the oven), or one at a time to the peel. Slash the tops with the serrated knife. Spray the bread all over with water. Put the tray into the oven, or slide each loaf on to the baking stone, pour some boiling water into the roasting tin and close the door as quickly as you can.

Turn the heat down after about 10 minutes to 200°C/Gas Mark 6 if the crust is still very pale; 180°C/Gas Mark 4 if the crust is noticeably browning; or 170°C/Gas Mark 3 if the crust seems to be browning quickly. Bake until the loaves are well browned and crusty, and feel hollow when you tap them: in total allow 30–40 minutes for small loaves; 40–50 minutes for large loaves. If in doubt, bake for a few minutes longer. Leave to cool on a wire rack.

Pumpernickel

Pumpernickel originated in the Westphalia region of Germany, invented by bakers as a way of making the most of the residual heat of their wood-fired ovens once the usual bread had been baked. The recipe includes rye or wheat berries, which you can buy in many health food shops. Please make this once, at least, just for the experience. It is a drawn-out affair, to say the least (two and a half days from start to finish), but each stage is very simple.

Use a medium cast-iron (Le Creuset-type) casserole dish with lid, or something similar, for baking this bread. Alternatively, you could use a couple of loaf tins.

Makes 1 loaf

For the soaker
200g rye bread, or other brown bread, sliced (stale is fine)
200g rye berries (or wheat berries)
Enough water to cover

For the sponge
300g rye flour
300ml warm water
About 1 tbsp sourdough starter (see p.110)

For the dough
300ml warm water (use the water from the soaker)
250g rye flour
250g rye flakes
20g salt
50g blackstrap molasses
A little oil

The evening before baking, make the soaker: preheat the oven to 200°C/Gas Mark 6 and lay the slices of bread on a baking tray. Bake until they are brown all the way through to the middle – snap one in half to check. Go as dark as you dare without burning. When you are happy, place the bread in a bowl with the rye berries and cover with cold water. Press the bread down every now and then to get it nice and soggy. In a separate bowl, make the sponge: beat together the flour, water and starter until smooth. Cover and leave both, at room temperature, until the morning.

The next morning, strain the soaker in a sieve set over a bowl, squeezing the bread out and reserving the liquid. Measure 300ml of this liquid (or make it up to 300ml with water if you don't have enough). Heat in a pan until tepid, then pour into a large mixing bowl and add the bread and rye berries, the sponge, rye flour, rye flakes, salt and molasses. Mix, stickily, until it all comes together. Oil your baking container(s), then scoop the mixture in, filling no more than half-full. Cover with a plastic bag (or lid) and leave to double in size – this could take up to 4 hours.

When you are nearly ready to bake, cover tightly with a double layer of foil (if your container doesn't have a lid). Preheat the oven to 200°C/Gas Mark 6. Place the tins on the middle shelf and bake for an hour. Turn the oven down to 190°C/Gas Mark 5 and bake for another 30 minutes, then at 180°C/Gas Mark 4 and 170°C/Gas Mark 3 for 30 minutes each. Finally, bake at 150°C/Gas Mark 2 for 3 hours, then switch the oven off and leave the pumpernickel inside until morning.

If you are baking your pumpernickel in a clay oven, put the tins in when it is nice and hot, seal the door and chimney up, and leave to bake until morning.

The morning after, remove the almost-black breads from the tins (they may be quite well stuck – running a knife around the sides will help), wrap them in greaseproof paper and leave to mature at room temperature for a day before eating. Delicious with cheese, cold meats and smoked fish.

Bread Made without Yeast

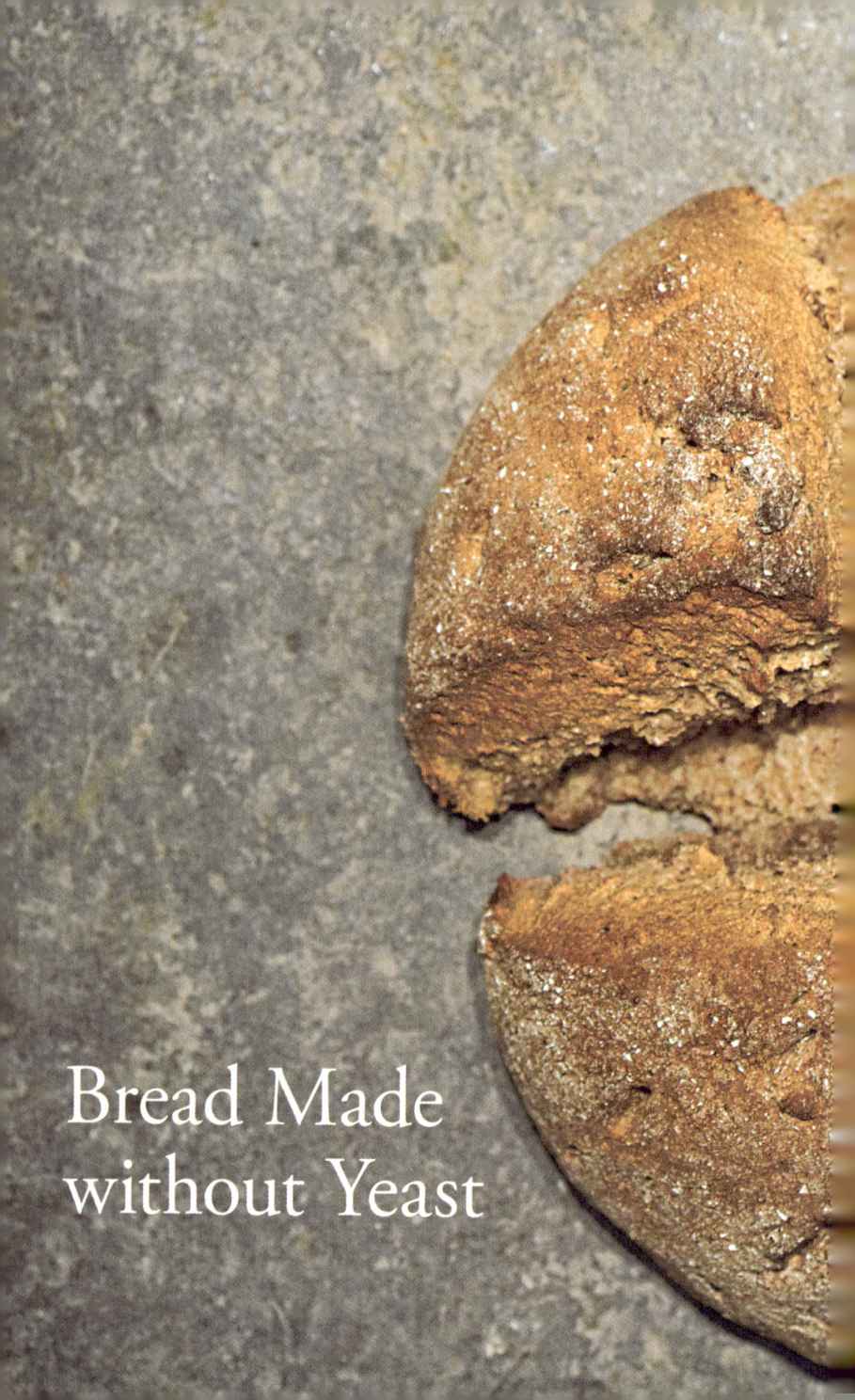

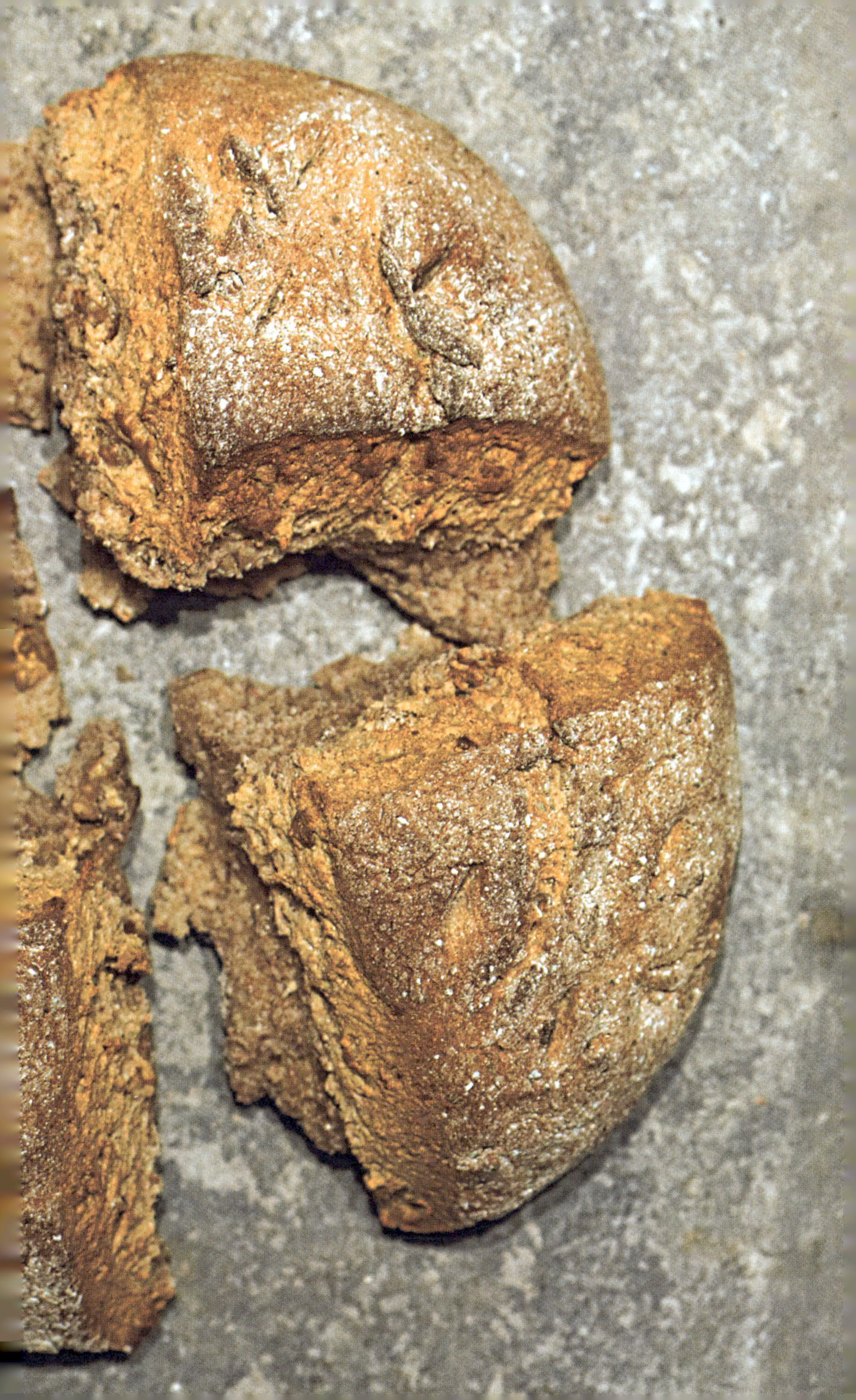

If time is tight,
or it's lunchtime and you've forgotten to go shopping, then this is the chapter for you. Yeast-free breads are much easier and far less demanding of your time than the yeasted kind. For most of these recipes, you simply mix everything together and cook it.

There are also a few flat breads in here. These are unleavened, meaning they contain no raising agent at all. However, roti, the staple bread of southern Asia, still manage to puff up impressively all by themselves.

As you become confident with these recipes, you can adapt them to suit yourself – adding a few herbs, spices or some dried fruit perhaps. If there was ever a good place to spread your floury wings, it is here. These are such simple, basic breads that before long, making them – and your own variations – will become second nature.

Bread made without yeast

- Soda bread (p.130)
- Walnut and honey bread (p.131)
- Roti (p.133)
- Tortillas (p.134)
- Bannocks (p.137)

Reminder: Oven timings in the recipes relate to fan-assisted ovens.
If using a conventional electric or gas oven (without a fan), increase
the temperature by 15°C (1 Gas Mark). Use an oven thermometer to check
the accuracy of your oven.

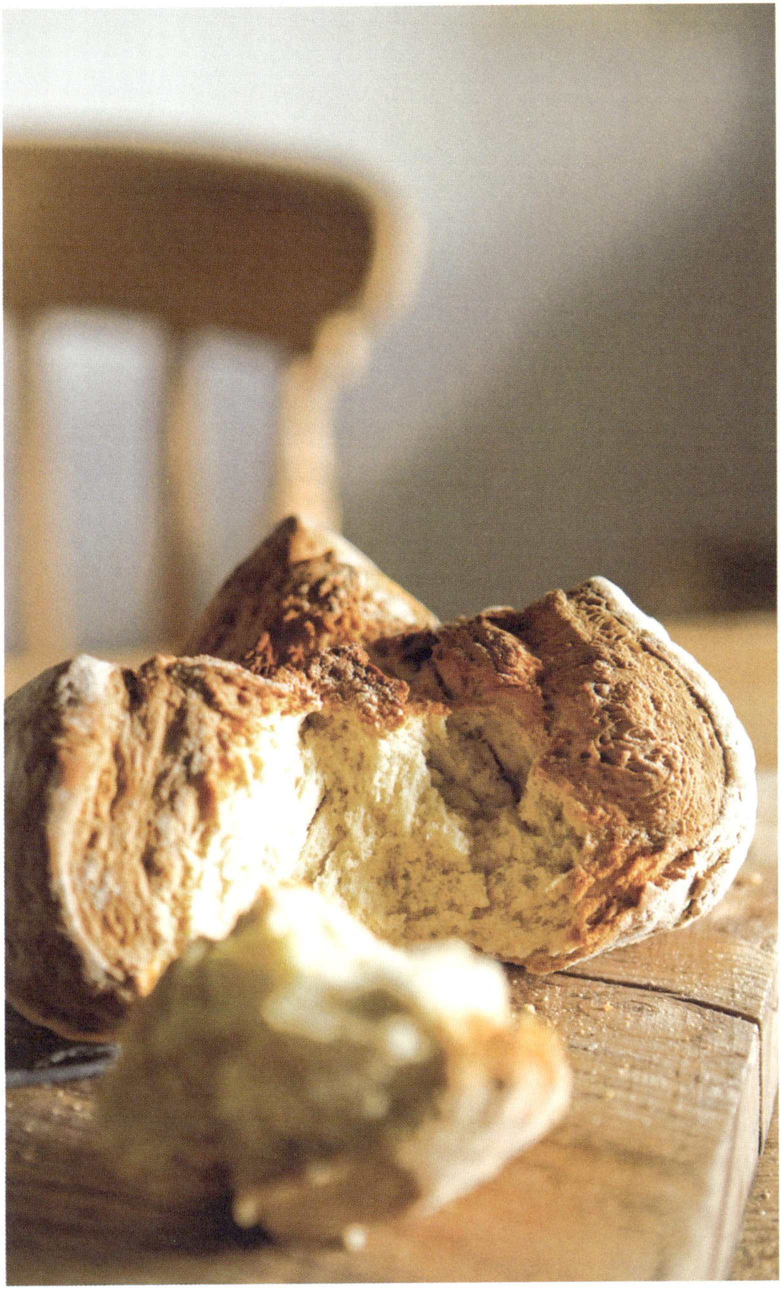

Soda bread

Soda bread is so easy to make. No kneading, no proving – just mix the ingredients together, shape into rough rounds and throw in the oven. Buttermilk is relatively easy to buy, but you can also make this bread with thin yoghurt, milk or water, or any combination of these.

Makes 2 loaves
500g plain white flour, plus extra
 for dusting
10g salt
4 tsp baking powder
300ml buttermilk, thin yoghurt,
 milk or water

For coating
A little flour (rye would be good)

Preheat the oven to 200°C/Gas Mark 6. Combine the dry ingredients in a bowl and mix in the buttermilk or other liquid to make a dough.

Knead briefly, divide into two, then shape into rough rounds. Pat to flatten until about 5cm high, flour the loaves all over and place on a baking tray. Now cut a cross in the top of each loaf, almost through to the bottom, then stab lightly all over.

Bake for 20–25 minutes or until the bread sounds hollow when tapped on the base, then allow to cool for a few minutes on a wire rack. Best eaten warm, with butter.

P.S. If you have time, try making your own buttermilk, which will also give you fresh butter to spread on your bread. Cream will eventually turn to butter when beaten, but it takes a while. Using a food mixer, beat 1 litre double cream until it thickens, then stiffens, then eventually (and very suddenly) separates. When it does, pour it through a fine sieve into a bowl. The liquid in the bowl is buttermilk. The residue in the sieve is butter. Squeeze and squidge the butter together, then hold it under cold running water and squeeze it a bit more to rinse off any buttermilk.

Variation
To make brown soda bread, replace the white flour with wholemeal and add a good tablespoonful of black treacle. This makes a sweeter, slightly heavier bread – excellent with a pint of Guinness and an Irish stew.

Walnut and honey bread

This is a lovely flavoured soda bread to serve with cheese. To vary the flavour, you could replace the honey with the same quantity of dried fruit (dates are excellent), and replace half the water with apple juice.

Makes 2 loaves
200g honey
200g walnuts
500g plain wholemeal flour, plus extra for dusting
10g salt
4 tsp baking powder
300ml water

Preheat the oven to 200°C/Gas Mark 6. Soften the honey in a pan over a gentle heat. Using a pestle and mortar, crush half of the walnuts very finely, almost to a powder. Crush the other half very coarsely. This gives the ideal combination – lots of flavour from the crushed nuts, and texture from the large pieces.

Combine the flour, salt, baking powder and walnuts in a bowl. Add the honey and water, and mix together until evenly combined. Knead briefly to a firm dough.

Divide the dough in two and shape into rough rounds. Flatten to about 5cm high and cut a deep cross in each, almost through to the base. Bake for 20–25 minutes or until the bread sounds hollow when tapped on the base.

Allow the bread to cool a little on a wire rack. If you're wondering what to have it with, a lump of Stilton and a ripe juicy pear would be perfect.

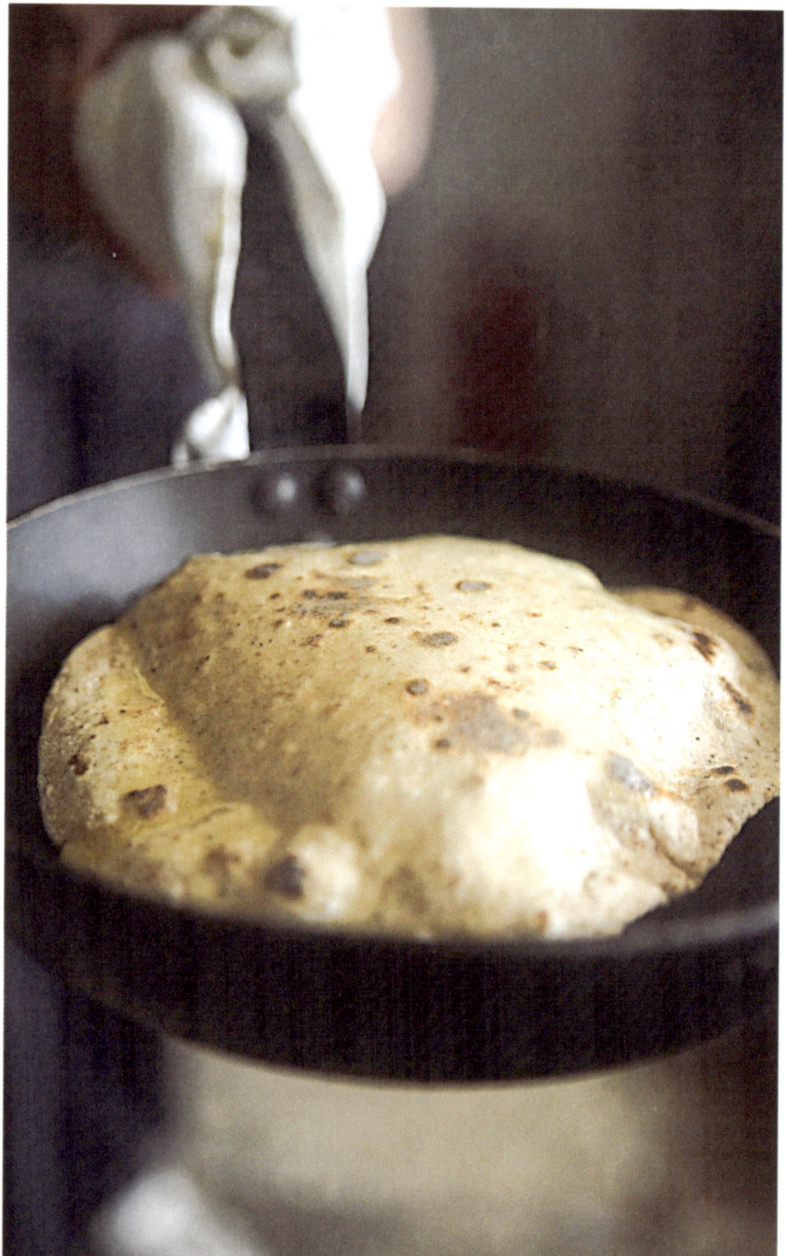

Roti

This is daily bread in India and Nepal, perfect for scooping up stews and curries, and lentils. Once you've grasped the method you will make roti all the time – it is so easy, and the way the bread balloons in the pan will delight and amaze you. If you use wholemeal flour, as I often do, sieve it to remove the coarser bits; your roti will puff up better.

Makes 6
**100g strong brown or wholemeal flour, plus extra for dusting
A small pinch of salt
60ml water
A large knob of butter, melted**

Mix the flour, salt and water together in a bowl and knead between your hands for a couple of minutes until smooth. Divide the dough into six and roll into balls, as round as you can. Place a heavy-based frying pan over a medium heat. Using plenty of flour, roll each ball out to a thin circle, about 15cm across.

When the pan is hot, lay the first roti in. After about half a minute, you should see a few bubbles. Flip the roti over – it should be slightly browned, with the odd dark spot. Cook the other side for another 30 seconds; the bubbles should get bigger. Flip again, and the whole thing should puff up. I say should – about one in three of mine don't quite make it. Turn a couple more times, if you want a bit more colour, then remove and brush with melted butter.

Keep the roti warm, wrapped in a tea towel, while you cook the rest. Serve as soon as they are all ready.

Tortillas

Perfect for wrapping around any food you like for a portable lunch, tortillas are quick and easy to make. This Mexican flatbread was so called by the Spanish conquistadors because it reminded them of the classic omelettes from their homeland. If your tortilla reminds you of an omelette, throw it away and start again... it has gone badly wrong.

Makes 8
250g plain white flour, plus extra for dusting
5g salt
150ml water

Mix the ingredients together in a bowl to form a rough dough. Knead for a few minutes, until the dough is smooth and no longer sticky. Cover and leave to rest for about half an hour; this relaxes the gluten and makes the dough easier to roll out.

Divide the dough into eight and shape each piece into a round. Lightly flour the work surface and roll the rounds out thinly – to a 2–3mm thickness. Place a large frying pan over a medium heat, and have ready a clean tea towel.

When the pan is hot, lay a tortilla in it and cook for half a minute or so, until the underside is patched with dark brown. Flip over and cook for another 30 seconds, then wrap it in the tea towel while you cook the next one. Keep adding the tortillas to the tea towel as you cook them – this holds the steam in as they cool, and keeps them soft.

If you are not planning on eating the tortillas straight away, wrap them in foil to stop them drying out. When ready to serve, reheat in a low oven at 140°C/Gas Mark 1, still wrapped in foil, until just warm.

Variation

Corn tortillas are made in the same way – just substitute cornmeal (maize meal) for wheat flour. To turn corn tortillas into nachos, cut them into wedges. Heat some oil for deep-frying in a suitable pan to 175°C (the temperature at which a cube of bread will turn golden brown in a minute). Deep-fry the nachos for up to a minute, until crispy. Drain on kitchen paper and serve with a dip or two, such as beetroot houmous (see p.178) or taramasalata (see p.179).

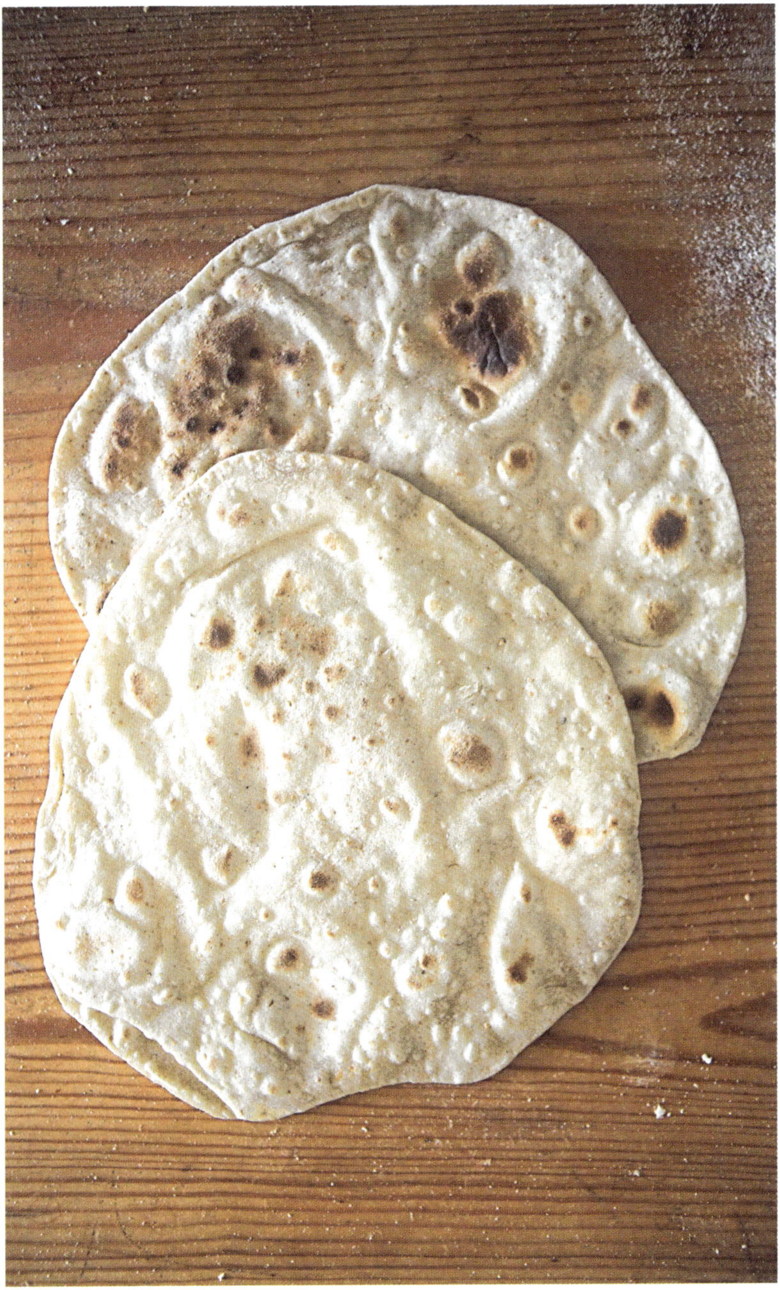

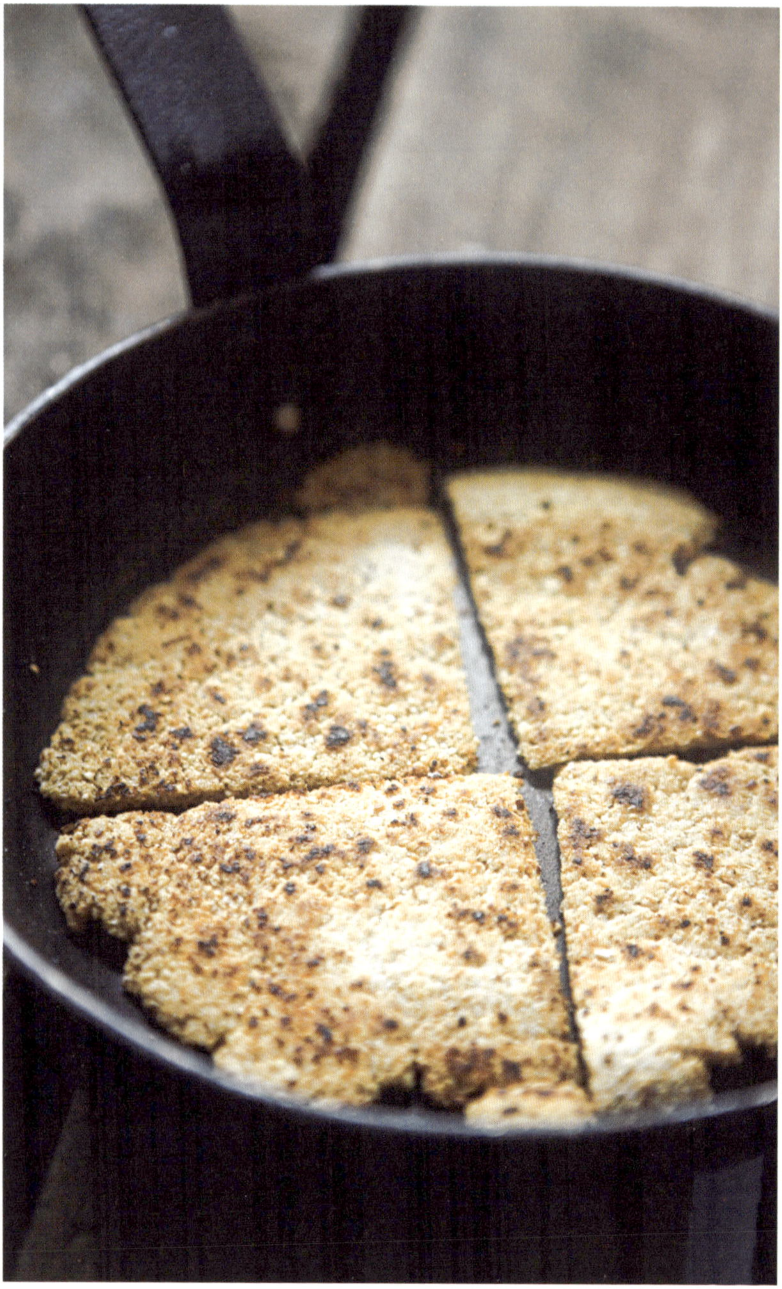

Bannocks

This Scottish, oaty, frying-pan bread should be made fast and eaten warm. You can store bannocks and reheat them later, but they are better served straight away. I love to eat them in winter, with butter and thick soup. Have the rest of your lunch ready and make the bannocks at the last minute.

Makes 2
125g medium oatmeal, plus extra
    for dusting
A small pinch of salt
A slightly bigger pinch of
    baking powder
About 2 tsp melted bacon fat (or lard,
    butter or oil), plus a little extra for
    greasing the pan
3–4 tbsp hot water

Mix the oatmeal, salt and baking powder together in a bowl and pour in the melted fat, along with enough water to mix to a stiff paste. Place a heavy-based frying pan over a medium heat.

Dust your work surface with oatmeal and scrape the mixture on to it. Sprinkle with more oatmeal and divide the dough in two. Roll each out to a round, a little less than ½cm thick. You'll need to work fast because the dough stiffens as it cools. Cut each round into quarters.

Add a little fat to the hot pan, and cook the bannocks, one at a time (that is four quarters together), for a couple of minutes on each side. Eat warm, with butter.

Buns, Biscuits & Batter Breads

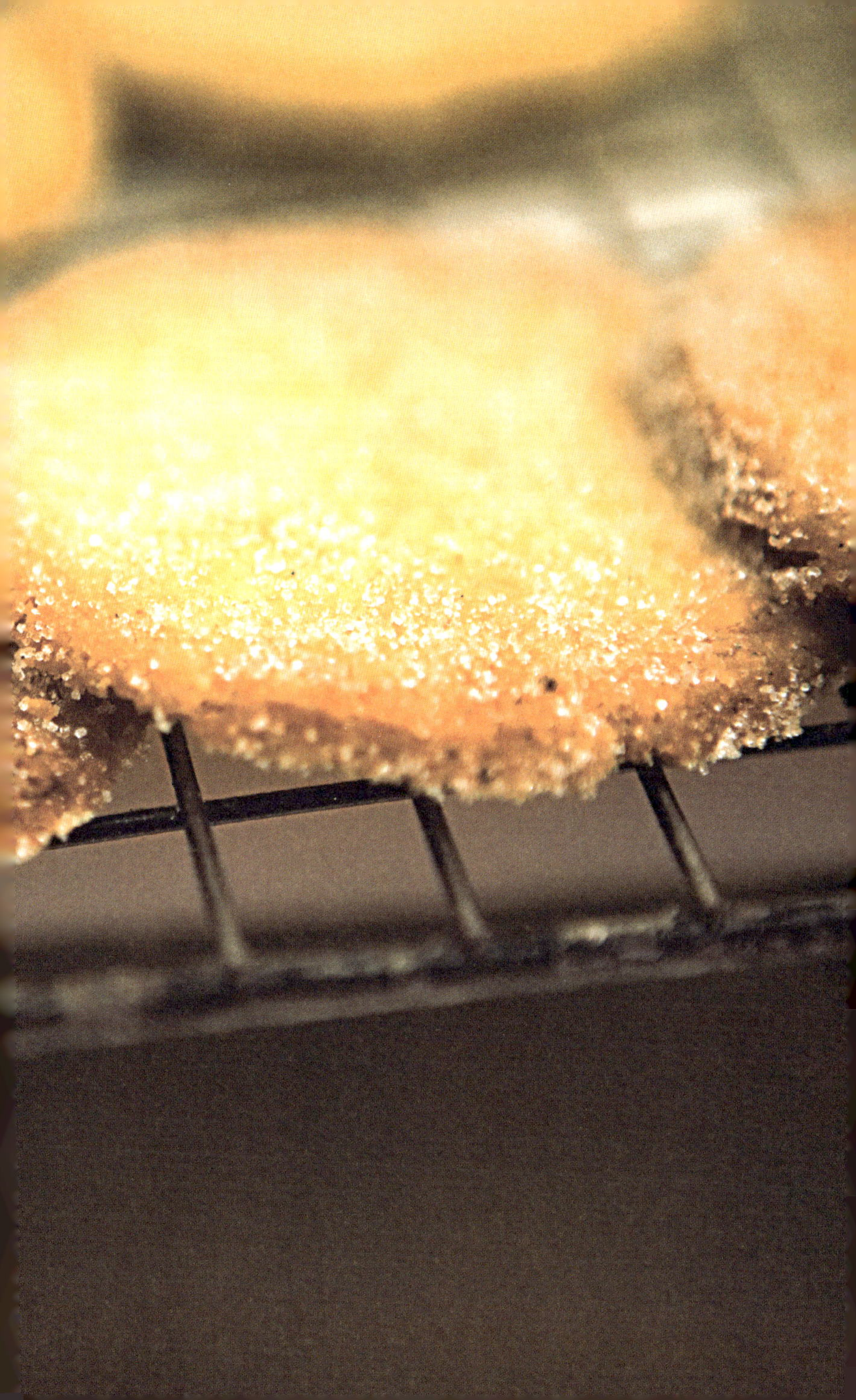

This collection

of recipes goes beyond a basic flour-and-water dough, to include enriched doughs and batter breads. I've also been liberal with the definition of 'bread' here by including a few biscuits, which is entirely for your benefit, of course. Guests will be awestruck when you offer handmade oatcakes and spelt digestives with the port and Stilton, rather than 'assorted biscuits for cheese'… with the best ones gone.

Now is the time to try your hand at English teatime classics, such as lardy cake, hot cross buns and Chelsea buns. Enriched with eggs and butter (or lard) and enlivened with fruit and spice, these are truly delicious. And everyone should know the pleasure of a homemade doughnut – still hot and buried in sugar. Doughnuts are made in much the same way as bread rolls, up to the point where you deep-fry them, of course.

Croissants are rather more time-consuming and a little tricky, but perhaps not as difficult as you might think. Get it right, and it may well be the proudest moment of your culinary life. But take my advice – do not make croissants if you are in a really hot kitchen, in a hurry, or in a bad mood. They will not work.

The batter breads, which include crumpets and blinis, are all cooked in a frying pan or on a griddle and are relatively easy to make. There is no kneading, or concern about perfect rising. In truth, you can wow your friends with little skill or precision on your part. Not that I'm suggesting you lack skill or precision, of course… I'm just suggesting you save it for the croissants.

Buns, biscuits & batter breads

- Doughnuts (p.142)
- Churros (p.144)
- Croissants (p.147)
- Lardy cake (p.151)
- Hot cross buns (p.152)
- Chelsea buns (p.154)
- Scones (p.156)
- River Cottage shortbread (p.158)
- Spelt digestives (p.161)
- Poppy and caraway crackers (p.163)
- Scottish oatcakes (p.164)
- Crumpets (p.165)
- Cornbread (p.167)
- Blinis (p.168)
- Staffordshire oatcakes (p.171)
- Socca (p.172)

Reminder: Oven timings in the recipes relate to fan-assisted ovens.
If using a conventional electric or gas oven (without a fan), increase
the temperature by 15°C (1 Gas Mark). Use an oven thermometer to check
the accuracy of your oven.

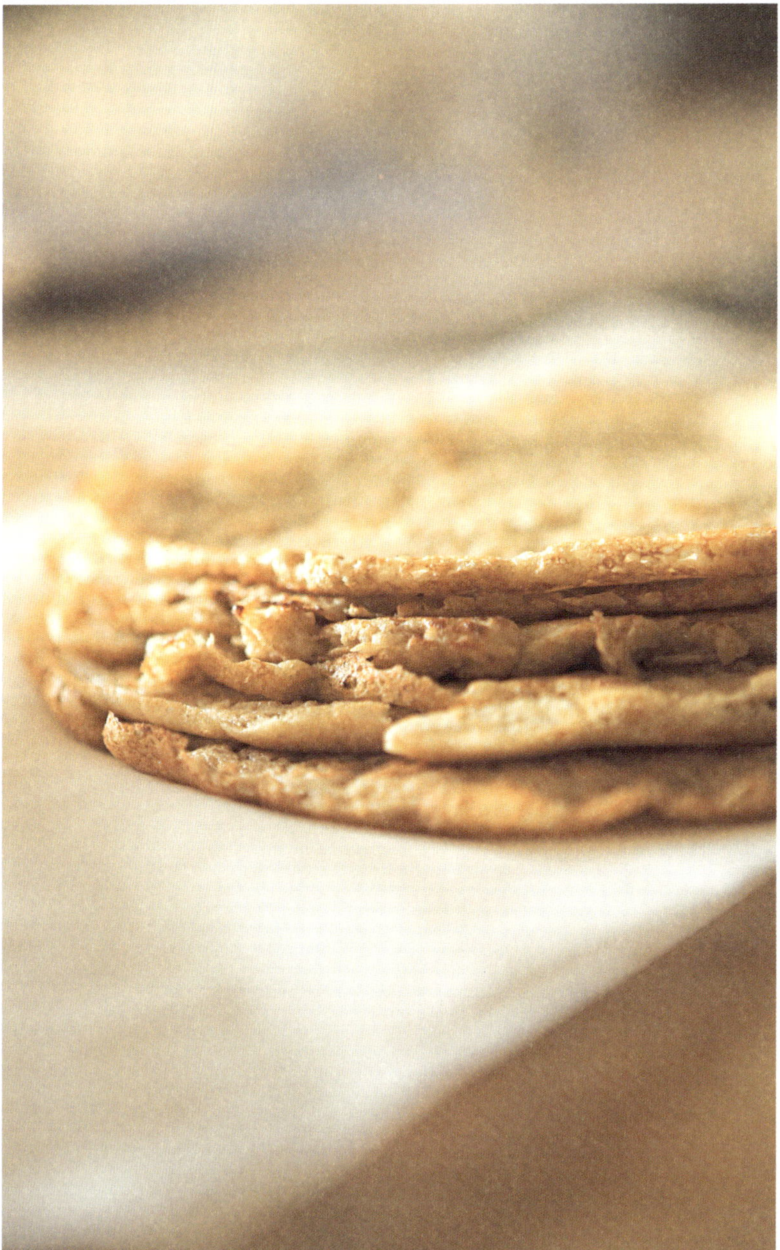

Doughnuts

This method will give you tangerine-sized doughnuts, but you can make them any size you like – simply adjust the frying time accordingly. Little golf-ball-sized doughnuts make a brilliant pudding with something to dip them into – try sieved raspberries and cold custard.

Makes 20

250g strong white bread flour
250g plain white flour
200ml warm milk
100g unsalted butter, softened
100g caster sugar, plus extra for dredging
2 medium free-range eggs
5g powdered dried yeast
10g salt
At least 1 litre sunflower or vegetable oil, for deep-frying

You really need to use a food mixer fitted with a dough hook for this recipe. Mix by hand if you like, but it will be a rather sticky affair. Put the flours, milk, butter, sugar, eggs, yeast and salt into the bowl of the mixer and knead with the dough hook for approximately 10 minutes. Dust the dough with a little flour, turn it out on to a floured surface and shape into a round (see p.48).

Clean and dry the mixing bowl, put the dough back in it and cover with cling film or a plastic bag. Leave to rise until it has doubled in size.

Turn the risen dough out on to the work surface, press out all the air and divide into 20 equal pieces. I find it easiest to weigh them – each piece should be around 50g. Roll them into balls and place on a floured cloth or board. Cover with cling film or a plastic bag and leave to prove until doubled in size.

Heat a 5–8cm depth of oil in a deep, heavy-based saucepan to 175°C; the oil must not fill the pan by more than a third. If you do not have a frying thermometer, check the oil temperature by dropping in a cube of bread; it should turn golden brown in a minute. Deep-fry the dough balls in batches for about 5 minutes, turning them over every now and then so they brown evenly.

Remove the doughnuts from the oil with a slotted spoon and drain well on kitchen paper for half a minute or so. While they are still warm, toss in caster sugar to coat generously. Keep warm while you deep-fry the rest, then enjoy your doughnuts – as soon as possible.

Variations

Add any of the following to the mixer along with the other ingredients:
- Finely grated zest of 1 lemon or orange
- 1 tsp natural vanilla extract (or use vanilla sugar rather than caster sugar)
- 2 tsp ground cinnamon (ideally freshly ground in a spice mill)

You could also flavour the sugar the doughnuts are tossed in with ground cinnamon, ground star anise, or ground mixed spice. Or fill your doughnuts with some runny jam, using a syringe or small piping bag fitted with a thin nozzle.

Churros

Traditionally eaten for breakfast in Spain, churros are deep-fried and tossed in sugar like doughnuts, but they are made with a thick, non-yeast batter rather than a risen dough. Eat them with coffee or dipped in hot chocolate, as the Spanish do.

Serves 4
300g plain white flour
1 tsp baking powder
A good pinch of salt
375ml boiling water
At least 1 litre sunflower or vegetable oil, for deep-frying
Caster sugar, for dredging

Mix the flour, baking powder and salt together in a mixing bowl. Add the boiling water and beat with a wooden spoon until smooth. Transfer to a saucepan and cook gently for a couple of minutes, stirring, until the mixture comes away from the side of the pan. Cover and leave to rest for half an hour.

Heat the oil in a suitable deep, heavy-based saucepan to 175°C; it must be at least 3cm deep, but not fill the pan by more than a third. If you do not have a frying thermometer, check the oil temperature by dropping in a cube of bread; it should turn golden brown in a minute.

Traditionally, the mixture is piped straight into the oil and you can do this if you wish, using a piping bag fitted with a 3cm nozzle. You'll need to deep-fry the churros a few at a time. Carefully pipe lengths (as long as you like), straight into the hot oil. Alternatively, drop tablespoonfuls of the mixture into the oil. Fry, turning every now and then, for 3–4 minutes until golden all over.

Remove the churros with a slotted spoon and drain on kitchen paper, then toss in a bowl of caster sugar. Serve as soon as possible, while still warm.

BUNS, BISCUITS & BATTER BREADS 145

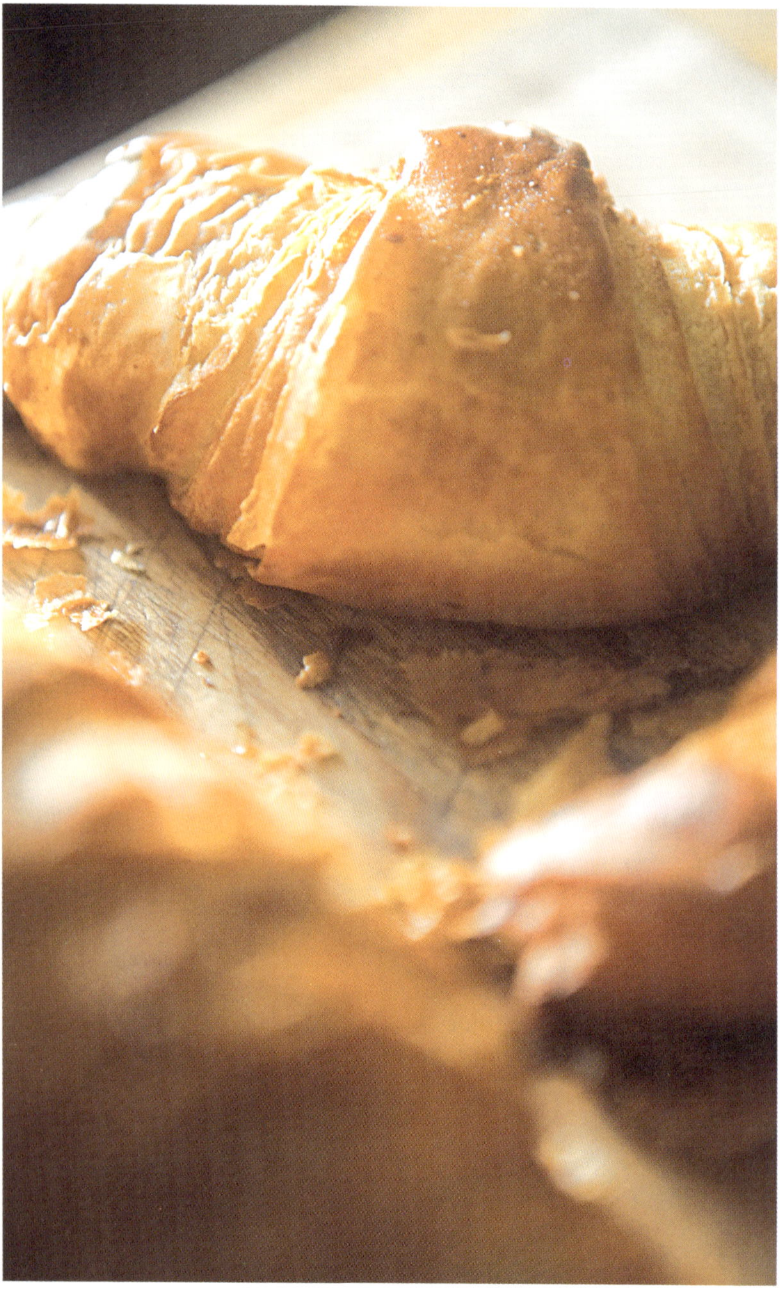

Croissants

I love croissants and everything about them. They take their name, which translates as 'crescent', from their shape of course. It also means growing or rising, which fits nicely because they billow beautifully in the oven.

The technique for making croissants is somewhat similar to puff pastry in that a sheet of butter is sandwiched in the dough, which is repeatedly rolled and folded to produce hundreds of wafer-thin layers. It is best to start the night before, as you need the dough to be cold when you roll it. If too warm and soft, it ruptures easily squeezing out butter everywhere.

Makes about 24–28
1kg strong white bread flour, plus extra for dusting
20g salt
330ml warm water
330ml warm milk
10g powdered dried yeast
140g caster sugar
500g unsalted butter

For the glaze
2 medium free-range egg yolks
50ml milk

It is best to use a food mixer for the first stage as the dough will be soft, sticky and difficult to knead by hand. So, put all the ingredients, except the butter, into the mixer bowl and fit the dough hook. Knead on low to medium speed until the dough is soft, stretchy and satiny – about 10 minutes. Put the dough in a decent-sized polythene bag (it needs room to rise), suck out the air, tie a knot in the bag and put it in the fridge to rest overnight.

First thing in the morning, get the butter out of the fridge. You need it to warm up a bit so it is workable, but not soft. The idea is that the dough and butter have a similar degree of firmness.

As soon as it seems ready, lightly flour the butter, lay it between two sheets of cling film and bat it out with a rolling pin to a fairly neat square about 1cm thick. Take your time to get the thickness and shape as even as possible, then put to one side.

Take your dough out of the fridge, flour it and roll out to a rectangle, a little more than twice the size of the butter (allow a couple of centimetres extra all round). Now lay the butter on one half leaving a border, fold the other half over and press down all the way round to seal the butter in.

(continued overleaf)

1

2

3

4

148 BREAD

Next, roll the dough away from you until it is twice its original length, then fold the top and bottom edges in by one-sixth. Fold them in again by another sixth, so the folds meet in the middle, then fold one on top of the other.

Give the dough a quarter-turn and roll it out again to about the same size as before. Fold the top and bottom edges in to meet at the middle, then fold one on top of the other. Roll this out slightly and seal the edges with the rolling pin.

Put the dough back in the plastic bag and return it to the fridge to rest for an hour or so. (You've given the gluten a good workout and it must relax now, otherwise it will be resistant and uncooperative later.)

In the meantime, you need to cut a template from a piece of cardboard (the back of a cereal box or something similar). You want an isosceles triangle, measuring 20cm across the base and 25cm tall. (The easiest way is to draw an upside down capital T and join the points, like a cartoon sail.)

When your dough has rested, unwrap and roll it out to a neat rectangle, a little larger than 140 x 50cm (pic 1). Now trim the rectangle to these measurements, leaving perfectly straight edges. Cut the rectangle in two lengthwise, to give two 25cm wide strips. Now using your template as a guide, cut 12–14 triangles from each strip (pic 2).

Lay each triangle pointing away from you and roll up from the base (pic 3). Wet the pointed end and seal it. Curl the tips around to form a crescent and pinch them together to hold them in place (pic 4); or you can leave them straight if you prefer. (At this point you could freeze some if you like. Space them out on a tray and freeze, then pack into bags. Allow an extra hour for rising when you come to use them.)

Lay your croissants, with the sealed point underneath, on baking trays lined with greased baking parchment or (better still) silicone mats. Cover with cling film or a bin liner and leave to rise until doubled in size. As the dough is cold, this could take a couple of hours, or longer.

When ready to bake, preheat the oven to 200°C/Gas Mark 6. Beat the egg yolk and milk together, then gently brush all over the croissants. Bake for about 10 minutes, then lower the setting to 170°C/Gas Mark 3 and bake for a further 5–10 minutes until they look beautifully golden. Transfer to a wire rack and let cool slightly, while you make coffee.

P.S. If your work surface isn't large enough to roll the dough out to a 140 x 50cm rectangle, cut it in half. Roll out one portion at a time to a rectangle a little bigger than 70 x 50cm, then cut into strips as above and cut 6 or 7 triangles from each strip, using your template as a guide.

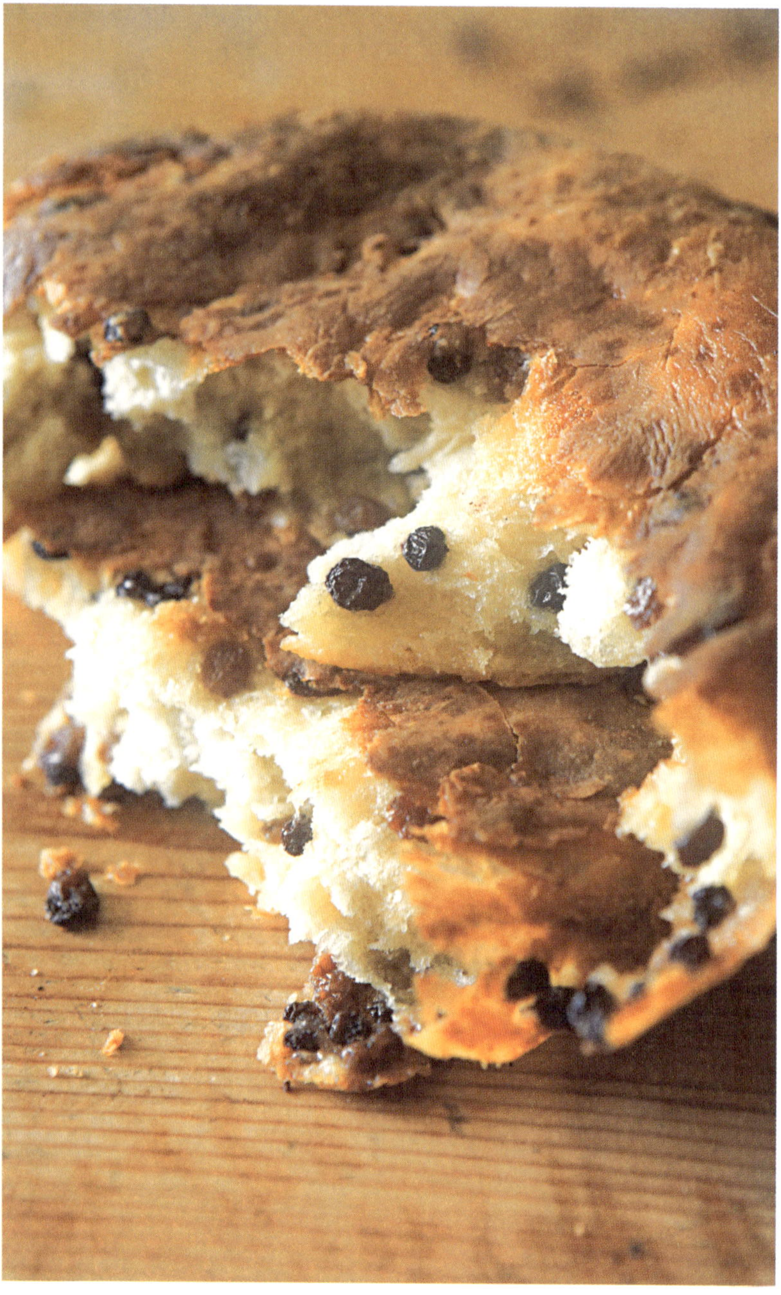

Lardy cake

Apparently, Northumberland lardy cakes are made with milk and currants, while Hampshire lardy cakes have no fruit at all. I have seen Wiltshire lardy cake made with various combinations of dried fruit and spices. Call it what you will, you can be sure of two things: plenty of lard, but no cake – lardy cake is bread. A footnote in Elizabeth David's *English Bread and Yeast Cookery* makes me smile: 'If you can't lay your hands on pure pork lard, don't attempt lardy cakes.' Say no more.

Serves 8

- 250g strong white bread flour, plus extra for dusting
- 150ml warm water
- 5g powdered dried yeast
- 5g salt
- 160g lard
- 50g sultanas
- 50g currants
- 50g chopped candied peel
- 50g caster sugar
- 1 tsp ground cinnamon (ideally freshly ground in a spice mill)

Put the flour, water, yeast and salt into a bowl and mix to a soft dough. Melt 10g of the lard and incorporate it into the dough, then turn out on to a floured surface and knead until smooth and elastic. Put into a clean bowl, cover and leave to rise until doubled in size.

In a separate bowl, toss the dried fruit and candied peel together with the sugar and cinnamon. Cut the rest of the lard into small dice.

Tip the dough out on to a clean work surface and press all over with your fingertips to deflate. Roll out to a rectangle, about 1cm thick. Scatter over half of the dried fruit mixture and lard pieces, then roll up from a short side to enclose the filling.

Give the dough a quarter-turn and roll it out again to a rectangle, as before. Scatter over the remaining fruit and lard and roll up again. Now roll out the dough to a 20cm square and place in a greased deep 20cm square baking tin. Leave to rise for another 30 minutes.

Preheat the oven to 200°C/Gas Mark 6. Bake the lardy cake for 30–40 minutes until well risen and golden brown. Leave to cool slightly in the tin for 10–15 minutes, then invert on to a wire rack to finish cooling. Placing the lardy cake upside down will allow the melted lard to be reabsorbed into the dough as it cools. Serve warm or cold, cut into slices.

Hot cross buns

Freshly baked or toasted, I love these buns and bake a batch whenever it takes my fancy, leaving off the crosses if it isn't Easter. I also like to vary the dried fruit – a mix of chopped dates, cranberries, apricots and cherries is particularly good.

Makes 8

250g strong white bread flour, plus extra for dusting
250g plain white flour
125ml warm water
125ml warm milk
5g powdered dried yeast
10g salt
50g caster sugar
1 medium free-range egg
50g butter
100g raisins, currants or sultanas (or a mixture)
Finely grated zest of ½ orange
1 tsp ground mixed spice

For the crosses
50g plain white flour
100ml water

To finish
1 tbsp apricot (or other) jam, sieved
1 tbsp water

If you have a food mixer, combine the flours, water, milk, yeast, salt and sugar in the bowl and fit the dough hook. Add the egg and butter and mix to a sticky dough. Now add the dried fruit, orange zest and spice and knead on low speed until silky and smooth. (You can do this by hand, but it will be sticky to handle.) Cover the dough and leave to rise in a warm place for about 1 hour until doubled in size.

Knock back the risen dough and divide into 8 equal pieces. Shape into rounds (see p.48) and dust with flour. Place on a floured board, cover with plastic or linen and leave to prove for about half an hour until roughly doubled in size.

Preheat the oven to 200°C/Gas Mark 6. To make the crosses, whisk together the flour and water until smooth, then transfer to a greaseproof paper piping bag and snip off the end to make a fine hole (or use a plastic food bag with a corner snipped off, as I do). Transfer the risen buns to a baking tray and pipe a cross on top of each one, then bake in the oven for 15–20 minutes.

Meanwhile, melt the jam with the water in a pan. Brush over the buns to glaze as you take them from the oven. Transfer to a wire rack to cool. Serve warm, cold or toasted.

BUNS, BISCUITS & BATTER BREADS 153

Chelsea buns

According to Mrs Beeton, Chelsea buns are sweet rolls made with dried fruit... similar to hot cross buns but without the cross. However, these are Chelsea buns as we know them – sticky, curranty, swirly and square.

Makes 9

550g strong white bread flour, plus extra for dusting
50g caster sugar, or vanilla sugar
5g powdered dried yeast
10g salt
150ml warm milk
225g butter, melted
1 medium free-range egg

For the filling
25g butter, melted
100g caster sugar
200g currants

For the glaze
50ml milk
50g caster sugar

In a bowl, combine the flour, sugar, yeast and salt, then add the milk, butter and egg and mix to a sticky dough. Turn out on to a floured surface and knead until smooth and silky. Return to the cleaned bowl, cover and leave to rise for about an hour until doubled in size.

Brush the base and sides of a deep 30cm square baking tin with a little of the melted butter and coat with a little of the sugar (for the filling), shaking out the excess.

Tip the dough out on to a floured surface, dust with flour and roll out to a rectangle, about 60 x 40cm. Brush the melted butter all over the dough to the edges, leaving a 2cm margin free across the top (long) edge. Sprinkle with the sugar and scatter the currants evenly on top, right to the edges, but leaving the top margin clear.

Press the currants into the dough, then starting from the edge closest to you, roll up the dough to enclose the filling and form a long sausage. Moisten the margin at the top with water and press to seal. Cut the roll into 9 equal pieces. Turn each piece on its end and press with your hand to flatten slightly, until no more than 3cm high. Arrange in rows of three in the baking tin – they should just touch each other.

Preheat the oven to 200°C/Gas Mark 6. Leave the buns to prove for about half an hour until doubled in size again. Sprinkle a little of the sugar for the glaze over them and bake for about 20 minutes until golden brown.

Warm the milk and remaining sugar together in a pan until dissolved, then brush over the buns to glaze when you take them out of the oven. Best served warm.

BUNS, BISCUITS & BATTER BREADS 155

Scones

Of course you can put what you like on your scones, but I'll usually opt for a cream tea. Cream tea etiquette is fiercely disputed in the West Country. The Cornish put strawberry jam on their scones first, then the cream; in Devon and Dorset it is customary to do it the other way round. Personally, I prefer raspberry jam and I always put jam on first… even though I live on the Devon/Dorset border.

Makes about 8

300g plain white flour, plus extra for dusting
2 tsp baking powder
A good pinch of salt
75g unsalted butter, at cool room temperature (neither fridge-cold nor soft), cut into cubes
50g caster sugar
1 medium free-range egg
1 tsp natural vanilla extract
120ml double cream
A little milk, for brushing

Preheat the oven to 200°C/Gas Mark 6. Using a food processor if you have one, whiz together the flour, baking powder, salt, butter and sugar until the mixture resembles fine breadcrumbs. (Otherwise, sift the flour, salt and baking powder into a mixing bowl, rub in the butter with your fingers, then stir in the sugar.)

In a separate bowl, beat the egg, vanilla and cream together, then add to the rubbed-in mixture and bring together with your hands to form a soft dough.

Turn the dough out on to a floured surface and knead very briefly, for 10 seconds or so, to make it a little smoother. Now, using a little more flour, pat or gently roll out to a thickness of about 4cm.

Using a 6 or 7cm pastry cutter (or a larger one, if you like), cut out about 8 scones – pressing the cutter straight down, rather than twisting it, as this gives the scones a better chance of rising straight up.

Lay the discs on a lightly greased baking sheet, brush the tops with milk and bake for about 15 minutes, or a little longer if the scones are large. To check that they are cooked, insert a wooden cocktail stick into the middle; it should come out clean. Transfer to a wire rack to cool for a few minutes, then serve warm.

BUNS, BISCUITS & BATTER BREADS 157

River Cottage shortbread

This is quite different from a traditional thick Scottish shortbread. Rather than rubbing butter into flour then adding sugar in the usual way, we cream the butter with the sugar first as you would for a sponge cake, which makes the mixture really light. We also add egg yolks, and roll the dough out thinly – to make rich, delicate biscuits.

Makes about 24
175g butter, softened
90g caster sugar, plus extra
    for sprinkling
A generous pinch of salt
2 medium free-range egg yolks
200g plain white flour, plus extra
    for dusting

Flavourings (optional)
One (or more) of the following:
    1 tsp natural vanilla extract
    Grated zest of 1 lemon or orange
    1 tsp ground cinnamon (ideally
        freshly ground)

In a food mixer fitted with the paddle beater, or using a hand-held electric beater, cream the butter and sugar together on medium-high speed until very pale (almost white) and fluffy, scraping the sides down regularly with a spatula.

Lower the speed to medium, and add the salt, egg yolks and any extra flavourings at this stage. Beat for another half a minute, then switch the machine off. Fold the flour into the mixture, using a spatula. You will have a very soft sticky dough.

With floured hands, scrape the dough out of the bowl on to a floured surface. Pat it into a wide, flat disc, using more flour if you need to, then wrap in cling film and refrigerate for about 1 hour, as the dough needs to firm up before you can roll it out.

Preheat the oven to 180°C/Gas Mark 4. Unwrap the dough and roll it out on a floured surface to a thickness of about 3mm. Using a 6cm pastry cutter, cut out about 24 rounds. With a palette knife, carefully transfer them to a non-stick baking sheet, or one lined with baking parchment.

Bake for 7–10 minutes, until just golden around the edges, but pale on top, checking every minute after 7 minutes. The shortbread biscuits will still be soft; they firm up on cooling. As you remove them from the oven, sprinkle generously all over with caster sugar. Leave on the baking sheet for a minute or two, then carefully transfer to a wire rack to cool.

P.S. These delicate biscuits will keep for a couple of days in an airtight container.

BUNS, BISCUITS & BATTER BREADS 159

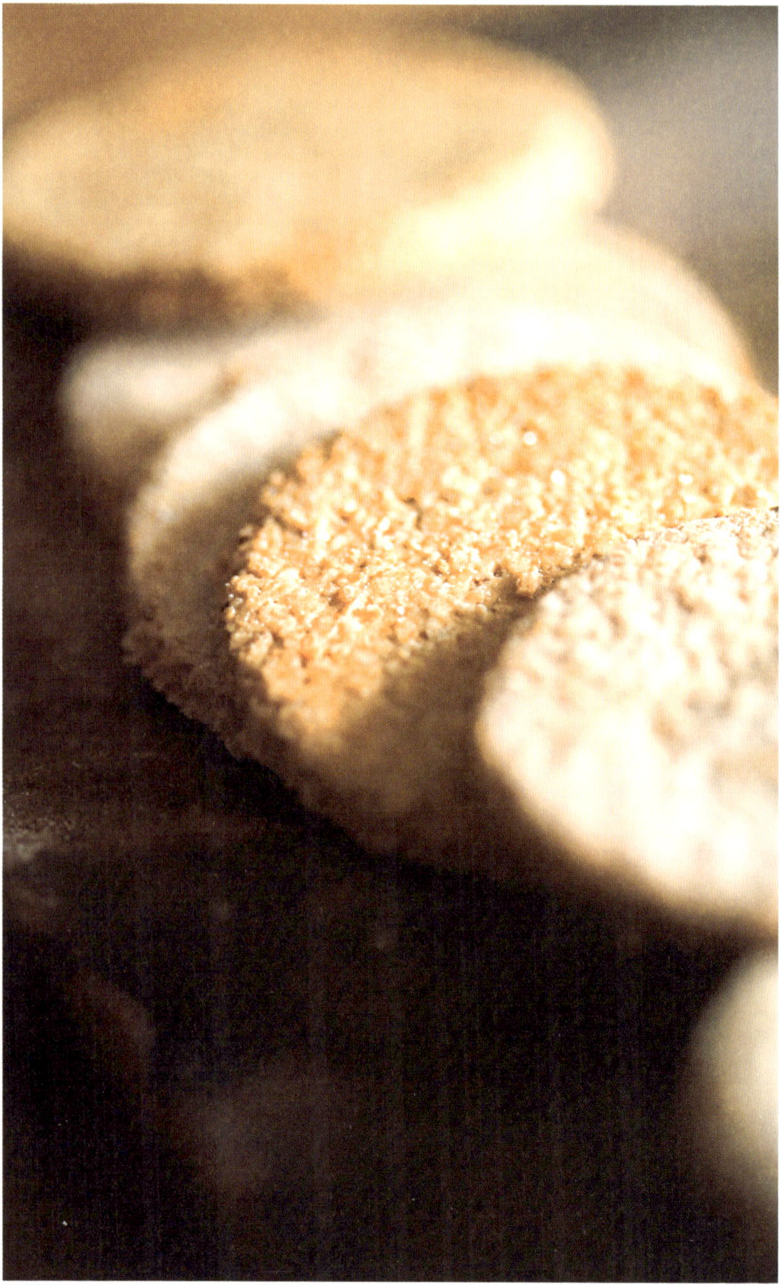

Spelt digestives

We often make these at River Cottage, usually to serve with cheese, but they are also delicious with cold meats, particularly pâtés and terrines. We prefer a less sweet biscuit with meats, so we reduce the sugar content slightly. I have given both options here.

Makes about 40
250g unsalted butter, softened
250g spelt flour, plus extra for dusting
250g medium oatmeal
125g soft brown sugar (or 100g for a less sweet biscuit)
10g salt
2 tsp baking powder
A little milk, to mix

Rub the butter into the flour until it resembles fine breadcrumbs; the easiest way to do this is in a food processor, if you have one. Add the oatmeal, sugar, salt and baking powder, and mix together until evenly combined. Add enough milk, a few drops at a time, to bind the mixture and form a slightly sticky dough.

Turn the dough out on to a lightly floured surface and dust with more flour, then press into a round, flat disc. Wrap in cling film and refrigerate for at least half an hour, to rest and firm up a bit. (This dough will keep well in the fridge for a few days, but it will become rock-hard, so if prepared ahead you'll need to let it soften out of the fridge before you roll it out.)

When ready to cook, preheat the oven to 180°C/Gas Mark 4. Flour the dough well and lay it between two sheets of greaseproof paper or cling film. (As the dough is sticky and brittle, this makes it much easier to handle.) Roll it out carefully to a thickness of 3–4mm, dusting regularly with flour to stop it sticking.

Using a 7cm pastry cutter, cut out about 40 rounds and lay them on non-stick baking sheets, or ones lined with baking parchment. Bake for 7–10 minutes, checking regularly after 7 minutes; the biscuits should be brown around the edges and lightly coloured on top. Leave on the baking sheet for a minute or two, then carefully transfer to a wire rack to cool.

P.S. These biscuits will keep for several days in an airtight container.

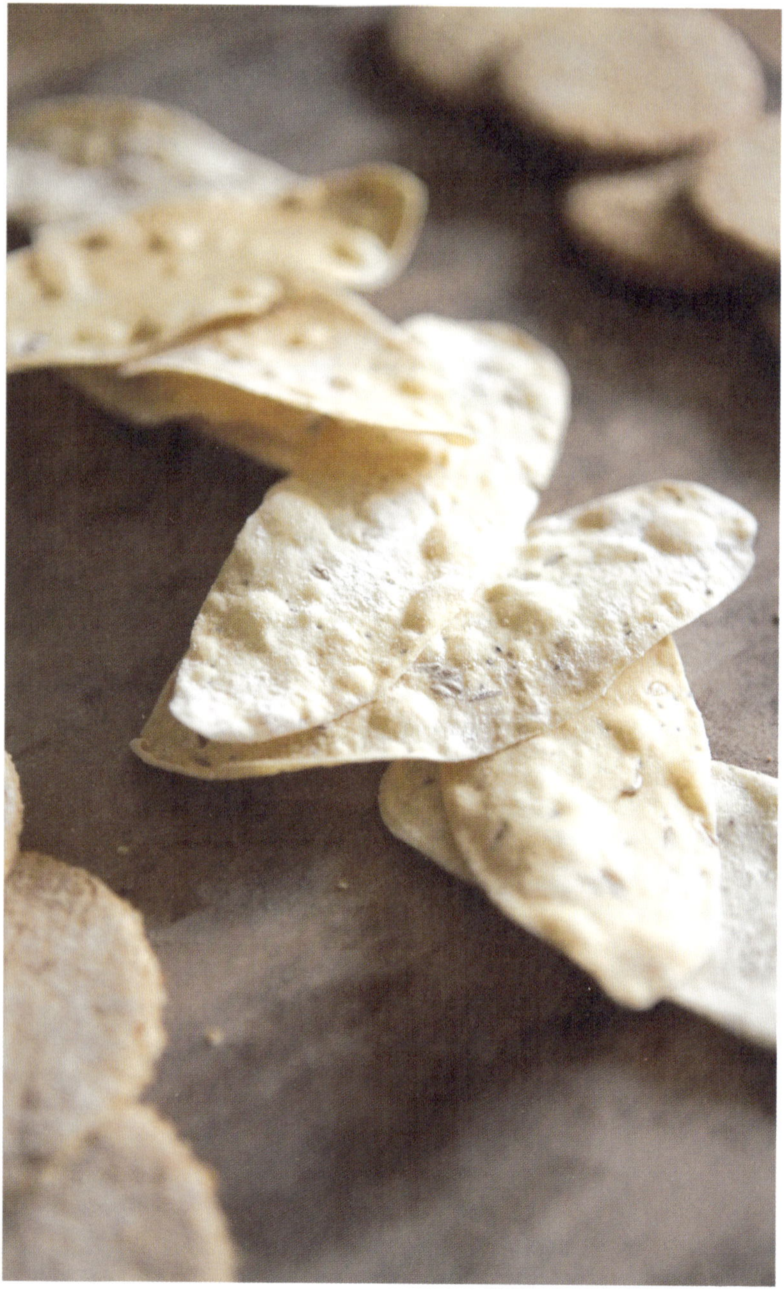

Poppy and caraway crackers

These are tasty, crispy and light as a feather. So light, in fact, that you should switch the oven fan off if you have one – they have a tendency to take off.

Makes about 25

250g plain white flour, plus extra for dusting
½ tsp baking powder
½ tsp poppy seeds
½ tsp caraway seeds
½ tsp salt
40ml olive or sunflower oil
100ml water

In a bowl, mix all the dry ingredients together, then make a well in the middle and add the oil and water. Gradually mix together until evenly combined and bring together to form a rough dough. Knead briefly, using more flour if you need to; the dough should be soft, but not sticky. Wrap in cling film and leave to rest in the fridge for half an hour or so.

Preheat the oven to 180°C/Gas Mark 4. Lightly flour your work surface, then roll the dough out until about 5mm thick. Using a 5cm cutter, cut out about 25 rounds, then roll out each round again, in one direction, as thinly as you can. Lay them on baking sheets and bake for up to 10 minutes, but be watchful – it is easy to overcook these crackers. They are ready when they are just showing the first signs of browning, but still predominantly pale.

P.S. These crackers don't keep very well once cooked, so if you don't think you need this quantity, it is best to freeze half of the dough.

Scottish oatcakes

This is one version – and there are many – of the classic Scottish biscuit. I have made oatcakes simply with oatmeal and cold water, as I suppose was once customary. I quite liked them, but they were terribly fragile. Using hot water softens the oats, and the oil helps to bind them.

Makes about 20

140g medium oatmeal, plus extra for dusting
140g porridge oats
A little pinch of salt
75ml sunflower oil
About 2 tbsp just-boiled water

Preheat the oven to 180°C/Gas Mark 4. Mix all the dry ingredients together in a bowl. Add the oil and enough hot water to mix to a firm dough. Pat into a flat disc, cover and leave for 10 minutes or so – this makes the dough a little easier to roll.

Dust your work surface and the dough with oatmeal and roll out until it is about 5mm thick. Using a 6cm cutter, cut out about 20 discs. Place on baking sheets and bake for about 20 minutes until just browned at the edges. Leave on the trays for about 5 minutes to firm up, then transfer to a wire rack to cool. Either eat straight away, with cheese if you like, or keep for up to a few days in an airtight container.

Crumpets

Crumpets are an English teatime classic, not for a refined cucumber-sandwich-and-best-china tea, but eaten fireside with a big pot of tea – and very likely butter down your shirt. To make real crumpets, you need metal crumpet rings to hold the batter in while they are cooking. If you don't have any suitable metal rings, try the variation for pikelets below.

Makes about 12

450g plain white flour (approximately)
350ml warm milk
350ml warm water (approximately)
5g powdered dried yeast
10g salt
1 tsp baking powder
A little sunflower or vegetable oil

In a bowl, whisk together the flour, milk, water and yeast. You will end up with a rather runny batter (the consistency of single cream). Cover with cling film or a plastic bag and leave to one side for at least an hour, until it is really bubbly. You can leave it for 3 or 4 hours if it suits you.

When you are ready for tea, heat a large, heavy-based frying pan or flat griddle over a medium-high heat. Whisk the salt and baking powder into the batter. Grease your crumpet rings and pan, using a scrunched-up piece of kitchen paper dipped in oil.

Now I suggest you do a test run. Put one crumpet ring in the pan, fill to just below the top and see what happens. If the batter is the correct consistency, it should stay contained within the ring and lots of holes should appear on the surface after a minute or two. (If it dribbles out underneath, the batter is too thin so whisk in a little more flour. If lots of holes don't appear, the batter is probably too thick, so whisk in a little water.) Do another test run if necessary.

After 5 minutes or so, when the surface is just set, flip the crumpet over, ring and all. (If the base is too dark, turn the heat down.) Cook for 2–3 minutes until golden on the other side. Once you have a successful test run, cook your crumpets in batches. Either butter and eat straight away, or cool on a wire rack for toasting later.

Variation

To make pikelets, whisk another 50g flour into the batter to stiffen it, so you won't need to use crumpet rings to prevent it spreading out like a pancake. Dollop spoonfuls of this batter into your greased pan and cook for a couple of minutes only on each side. Pikelets will be less than half the thickness of crumpets.

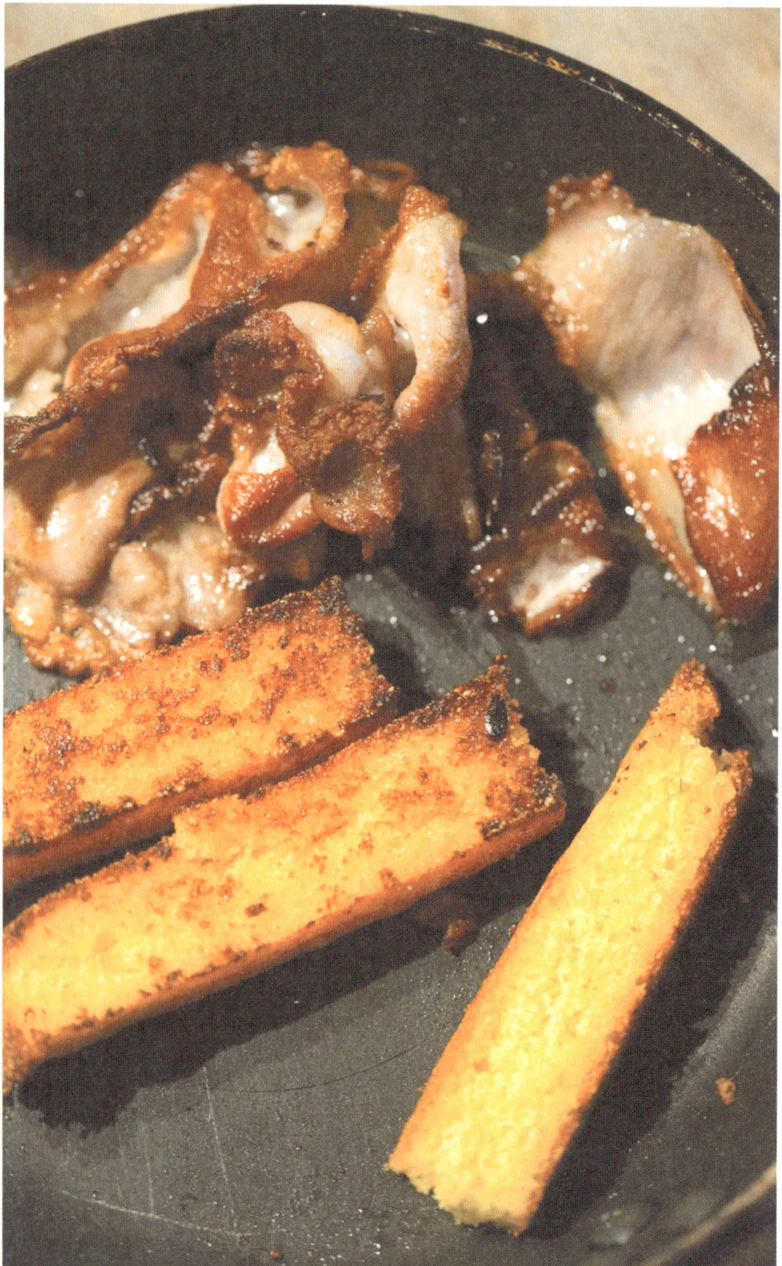

Cornbread

Cornbread is delicious, one of the defining tastes of the Deep South of America. It is traditionally made with bacon fat, but butter and lard are both excellent substitutes. Eat it warm with butter, or fry slices in butter or bacon fat. Cornbread would be at home at a barbecue – alongside a sticky rack of ribs and a big salad. Or try it my favourite way (see below).

Makes 1
250g cornmeal (maize meal)
10g baking powder
5g salt
1 tbsp bacon fat, butter or lard,
    plus an extra 1 tbsp for cooking
125ml milk
125ml yoghurt

Preheat the oven to 180°C/Gas Mark 4. Place a good heavy-based medium ovenproof frying pan over a medium heat to warm up.

Meanwhile, mix the cornmeal, baking powder and salt together in a large bowl. Melt the bacon fat or other fat in a small saucepan, then add the milk and yoghurt. Warm through, then add to the dry ingredients and stir it all together.

Melt the 1 tbsp fat for cooking in the frying pan, then immediately pour in the cornbread mixture. Let it cook for a minute, then transfer to the oven and bake for about 20 minutes, until firm and golden. You can eat it straight away or leave it to cool for a while if you prefer.

P.S. To make my perfect breakfast (for one or two, depending on appetite): wipe out the pan you made the cornbread in and cook 5–6 rashers of smoked dry-cured bacon until crispy; remove and keep warm. Add ½ finely diced small onion to the pan with a knob of butter and fry over a medium heat until soft and golden. Meanwhile, strip the kernels from a corn cob and cook in boiling water for 2 minutes. Drain and toss with the onions. Season with salt and a good grinding of pepper, and serve with the bacon, cornbread and maple syrup. To turn breakfast into supper, serve after sundown with a large sip of bourbon.

Blinis

These traditional Russian pancakes are properly made with buckwheat flour. At River Cottage, we love to make blinis but rarely have buckwheat, so we use a mix of rye and wheat flours. They are totally delicious.

Makes about 12 (or 50 mini-blinis)

- 225ml milk
- 200ml natural yoghurt or crème fraîche
- 2 large free-range eggs, separated
- 100g rye flour
- 100g strong white bread flour
- 1 tsp salt
- 5g powdered dried yeast
- A little melted butter or sunflower oil, for greasing

Warm the milk and yoghurt or crème fraîche together in a pan until just tepid, then remove from the heat and whisk in the egg yolks.

In a mixing bowl, whisk together the flours, salt, milk mix and yeast until smooth. Cover with cling film and leave for at least an hour to ferment. You can leave it for 3 or 4 hours, if you like.

When ready to cook, heat a large, heavy-based frying pan or flat griddle over a medium-high heat. Whisk the egg whites in a separate bowl until stiff, then stir a spoonful into your bubbling batter to loosen it. Now gently fold in the rest of the egg whites.

Grease the pan with a scrunched-up piece of kitchen paper dipped in melted butter or oil. Dollop tablespoonfuls of the batter into the pan – as many as you can fit, but not too close together as they will spread slightly. Cook for a minute or so, then flip over and cook for another minute. Remove and keep warm, wrapped in a cloth, while you cook the rest. Serve hot, with butter or savoury toppings.

Variation

'Mini-blinis' – teaspoonful-sized dollops that cook in half the time – make excellent party food. Top them with smoked salmon and crème fraîche, or caviar perhaps, or the River Cottage way – with slices of home-cured mackerel and a little dill yoghurt.

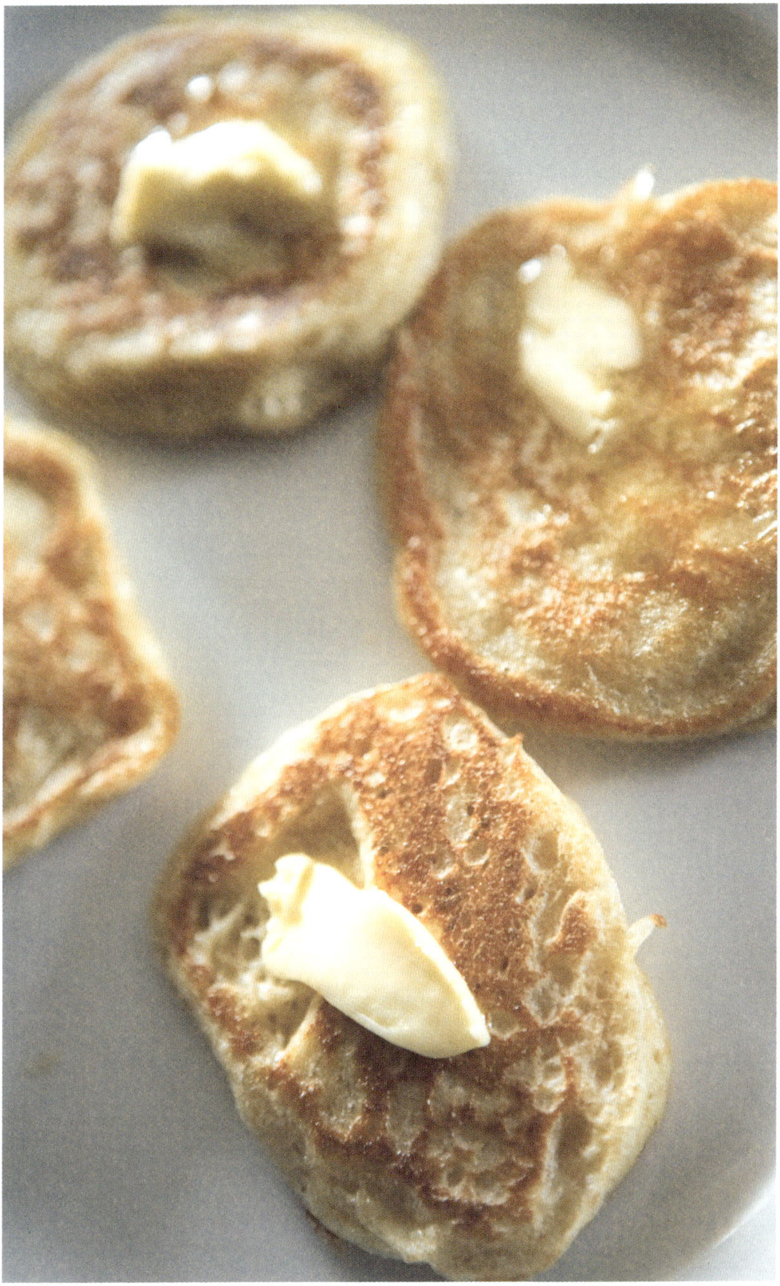

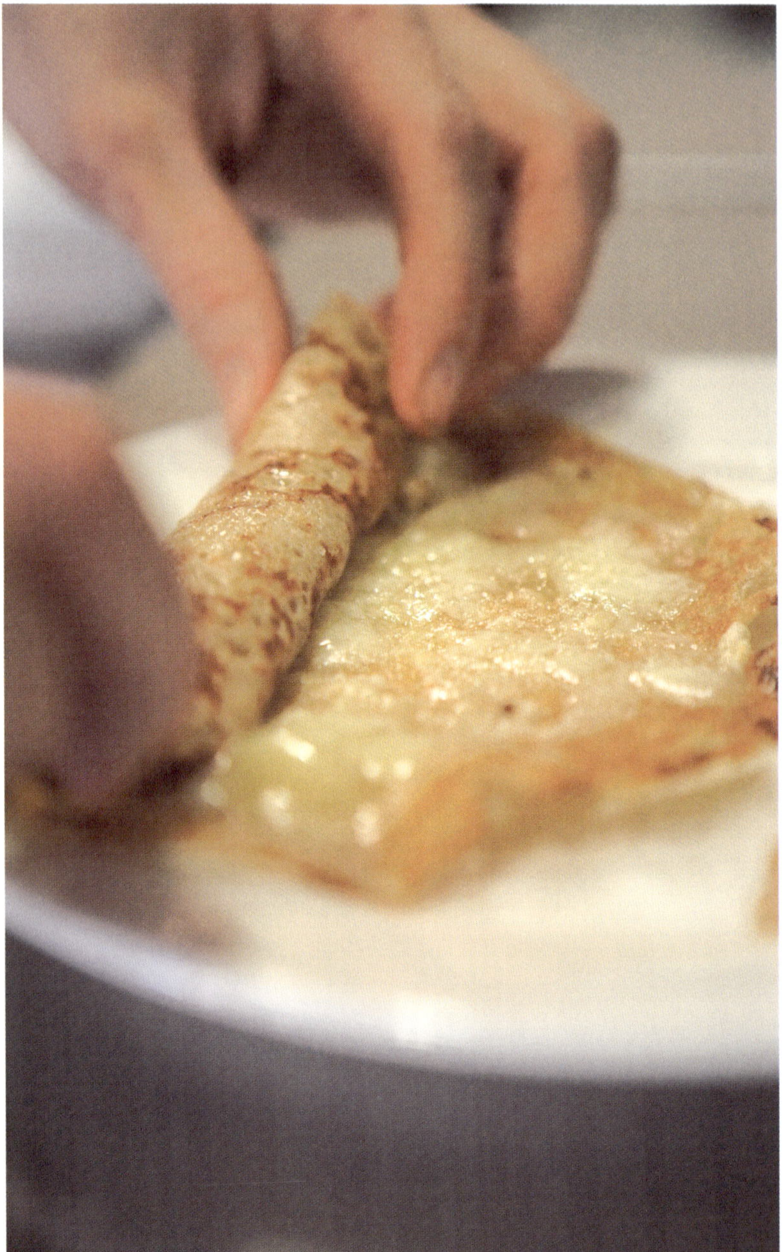

Staffordshire oatcakes

My best friend at university came from a village near Stoke-on-Trent. He loved Staffordshire oatcakes, which we ate for breakfast on Sundays – three each, stacked up with the 'full English', plus loads of ketchup. They also make a great lunch (two is more than enough) rolled around cheesy béchamel sauce and bacon lardons, with some salad on the side. Make a whole batch and cook as many as you need – the batter keeps well in the fridge or freezer. I've also found that cooked oatcakes can be warmed in the oven or in a pan successfully.

Makes 10–12
225g wholemeal flour
225g fine oatmeal
500ml warm water
500ml warm milk

5g powdered dried yeast
10g salt
A little sunflower (or other) oil

Whisk everything together, except the oil, in a large bowl until smooth. At this stage the batter will seem too thin, but it will thicken as the oatmeal swells. Cover and leave for at least an hour, until the batter is really bubbly and frothy.

Heat a large, heavy-based frying pan over a medium-high heat, then grease it with a scrunched-up piece of kitchen paper dipped in oil. Give the batter a good whisk then pour a ladleful into the pan, tipping and swirling the pan so the batter thickly coats the base.

Cook for a couple of minutes, during which time the surface will become pocked with holes. Flip over and cook for a further minute, then remove from the pan. Wrap in a clean tea towel to keep warm. Cook enough oatcakes for breakfast (or lunch); keep the rest of the batter in the fridge or freeze for later.

Socca

Made with chickpea flour, this thick pancake from the South of France is summer tearing and sharing food. Serve it outdoors, with some good tomatoes, cheese, salad leaves, salami and olives, perhaps, or a ragu of beans. You could try adding flavours to the pancake batter too: finely chopped rosemary and black pepper would be excellent. You'll notice the recipe uses equal volumes of flour and water, and the flour is measured by volume, not weight for convenience. Use a measuring cup, or a jug, or any other container, to measure first the flour, then the water. The quantities are easily adjusted to make the number of pancakes required.

Makes 1
About 100ml chickpea flour
About 100ml water
Small pinch of salt
Extra virgin olive oil, for frying

Tip the flour and water into a mixing bowl. Add a pinch of salt, then whisk until most of the lumps have gone.

Heat a slug of olive oil in a small frying pan. When it is hot but not smoking, pour in enough batter to give a 5mm thickness. Cook until it has set, but keep checking the underside.

When it is dark in patches, even very slightly charred, flip the pancake over, trickle a little more oil round the side of the pan and give it a shake. Cook for another couple of minutes, until the other side is similarly coloured. Tear a bit off the side to check it is cooked through.

Serve the pancakes straight away, or keep warm while you cook some more.

P.S. You can buy chickpea flour from health food shops, or Asian food stores where it may go by the name of *besan* or gram flour.

BUNS, BISCUITS & BATTER BREADS 173

Using Leftover Bread

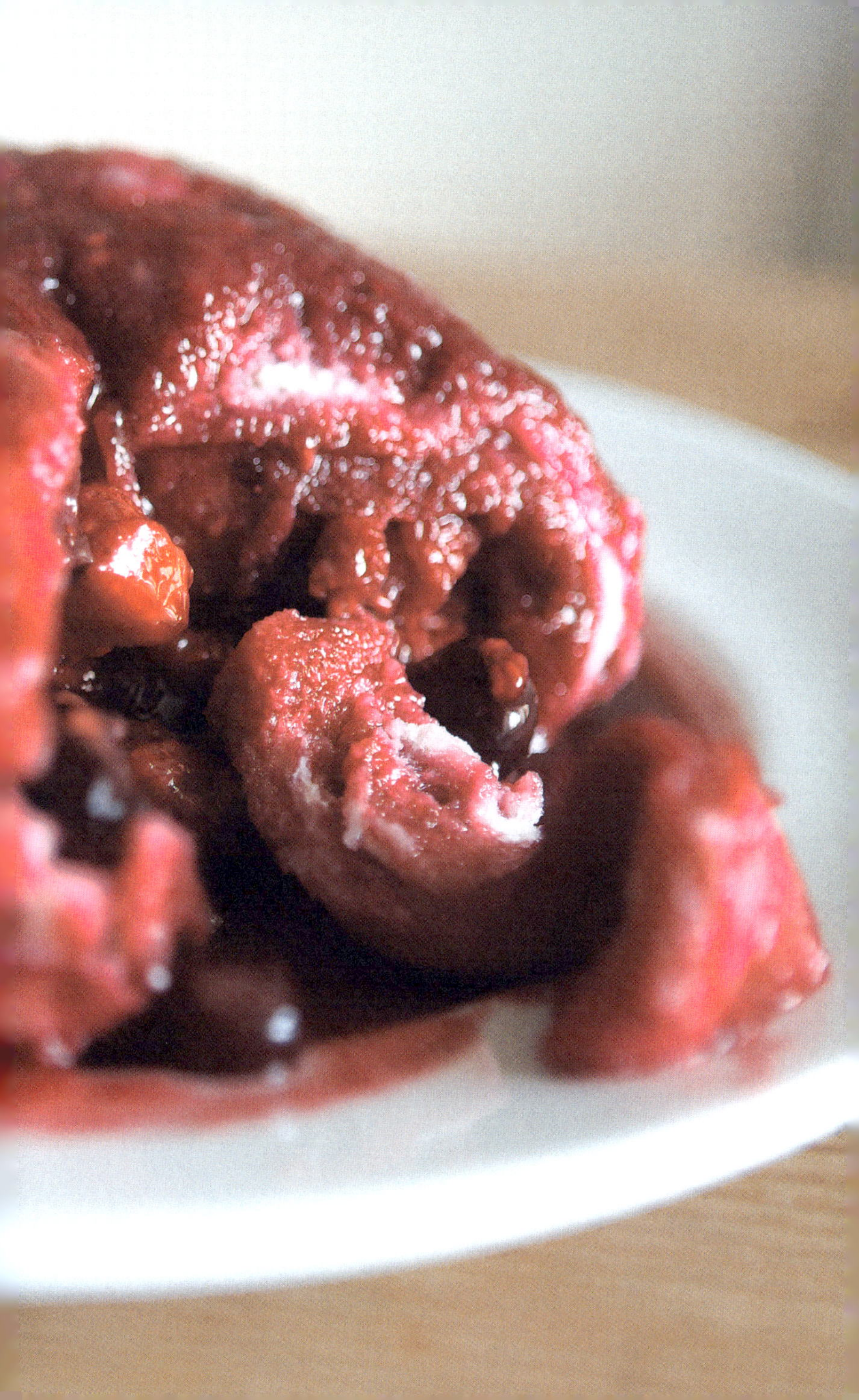

I never throw bread in the bin and neither should you

– unless, of course, it is mouldy, which it shouldn't be if you've stored it properly. Consider these possibilities for your ageing loaf:

Cut the whole bottom crust off your loaf and use as a plate for a stew. Afterwards, eat the plate. It may sound silly, but this was an old English staple, known as a 'trencher'. A good, thick slice of stale bread in the bottom of a bowl of stew is still an excellent idea.

Rip bread up into big chunks keeping the crusts on. Toss them in olive oil and bake until golden for wonderful croûtons to drop into soup. You could add some grated cheese as you toss – for a tastier, more stuck-together affair.

Make a bread sauce to serve with roasted poultry or game. Remove the crusts, tear the bread into chunks and soak in just-boiled milk infused with a small onion, a bay leaf and a few cloves for half an hour. Reheat and season generously with sea salt and freshly ground pepper to serve.

Rip bread into smaller chunks to make Spanish *migas*. Fry the bread in lard or bacon fat until crispy, throwing in some bacon lardons and sliced onion for extra flavour if you like. Season with salt and pepper, and finish with chopped parsley. Serve topped with a fried egg for the perfect breakfast.

Make breadcrumbs by blitzing chunks of bread, a handful at a time, in a food processor to make coarse crumbs. Freeze any breadcrumbs you won't use straight away. They freeze brilliantly and you'll find endless uses for them:
- Use to thicken soups, or sprinkle over dishes to be flashed under the grill for a crisp topping.
- Or to coat fish: season fillets of fish, dip into flour, then into beaten egg, then into breadcrumbs and shallow-fry. (For a thicker, crunchier coat double-dip them in the egg and breadcrumbs.)
- Or to make 'poor man's Parmesan': shallow-fry breadcrumbs in olive oil with a little salt until crisp, drain on kitchen paper and scatter over pasta.

Dry breadcrumbs completely spread out on a tray, in a very low oven or somewhere else warm, then blitz again until super-fine.
- Use to make Scotch eggs: seal just-softer-than-hard-boiled eggs inside good-quality sausage meat (100g per egg), dip first in flour, then into beaten egg, then into fine, dry breadcrumbs to coat. Deep-fry in hot oil at 170°C for about 5 minutes, until the sausage meat is cooked through.

- Or, if you make your own sausages, use these dry breadcrumbs as rusk – they will soak up fat and moisture, keeping the sausages juicy.
- Or use to coat your own homemade fish fingers.

And don't forget toast – one- or two-day-old bread makes better toast than fresh bread. Or do as Benjamin Franklin once said, 'Give me yesterday's Bread, this Day's Flesh, and last Year's Cyder.' Sounds good to me... Or, try the recipes on the following pages.

Beetroot houmous

For this shocking-purple variation of the classic chickpea dip, bread is used as a thickener because beetroot makes a thinner purée than chickpeas. I've given exact quantities here, but the way to make houmous is to add the ingredients a little at a time, tasting and tweaking as you go, until you think it is perfect. You could make a larger batch – it will sit quite happily for several days in the fridge, ready to dip raw vegetables into when you fancy a snack. Illustrated on p.87.

Serves 4
1 tbsp cumin seeds
25g crustless, stale bread
200g cooked beetroot
1 large garlic clove, peeled and crushed
About 1 tbsp tahini
 (sesame seed paste)
Juice of 1 lemon
Salt and black pepper

Toast the cumin seeds in a dry frying pan over a medium heat, shaking the pan almost constantly, until they start to darken and smell amazing (less than a minute). While still hot, crush the seeds using a pestle and mortar, or a spice grinder.

Break the bread into chunks and whiz in a food processor to crumbs. Add the beetroot, most of the garlic, 1 tbsp tahini, a good pinch of the cumin, half the lemon juice, a sprinkling of salt and a good grinding of pepper. Blend to a thick paste.

Taste the houmous; you should be able to detect every flavour. If not, add a little more of whatever is lacking and blend again. Keep tasting and adjusting until you are happy. Serve with flatbread (see p.103) and/or vegetables for dipping.

Taramasalata

If pollack are obliging enough to come into the River Cottage kitchen laden with roe, we salt, poach and hang the roe in our cold smoker quicker than you can say taramasalata backwards. This is our recipe.

Serves 8

250g smoked pollack or other fish roe
About 100g stale white bread,
   crusts removed
150ml whole milk
1 garlic clove, peeled and crushed
100ml extra virgin olive oil
200ml sunflower oil
Juice of 1 lemon
Salt and black pepper

To serve
Smoked paprika, for sprinkling
About 1 tbsp finely chopped parsley
A little preserved lemon rind, cut into
   very thin strips (optional)

Cut the smoked roe open and scrape them out with a spoon, discarding the skins. Tear the bread into chunks and soak in the milk for a few minutes, then squeeze out excess moisture and put into a food processor, along with the fish roe and garlic.

With the machine on low speed, trickle in both oils through the funnel in a steady stream. Add the lemon juice a little at a time, tasting as you go, until you are happy. Season with salt if needed (this depends on the saltiness of the roe), and a generous grinding of pepper.

Transfer the taramasalata to a serving bowl, sprinkle with a little smoked paprika and scatter over the chopped parsley and preserved lemon if you have any. Serve with loads of flatbread (see p.103) or toast.

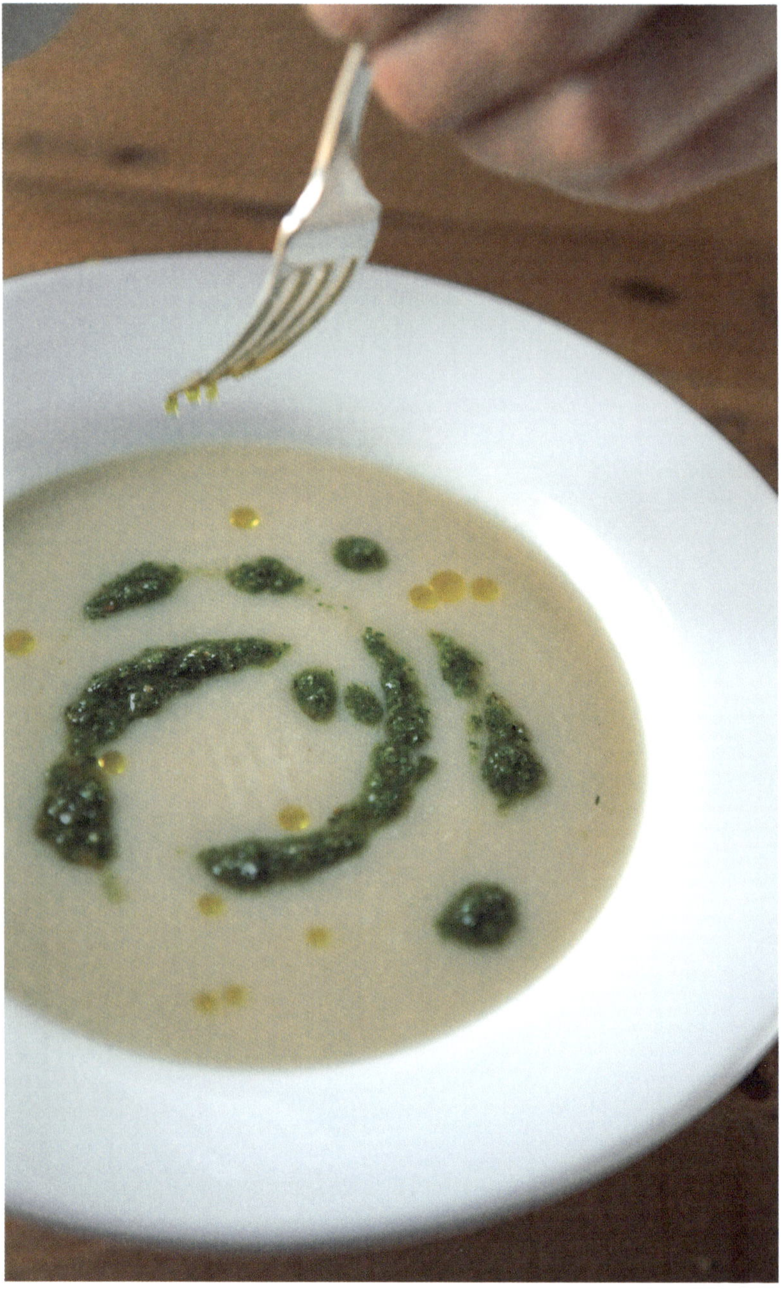

Nettle pesto

This is a rural Devon, River Cottage version of the classic Italian sauce. We substitute nettles, rapeseed oil, Cheddar and breadcrumbs for basil, olive oil, Parmesan and pine nuts. Use it wherever you would use pesto – it is excellent swirled on top of creamy soups, or tossed through pasta.

Makes about 450g
20g breadcrumbs
100g young nettles (or the top few leaves of older ones)
20g strong Cheddar, grated
½ garlic clove, crushed to a paste with a little salt
150–200ml rapeseed oil
Salt and black pepper

Preheat the oven to 180°C/Gas Mark 4. Scatter the breadcrumbs on a baking tray and bake for about 10 minutes until dry and golden, checking them frequently towards the end as they burn quite quickly. Tip on to a plate and allow to cool.

Wearing gloves, pick over the nettles, discarding all but the thinnest stalks, then wash well. Fill a bowl with iced water. Find a pan large enough to take the nettles and half-fill it with water. Bring to the boil and cram in the nettles, pushing them down with a wooden spoon to immerse them. Cook for just 1 minute, then drain through a sieve over a bowl to save the cooking water. Immediately plunge the nettles into the iced water. As soon as they are cold, remove and squeeze them as dry as you can – they will not sting you once they are cooked.

Put the nettles into a food processor along with the breadcrumbs, cheese and garlic. With the machine on low speed, trickle in enough rapeseed oil to make a loose paste. (Alternatively, you can grind the nettles, breadcrumbs, garlic and cheese to a paste using a pestle and mortar, then slowly incorporate the oil.)

Season your pesto with salt and pepper to taste. It is now ready to use. As for the nettle cooking water you saved, drink it – it's too good to waste.

Panzanella

This Tuscan bread salad is excellent eaten on its own for lunch, but also just right with barbecued food, or anything else you want to eat outdoors with a bottle of wine on a hot summer's day. As with all peasant food, there are limitless variations, so feel free to adjust this recipe. That said, I would never attempt to make it if I didn't have some really good ripe tomatoes and decent extra virgin olive oil.

Serves 4

About 500g stale white bread (ideally ciabatta or sourdough)
150ml extra virgin olive oil
1 large red onion, finely chopped
½ cucumber, chopped quite small
4 good-sized ripe tomatoes, chopped quite small
A handful of small capers
25ml good-quality white wine vinegar, or cider vinegar
A pinch of caster sugar
Flaky sea salt and black pepper
A big bunch of basil, leaves only

Preheat the oven to 180°C/Gas Mark 4. In a roasting tray, toss the bread with half the olive oil then bake it, shaking the pan occasionally, until golden and crispy. You can miss out this step – many Italians would – but it adds texture and flavour, which I like. Leave to cool, then toss with the onion, cucumber, tomatoes (including all their juices) and capers in a large serving bowl.

In another bowl, whisk the rest of the olive oil together with the wine vinegar and sugar. Pour this dressing over the salad and season generously with salt and pepper. Tear the basil over and toss it all together. Taste for seasoning.

You can either serve the salad straight away, or leave it to stand at room temperature for an hour or so, to let the flavours blend.

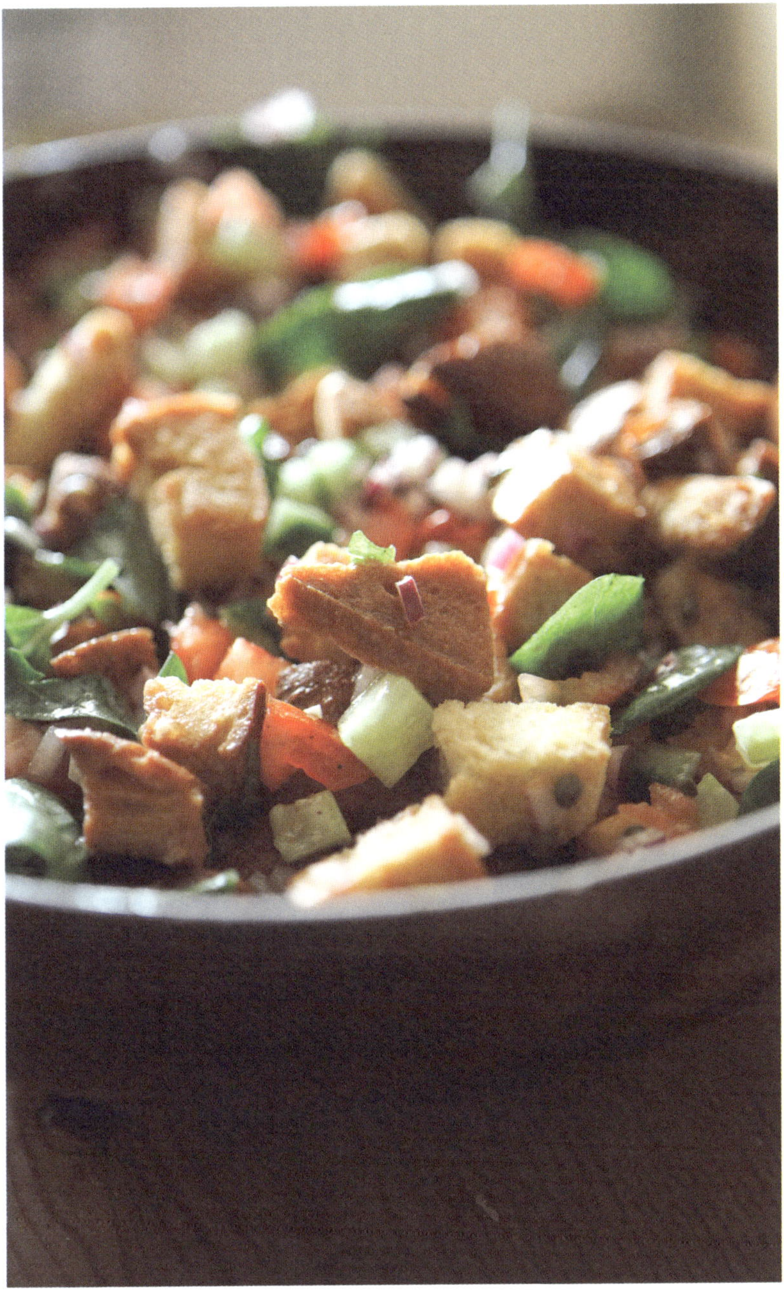

Pain perdu

This is a classic French dessert, which translates as 'lost' or 'forgotten' bread. Basically, it is sugary, eggy bread, which is truly delicious topped with seasonal fruit. Try it with poached rhubarb, or with summer berries – some of them puréed. Serve for dessert, or brunch if you prefer.

Serves 6
3 thick slices stale white bread, crusts removed
4 large free-range eggs
100g caster sugar
200ml whole milk

A few drops of natural vanilla extract
About 100g unsalted butter

To serve
Poached fruit or summer berries

Cut the bread slices in half diagonally. In a mixing bowl, whisk the eggs and sugar together for a couple of minutes to help dissolve the sugar, then add the milk and vanilla extract, and whisk again. Tip this mixture into a shallow dish (large enough to take all the bread in a single layer). Lay the bread slices in the dish, leave to soak for a minute, then turn them over and leave for another minute.

In the meantime, set a frying pan over a medium-low heat. Once the bread has soaked, add a generous knob of butter to the pan – enough to just cover the bottom of the pan once melted. As soon as the butter is frothing (don't let it brown), lay as many bread slices in the pan as will comfortably fit, and fry for 2–3 minutes on each side until golden brown.

Remove the *pain perdu* from the pan and keep warm while you fry the rest of the bread slices, adding more butter to the pan as necessary. Serve straight away, with poached fruit or berries.

Variation

You can flambé the bread, too, if you like. Add a splash of Cognac, Grand Marnier or whatever you fancy, right at the end. Set alight with a match and leave until the flame has subsided.

USING LEFTOVER BREAD

Bread and butter pudding

If you don't like bread and butter pudding, the chances are that you've never had one that's been made properly. This recipe should change your mind.

Serves 6

About 600g one- or two-day-old white bread
About 50g unsalted butter, softened
300ml double cream
300ml whole milk
1 vanilla pod
6 medium free-range egg yolks
200g caster sugar
A good handful of raisins

Butter a shallow oval baking dish, about 30 x 20cm. Cut the bread into medium-thick slices, butter them, then cut the crusts off and halve the slices on the diagonal to form triangles.

Pour the cream and milk into a saucepan. Split the vanilla pod lengthways, scrape out the seeds with a teaspoon and add them to the pan with the empty pod. Bring just to the boil over a medium heat, then take off the heat and leave to infuse for 10 minutes. In a large bowl, briefly whisk together the egg yolks and 150g of the sugar to combine. Pour in the hot milk and cream mix, including the vanilla, whisking all the time. This is your custard.

Arrange the triangles of bread in the baking dish – in rows, propped up and leaning on each other so they come just proud of the dish, sprinkling the raisins in between. Continue in this way until you've filled the dish and used all the bread, cutting the triangles up and tucking the pieces in as you need to. Don't try to be neat – the point of layering like this is that the propped-up ends, which stand clear of the custard, turn golden and crispy in the oven. Try not to leave too many raisins exposed, as they are liable to scorch during baking.

Now, pour over the custard, making sure you moisten all the pieces of bread. Let the pudding stand for 20 minutes or so, to allow the custard to soak in. Heat the oven to 180°C/Gas Mark 4 and boil the kettle.

When you are ready to bake, sprinkle over the rest of the sugar. Sit the dish in a roasting tin and pour in enough boiling water to come halfway up the side of the dish (this bain-marie will help to keep the pudding soft.) Bake for 20–30 minutes, until the custard is just set in the middle – prod the top with your finger to check. Serve hot or warm, with cream or ice cream.

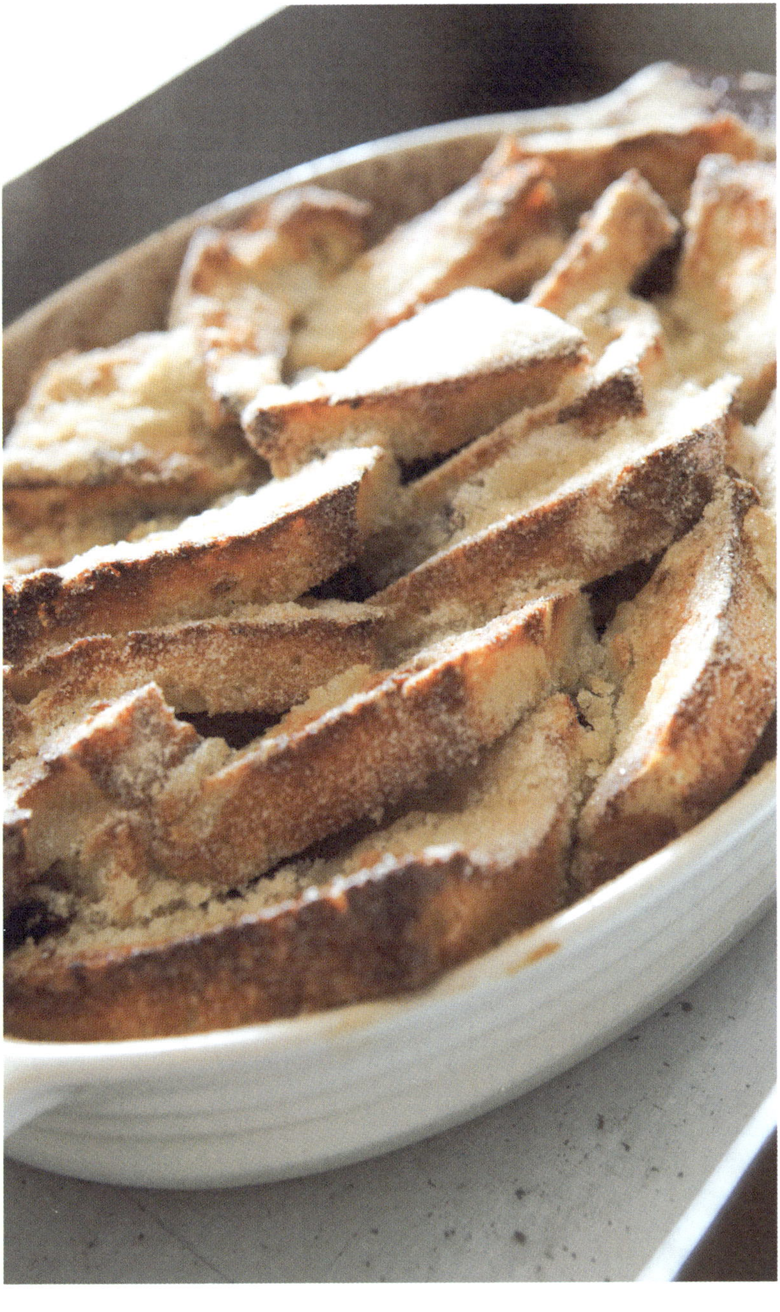

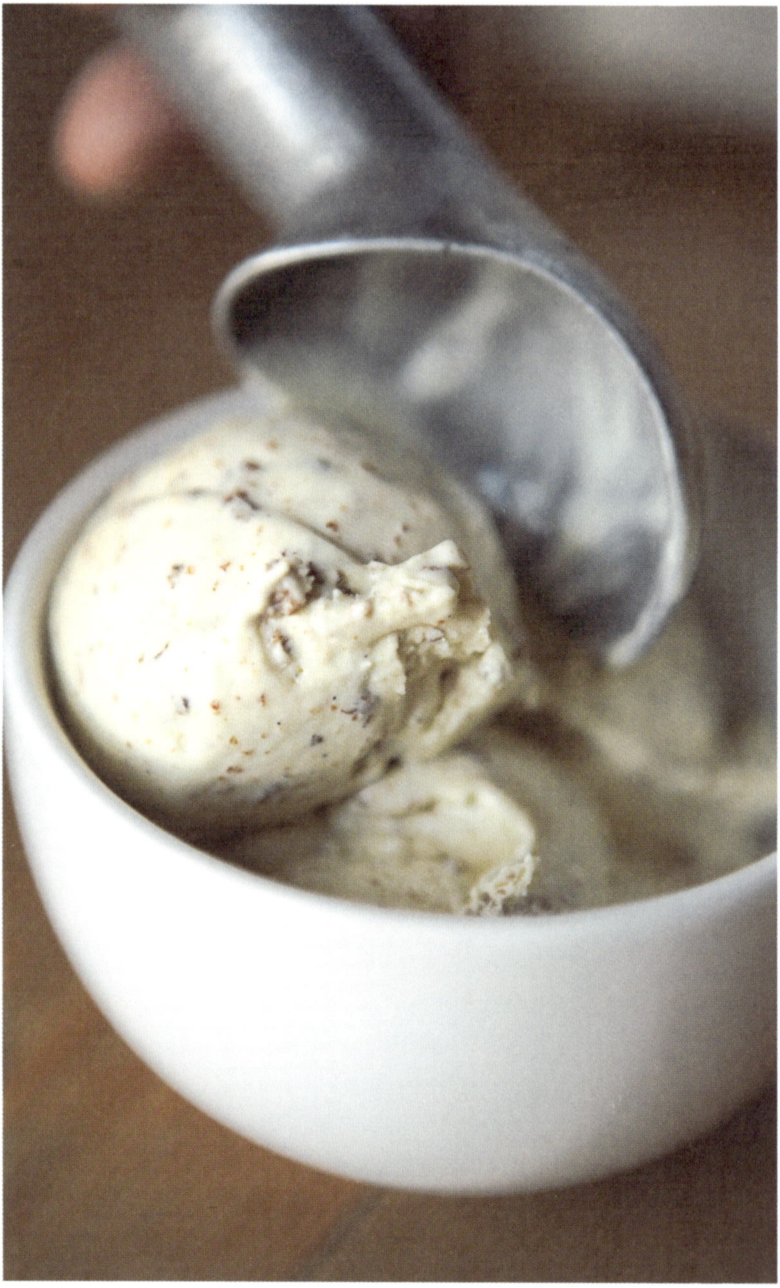

Brown bread ice cream

This is vanilla ice cream, dappled with little golden, sweet, nutty-tasting, chewy treats, so it tastes that much better. Ideally you would make this in an ice-cream maker, but if you don't own one, there is another way (see below).

Makes about 600ml

100g fresh or one- or two-day-old wholemeal bread
100g soft light brown sugar, or demerara
250ml whole milk
1 vanilla pod
6 medium free-range egg yolks
125g caster sugar
250ml double cream

Preheat the oven to 180°C/Gas Mark 4. Tear the bread into smallish pieces, toss with the brown sugar and scatter on a baking tray. Bake in the oven for 10 minutes or so, until quite dark and caramelised. Leave to cool on the tray.

Meanwhile, pour the milk into a heavy-based pan. Split the vanilla pod lengthways, scrape out the seeds with a teaspoon and add them to the milk together with the empty pod. Slowly bring just to the boil.

Meanwhile, in a large mixing bowl, briefly whisk together the egg yolks and caster sugar, then slowly pour in the hot milk, whisking constantly. Tip in the vanilla pod too. Pour the mixture back into the saucepan and set over a low heat. Stir constantly with a wooden spoon or silicone spatula for about 5 minutes until the custard is thick enough to coat the back of the spoon; do not let it overheat or it may curdle.

As soon as it is ready, pour the custard into a cold bowl, cover with cling film to prevent a skin forming, and leave to infuse for at least 10 minutes.

Remove the vanilla pod, stir in the double cream and churn the mixture in an ice-cream maker according to the manufacturer's instructions. When the ice cream is thickened and almost ready but still a little soft, crumble in the toasted bread and churn until frozen.

P.S. If you do not have an ice-cream maker, freeze the mixture in a suitable bowl in the freezer, taking it out and whisking or beating it every half-hour over the next few hours until it becomes too firm to beat, then allow to freeze completely. Ice cream made this way will be harder when fully frozen, so you will need to allow extra time for it to soften slightly before serving. It will be delicious nonetheless.

Summer pudding

This is a celebration of the English summer, so make it with homegrown fruit if you possibly can. The mix of fruits should be governed by what is in season. Try for a balance of sweet and tart fruits – say, strawberries, raspberries, redcurrants, blackcurrants and blueberries. You will need a 900ml pudding basin and a plate small enough to fit inside the rim. The whole pudding is illustrated on pp.174–5.

Serves 4
600g mixed ripe soft fruits (see above)
100g caster sugar

6–8 medium thick slices of one- or two-day-old white bread, crusts removed

Put the fruits and sugar into a heavy-based pan over a medium heat, stir together and bring just to the boil, stirring regularly. Simmer for 1 minute only, then remove from the heat. The fruits will release a fair amount of juice.

Line the base and sides of a 900ml pudding basin with slices of bread, overlapping them slightly and cutting them to fit as necessary. Reserve a slice or two for the lid.

Now fill the basin with all of the fruit and most of the juice, saving a few tablespoonfuls (or more) for serving. You may find you have more juice than you need; this depends on the fruit and its ripeness.

Cut the reserved bread to fit the top, sit a plate on top that just fits inside the rim and weight it with a couple of tins from the cupboard. Refrigerate for about 8 hours.

To serve, invert the pudding on to a large plate and pour over the reserved juice. Serve with cream.

USING LEFTOVER BREAD 191

Building a Clay Oven

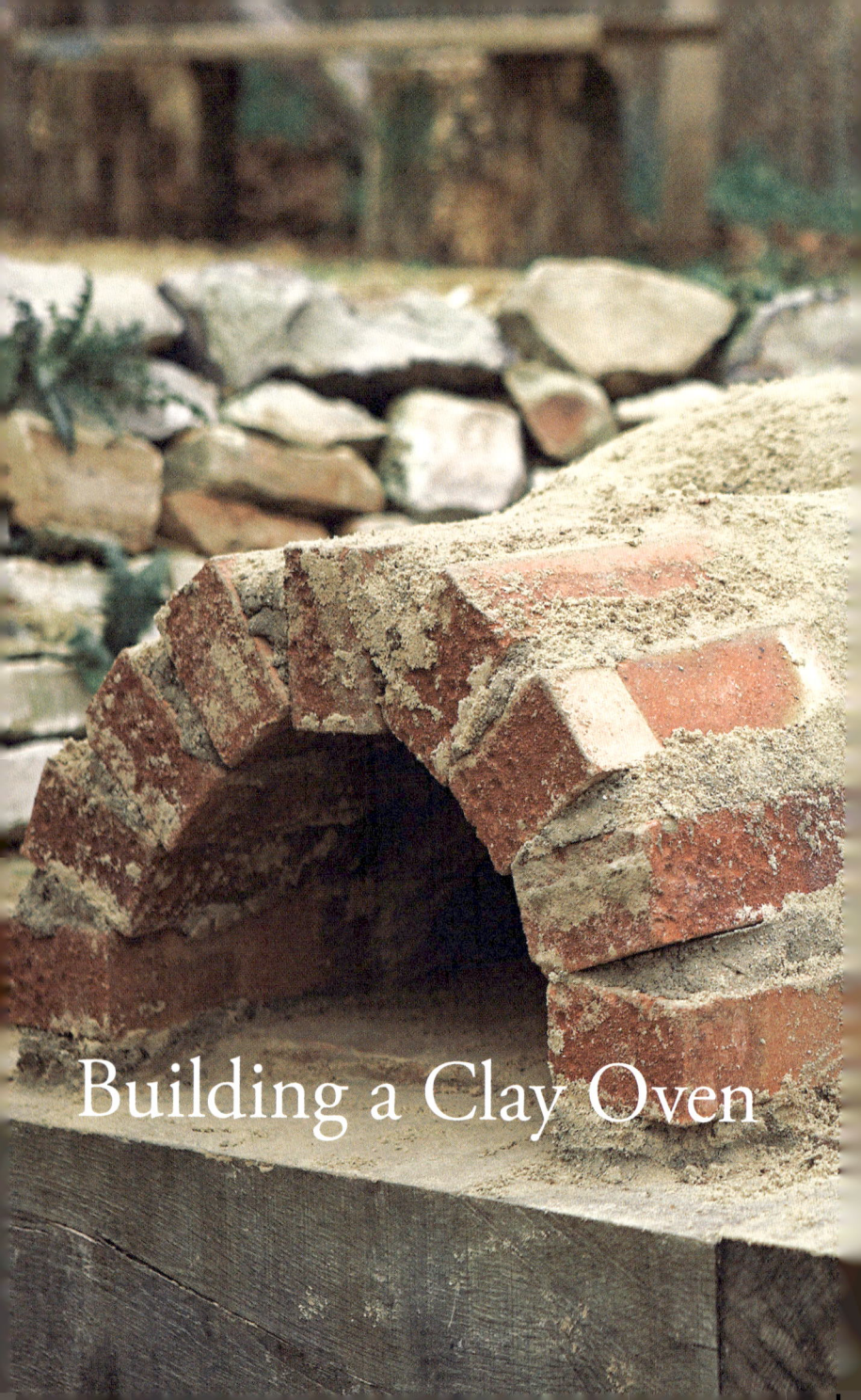

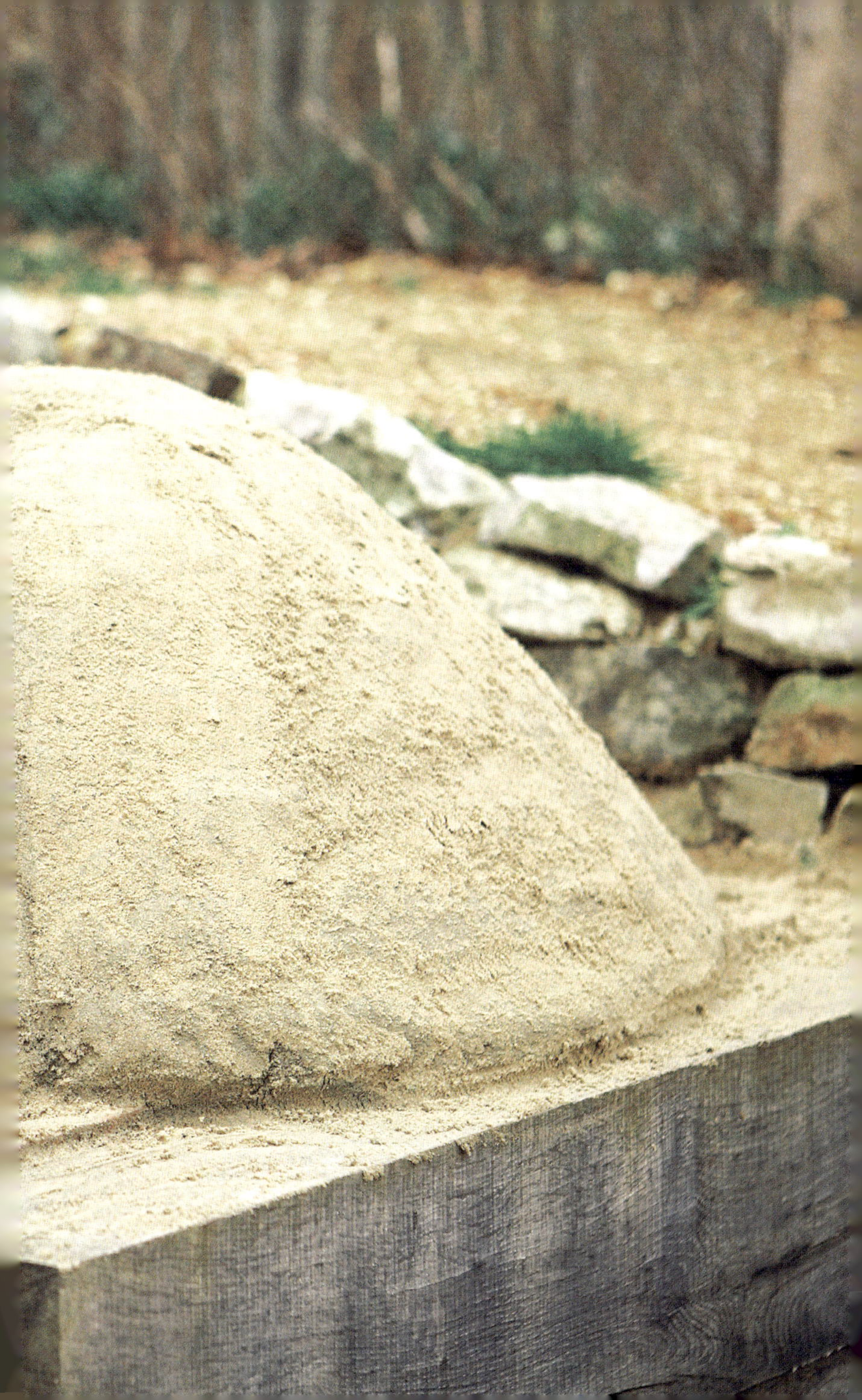

If I was a lump of dough, proving my final minutes away

and contemplating the manner of my passing, I'd choose the old-fashioned way to go – to be slipped, bare-bottomed, straight on to the ash-covered floor of a hell-hot wood-fired oven. However, these days I'd be hard pushed to find such an oven. A few small artisan bakers still use one, so do some authentic pizzerias; you might even find one in an old house – nestled in the side of an inglenook fireplace. Your best bet, however, is to build your own.

This is not as ridiculous as it may sound. With a little effort and not too much money, you can build yourself an oven from clay, sand and bricks in your back garden – an oven that is capable of reaching temperatures of 400°C and above, in which you could bake bread or pizzas, or even your Sunday roast.

Almost anything you can cook in your domestic oven, you'll be able to cook in a clay oven, and in most cases the food will be better for it. I would probably draw the line at a sponge cake, or a soufflé, which are fragile affairs that need a temperature dial and an airtight door. On the other hand, I would certainly give scones and Yorkshire puddings a go.

So, if you can find around two square metres in your garden, and three spare days in your life, you could build yourself something truly special. Your humble backyard could be transformed into a Mecca of gastronomy.

How a clay oven works

The principle is simple: you light a fire inside the oven and keep it stoked long enough for the heat to fully penetrate the walls and floor. You then remove some or all of the embers and bake using the residual heat. A well-built oven with a close-fitting door will retain heat for many hours, even with all the embers removed.

Building your oven

You will be building a simple igloo-shaped clay-and-sand oven, set on some sort of raised plinth. You can tailor the size of your oven to suit your needs, so consider what they will be. Will you be baking two or three loaves at a time, or a dozen? Do you want to be able to fit a whole shoulder of pork in it, or will you never cook anything larger than a leg of lamb?

There is more chance of scorching food in a small, cramped oven because the oven is hottest around the edges (as the heat radiates from the walls and floor). On the other hand, a large oven will take more fuel to heat, so I wouldn't make it any larger than you think you will need.

To make things simpler, I will give measurements for an oven that is a good size to bake a few loaves, or three or four pizzas at the same time, or take a large roasting tin. It will have an internal oven space about 80cm in diameter and 40cm high, and the oven will need to sit on a square plinth 150 x 150cm. In practice, it is quite straightforward for you to scale this up or down. The entire oven size is dictated by a single measurement: the diameter of a hemisphere of sand, which you will build, and around which your oven will be moulded.

The plinth

Technically, you could build an oven at ground level, but in practice you'd be bending down too far to see into it. The nearer to eye level you get, the easier it will be on your back, but an eye-level oven would mean an awful lot of plinth, which you may find rather obtrusive. You should also take into account the fact that you will be scraping hot embers out of the oven. These need to drop into something, and the further they have to fall, the more chance they will miss your container and land on your foot. Ideally, you want to raise the floor of the oven to somewhere between 1 and 1.5 metres.

There are any number of possible ways to build your plinth and I am sure you will want to think aesthetically as well as structurally. As it will be purpose-built, it may as well look good and be designed to fit in with your garden. As I'm not familiar with your garden, I can't tell you whether your finish should be timber, sandstone or jewel-encrusted mirrors, but I can tell you that the structure must be solid and stable – as indeed must be the ground you build it on.

You should allow yourself a good 1.5 metres of clear space in front of the place where your oven door will be sited: this area becomes your 'kitchen' and you will need room to move about in it. The top of the plinth should be made of brick, stone or concrete. Remember that this will become the floor of the oven, and as such, needs to be made as flat as possible.

Our plinth at River Cottage is 120cm square and 70cm high. The walls are railway sleepers, set on solid, level ground and fixed with right-angled brackets on the internal corners. The plinth is in-filled with rubble, the top of which is levelled with sand, to about 5cm below the top of the sleepers. Plain London bricks are set on this, upside down (flat side up), in a herringbone pattern, to form a level top. The gaps between the bricks are filled with more sand.

This construction works a treat, but there are other options. I once had an ugly square concrete-walled coal bunker in my garden, which would have made an ideal plinth. A stack of breezeblocks would do the job too.

Weather proofing

You may wish to construct a simple roof to protect your oven, though this is not essential; you could just keep it covered with tarpaulin when you are not using it. A roof can be anything you want it to be – it just needs to keep the worst of the rain off. A little water isn't going to hurt, but a soaking wet oven will not get hot enough, and badly weather-beaten clay will start to erode.

Bear in mind, too, that a lot of smoke will be coming out of the oven and your roof is bound to affect the airflow around it. I suggest it should clear the top of your oven by at least a metre. You may wish to make provision for a chimney if you feel the space is too enclosed – say, if you are building up against a wall. The roof over our clay oven at River Cottage is made of corrugated iron.

The three stages of building your oven

There will be three layers to your clay oven and you will need a separate day to build each one, as each layer needs to dry fully before you start the next one. Drying time depends largely on the weather, but you can – and should – accelerate the process by lighting a fire inside.

The oven consists of an inner skin, made of a mixture of sand, clay and water; an insulating layer, made of clay, wood shavings and water; and an outer wall, made again of sand, clay and water, with a brick-arch doorway, if you wish.

This is an uncomplicated project, but it does require some work, and I strongly recommend that you rope in a few able bodies to help with the grafting. A merry band of three or four helpers will make light of a job that you might find a little daunting alone. Plan roughly when you will tackle each of the stages and let them know, but ask them to be flexible, as the weather will determine how much time you'll need between the three building days.

Sourcing your materials

Before you begin, you will need to obtain 8 buckets of clay and 18 buckets of sand. By 'bucket', I mean a large metal pail, rather than a household mop bucket. You will also need two carrier bags full of wood shavings, a large heavy-duty tarpaulin, a newspaper, and a thin stick. This will become your measuring stick and you'll need to mark it 7cm from one end – with a pen or tape, or by cutting a notch. If you want to build a door and a chimney lid, you will need about half a square metre of wood (hardwood is best), 2–3cm thick, and a decent saw.

> Clay The easiest way to get hold of some clay is to go digging. It is very easy to find, though away from a source of water clay is likely to be pretty dry. At River Cottage we have a man-made pond in the lower field and we dig our clay from its banks. If you have access to such a pond, or a stream or small river, you will be able to do the same – with permission from the landowner, of course.
>
> Your clay should be squidgy, and reasonably free of other soils and stones; take a small piece and work it with your hands until it is supple, then roll into a snake and wrap it around your finger. It should not snap.
>
> You may prefer to buy your clay, of course. I am yet to find a nearby builder's merchant that sells it, but a friendly local potter or perhaps an art school should be able to point you in the right direction.
>
> Sand This is a natural material too, of course, and if you can get it for free so much the better. Otherwise, builder's merchants sell it pretty cheaply. Any grade will be fine.
>
> Bricks A builder's merchant again is probably your best option, or a reclamation yard if you happen to have one locally. Buy whatever bricks take your fancy.
>
> Wood shavings Any timber merchant or sawmill will probably be happy to sell you wood shavings. These should not be too coarse, or too fine – the texture of muesli would be good.

The first day

To do list:
- Mix the clay and sand
- Build the sand former
- Build the inner skin
- Remove the sand former
- Begin drying

Mix the clay and sand

Lay the tarpaulin out on the ground and tip 6 buckets of sand and 3 buckets of clay on to it (pic 1). This will give you enough for today's work, but if you want to get ahead of yourself, you could double the amount, which will give you enough for the outer wall too.

Now, stick a pair of wellies or stout boots on as many friends as you can muster and start stomping (pic 2). Throw out any stones as you come across them. Every so often, get hold of both corners of one end of the tarpaulin and pull it over to meet the other end (pic 3); this will turn the sand and clay over on itself, helping to mix it thoroughly.

You may feel the mix is just too firm, dry and difficult to work, in which case you need to add some water – this is likely if the clay was very dry to begin with. If you dug clay from a riverbank or pond, it will probably be wet enough already. The final consistency of the mix should be soft enough to mould and shape easily, and strong enough to hold its own weight.

When your mix is looking pretty well blended, test the consistency. Take a small piece of dough (the size of a lime) and spend a minute or so compacting it. Now hold it at shoulder height and drop it on to the ground. On impact it should crack, but roughly hold its shape (pic 4). If it crumbles, the mix is too sandy and you need to add more clay. If it 'splats', it is too wet and you should add more sand. When you are happy with the consistency, your building material – or 'mud' as I prefer to call it – is ready to use.

Build the sand former

The first stage of building is to make a dome of sand, which will be the 'former' around which you build the inner skin of the oven. First, trace a circle 80cm diameter, centrally on the plinth. Next, heap sand into the circle and start forming a dome – or almost a dome (p.200, pic 1). The mound should rise vertically to start with, to about a hand's depth, before it starts to curve inwards; this gives much more headroom for anything cooking next to the wall. The finished dome should be about 40cm high.

Mix the clay and sand

1

2

3

4

BUILDING A CLAY OVEN

Build the sand former

1

2

3

4

From time to time, stand on the plinth, centre your eyes over the dome and get a bird's-eye view of your work (pic 2) – it is much easier to spot imperfections from up there. When you are happy, the next step is to cover the dome with a layer of wet newspaper. You will be digging the sand out later; this newspaper layer tells you when to stop digging. Soak whole sheets and lay them over the dome (pic 3); you don't need to be neat, by any means – just make sure you completely cover the sand (pic 4). This is slightly harder in practice than it sounds, but only slightly; the paper won't stick to the sand as well as you might hope, but it will stick to itself.

Build the inner skin

You are now ready to start building your oven. The technique is simple. Pick up a good handful of your clay and sand 'mud' and pat and mould it into a rough brick shape. Sit this adjacent to the dome and, using the edge of one hand as a mallet and the other hand as a buffer, pack the brick down to a width of around 7cm (pic 1), using your measuring stick as a guide. Make a second brick and sit it alongside, packing down in the same way. The 'bricks' should merge into one (pic 2). Compacting is essential. Apart from giving the structure more solidity, it removes air pockets, which can expand with the heat of the oven and cause cracks.

Build the inner skin

1   2

Continue like this until you get all the way round, then start your second layer, and so on. You don't need to measure every time, but poke your stick in every now and then to make sure you maintain the thickness. And don't forget your bird's-eye view – this is still your best guide. Once you reach the top and close the gap, take some more time to depth-check and smooth your dome; the more even the structure, the stronger it will be.

When you are happy with the shape, have a cleanup. Your work is almost done. Save any leftover mud – splash a little water over it, shovel into plastic sacks or bin liners, tie the tops to stop it drying out and keep it for later. Now would be a good time to have lunch. You should leave your oven to settle on itself and firm up a bit for at least a couple of hours; you could even leave it overnight if it suits you better. You want it to get used to being there.

Remove the sand former

Now comes the fun bit: you are going to take away your oven's support. With a decent knife (a bread knife, funnily enough, is perfect), cut an arch where you want your door to be (pic 1). This will not be the finished doorway so don't worry about making it perfect. Decide how wide you want it. Do you have a particular roasting tray that needs to fit through? A reasonable size would be 30cm wide, and perhaps 20cm high.

Pull the mud out from the arch that you have cut (pic 2), then with one hand, start hollowing out the sand (pic 3). Keep digging, inwards, sideways and upwards. You won't be able to see what you're doing – your arm will be in the way – but at some point you will reach your layer of newspaper (pic 4). As you expose it, peel it away; this is too satisfying for words.

Keep digging and peeling, ignoring the little voice in your head that is telling you the whole thing will collapse at any minute. It won't. As you get deeper, be aware of your arm – it is easy to bash the side of the archway if you don't concentrate. When you finally scrape out the last bit of sand, take a step back and marvel at your oven. It really is still standing.

Begin drying

Over the next few days, you want your oven to dry out completely. Light a fire inside as often as you can. This can be tricky, as there is a lot of moisture inside and not much oxygen, but I suggest you resist using cheaty methods such as firelighters/barbecue fuel/petrol (unless you want your bread to taste of these). It is best to light a small fire near the doorway, where there is more air, then push it to the back once it is going strong. Your oven is fully dry when it has stopped steaming during firing; the colour will be considerably paler too.

Remove the sand former

1

2

3

4

BUILDING A CLAY OVEN

1

The second day

> **To do list:**
> - Build the door arch and chimney
> - Make a clay slip
> - Build the insulating layer
> - Continue drying

Build the door arch and chimney

You can form the door arch from your clay and sand mud, but I recommend that you make it from bricks. It will look more attractive and bricks are stronger, withstanding little knocks far better.

Build a sand former the same size as your doorway, extending forward a brick's length from the base of the oven. Now build an archway around the front section of the former, using some of your reserved clay and sand mix as mortar between the bricks (pic 1). Use more clay and sand to extend the doorway back to meet the receding wall of the oven (pic 2). Cut a hole in the top of this, roughly 20cm diameter, and form a chimney around the hole, around 20 cm high (pic 3). Remove the sand former after a few hours.

2

3

Make a clay slip

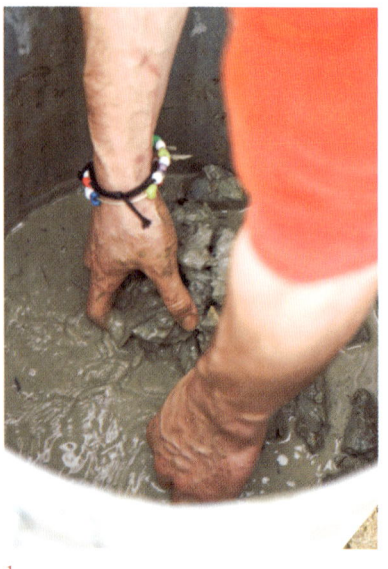

1   2

Make a clay slip
Get your wellies on again. Drag your tarpaulin out and empty one bucket of clay on to it. Tip about half a bucket of warm water on to the clay and start stomping. As the water gets blended in, keep adding more until you have a sludgy gloop, the consistency of thick yoghurt – this is called 'slip'. You can make the slip in a dustbin, mixing it with your hands (pic 1) if you prefer. Next, start to mix in the wood shavings with a shovel. Keep going until the whole thing looks like a stone giant's cornflake crunchie: the slip should bind the shavings together, just as the chocolate binds the cornflakes (pic 2).

Build the insulating layer
Using the same method as you used on the first day to build the inner skin (see pp.201–2), pack your wood and clay mixture over the dome, again to a thickness of about 7cm, using your measuring stick as a guide. Skirt around the doorway – you don't need to insulate the arch.

Continue drying
Dry this insulating layer out completely, building the odd fire as before (see p.202), over the next few days to hasten the process.

Build the insulating layer

The third day

To do list:
- Build the outer wall
- Make a door and chimney lid (optional)

Build the outer wall
You need to apply exactly the same method as you used to build the inner skin (see pp.201–2), though you'll find this stage much more satisfying. Keep fussing over your outer wall until it looks the way you want it to. You could decorate it, if you like – using some natural paints perhaps, or stud it with stones. The important thing is that the oven can breathe, or it will retain moisture – so don't smother it in tiles, or anything else that is not porous. Dry it out, building fires (see p.202), as before.

Make a door and chimney lid
Measure and cut a piece of wood to fit snugly inside the door arch. Cut a short baton for a handle and glue or nail it to the outside of the door. Cut a circle from another piece of wood to sit on the chimney. These will not be fireproof, of course; they are for retaining heat after the fire has been removed. Soaking them in water before every use will help stop them warping. Your oven is now ready to use.

Build the outer wall

Using your oven

The oven will need 3–4 hours' firing to get up to temperature. Start a small fire just inside the doorway, using paper and small kindling, then build it up with larger pieces of wood until it is burning well. When it is established, use sticks to slide the burning wood carefully right to the back, then keep feeding it with more wood as you need to, in order to maintain a good, rolling flame. The heat will become ferocious. I cannot give precise timings – you will get used to your own oven – but if the outer wall feels fairly warm you can be pretty sure the inside is scorching. For the last 10 minutes, spread the embers out to get extra heat into the whole floor.

When you are ready to cook, scrape or shovel all the embers out into a metal dustbin, or better still, something with a flat side that can sit flush to the wall of the plinth. At River Cottage we use a pig-feeding trough, which is ideal.

For most cooking, you will need to wait for the oven to cool a bit. The internal air temperature can be as high as 450°C, even with the fire removed completely. The surface temperature of the floor will be even hotter. This is perfect for cooking pizza, which will be ready in little over a minute, but nothing could withstand this heat for any longer. A loaf of bread would be black in no time. An oven thermometer would be helpful, but I have not found one that can measure above 300°C. In time, you will become a reliable temperature gauge. As you get to know your oven, you will get used to the searing heat – the feel of it on your skin as you reach in. I reckon if I can hold my hand just inside the doorway for a couple of seconds, I can probably bake a batch of bread without too much scorching. If I can't, I wait.

When I'm making bread, I shape a couple of small balls of dough (the size of a lemon) for testing. I put one into the oven and check it after a couple of minutes. If it shows signs of scorched patches, particularly on the bottom, I wait 5 minutes or so, then test the other ball. If this one is only turning golden after 2 minutes, I go for it. If it scorches again, I give it another 10 minutes or so before putting the loaves in.

To bake bread, follow your chosen recipe, then slip your loaves into the clay oven one at a time. Keep an eye on them; you will almost certainly want to shuffle them around so they colour more evenly. To bake pizza, follow the recipe (pp.104–6).

Once the bread is baked, I always feel it is a shame to waste the residual heat, so I almost always have something ready to follow it with – the temperature would now be perfect for a joint of meat, for example. Also, don't forget that your oven will make an effective, if rather immobile, patio heater.

As your oven settles into life, you may find cracks appearing. Don't worry unduly about this. If they become large, fill them in with clay, otherwise the efficiency of your oven may be affected. Some day, depending on how well it is sheltered and how often it is used, it will be time to knock your oven down and build a new one. Don't feel too downhearted about this. After all, everything returns to earth… in the end.

Useful Things

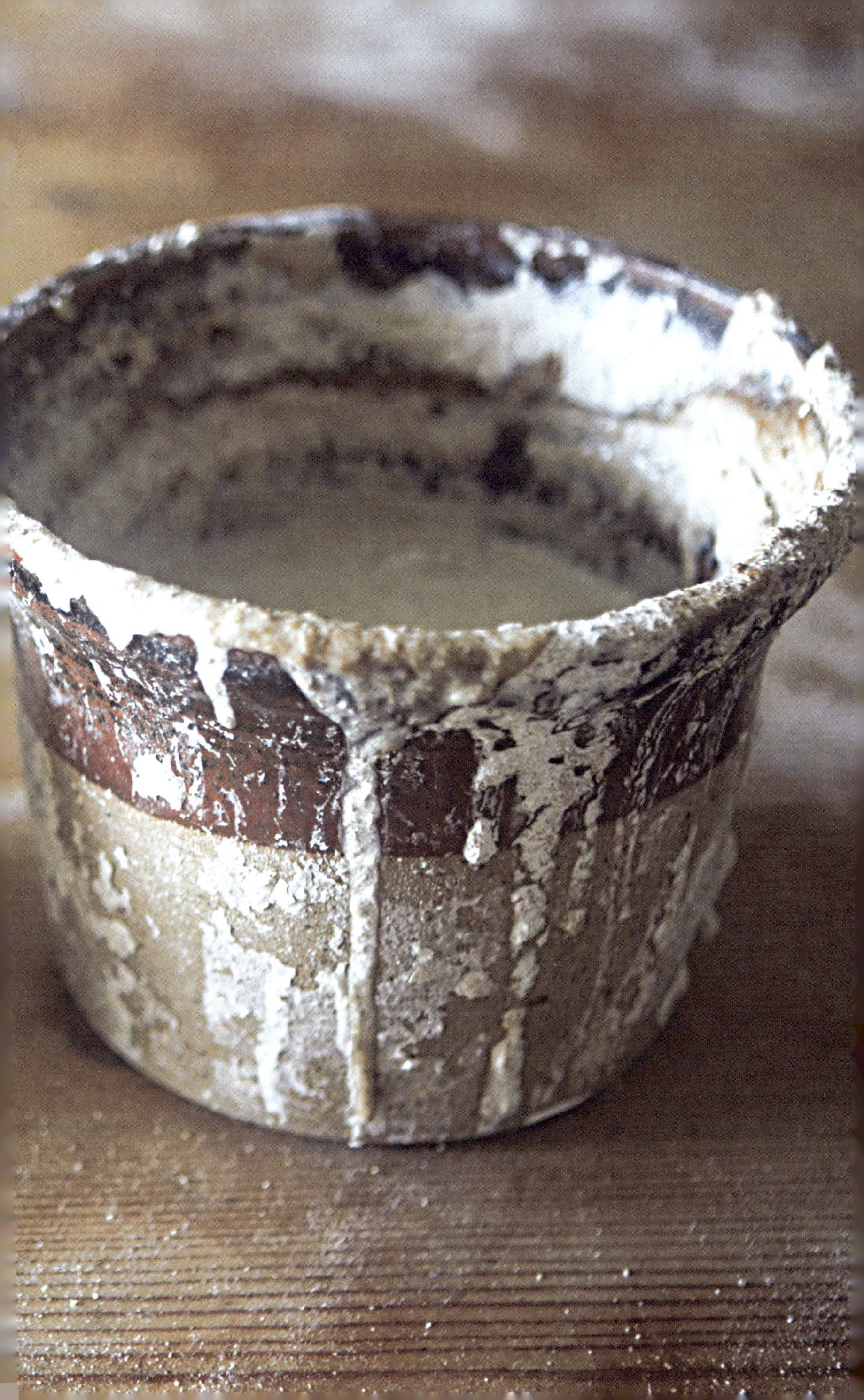

Directory

Flour suppliers

Doves Farm
Hungerford, Berkshire
www.dovesfarm.co.uk
01488 684880
Wide range of organic flours, including speciality and gluten-free

N R Stoate & Sons
Cann Mills, Shaftesbury, Dorset
www.stoatesflour.co.uk
01747 852475
Mainly organic flours, stoneground by Michael Stoate, a fifth-generation miller

Bacheldre Watermill
Churchstoke, Montgomery, Powys
www.bacheldremill.co.uk
01588 620489
Lovely range of stoneground flours, mostly organic

Shipton Mill
Tetbury, Gloucestershire
www.shipton-mill.com
01666 505050
Many organic and speciality flours

Sharpham Park
Glastonbury, Somerset
www.sharphampark.com
01458 844080
Spelt flour, grown and milled on an organic farm

Equipment suppliers

Creeds Ltd
Aylesbury, Buckinghamshire
www.creeds.uk.com
01296 658849
Suppliers of general baking equipment (including proving baskets and peels)

Nisbets
Avonmouth, Bristol
www.nisbets.co.uk
0845 140 5555
Full range of catering-standard kitchen equipment

Further reading

English Bread and Yeast Cookery
Elizabeth David
(Penguin Books, 1977)

The Tassajara Bread Book
Edward Espe Brown
(Shambhala Publications, 1970)

Baking with Passion (Baker & Spice)
Dan Lepard and Richard Whittington
(Quadrille, 2003)

McGee on Food and Cooking
Harold McGee
(Hodder & Stoughton, 2004)

USEFUL THINGS 213

Conversion charts

Metric quantities are given in the recipes. Use the following conversions if you prefer to work in imperial measures.

Weight

Metric	Imperial
25g	1oz
50g	2oz
100g–125g	4oz
170g	6oz
200g	7oz
225g	8oz
275g	10oz
340g	12oz
400g	14oz
450g	1lb
500g	1lb 2oz
900g	2lb
1kg	2lb 4oz

Liquid/volume

Metric	Imperial
150ml	5fl oz (¼ pint)
300ml	10fl oz (½ pint)
600ml	20fl oz (1 pint)
1 litre	35fl oz (1¾ pints)

1 tsp (1 teaspoon) = 5ml
1 tbsp (1 tablespoon) = 15ml

Oven temperatures

	°C	°F	Gas Mark
Very cool	130	250	½
Very cool	140	275	1
Cool	150	300	2
Moderate	160–170	325	3
Moderate	180	350	4
Moderately hot	190	375	5
Moderately hot	200	400	6
Hot	220	425	7
Hot	230	450	8
Very Hot	240–250	450–475	9–10

Acknowledgements

I could not have done this without…

Everyone at Bloomsbury:
Richard Atkinson, you have always had something good to say about me, your encouragement makes such a difference.
Janet Illsley, you have put so much work into this, thank you. I am so impressed by how you have brought it all together and made sense of my ramblings.
Will Webb, you have made such a good-looking book. Thank you for everything you've done. Oh, and I'm still waiting to try your bread…
Penny Edwards, thank you for your hard work and attention to the production of this book.
Erica Jarnes, thank you so much for your help, and for always looking pleased to see me.
And Natalie Hunt, you have guided me through this brilliantly. I have felt properly looked after… I will miss my trips to the big city. Thank you so, so much. I hope we have made a book you are proud of.

And everyone at River Cottage:
Thank you to Rob Love and Hugh Fearnley-Whittingstall, for giving me this opportunity, for believing in me, and for sticking by me.
And to Gill Meller, you have given me great help and massive support. I've run out of excuses now… I'd better get back in the kitchen. Cheers blood.
Thank you to Nikki Duffy for starting me off so well, for your time and energy and endless, endless patience.
Debora Robertson, you have been amazing. You have worked so hard for me, and given me so much encouragement, and so much belief in myself. Thank you also for 'conquistadors' – the best word in the book!

Not forgetting:
Aidan Chapman at the Town Mill Bakery: You have always been very generous with your knowledge. Thank you, I am a much better baker because of you.
Niamh, my lovely little bun. I hope you like the book I've made.
And Michelle Rose, Mia and Olivia… thank you for letting us cover your kitchen in flour. I had a wonderful day making wonderful bread with you.
Hazel Maxwell… thank you for everything. I wish I was more like you. I love you.

And last of all:
Thank you to Gavin Kingcome. Working with you was a complete pleasure. Your photographs are amazing... your camera makes the world so much more beautiful. This started out a word book with pictures; it ended up a picture book with words. It is our book.

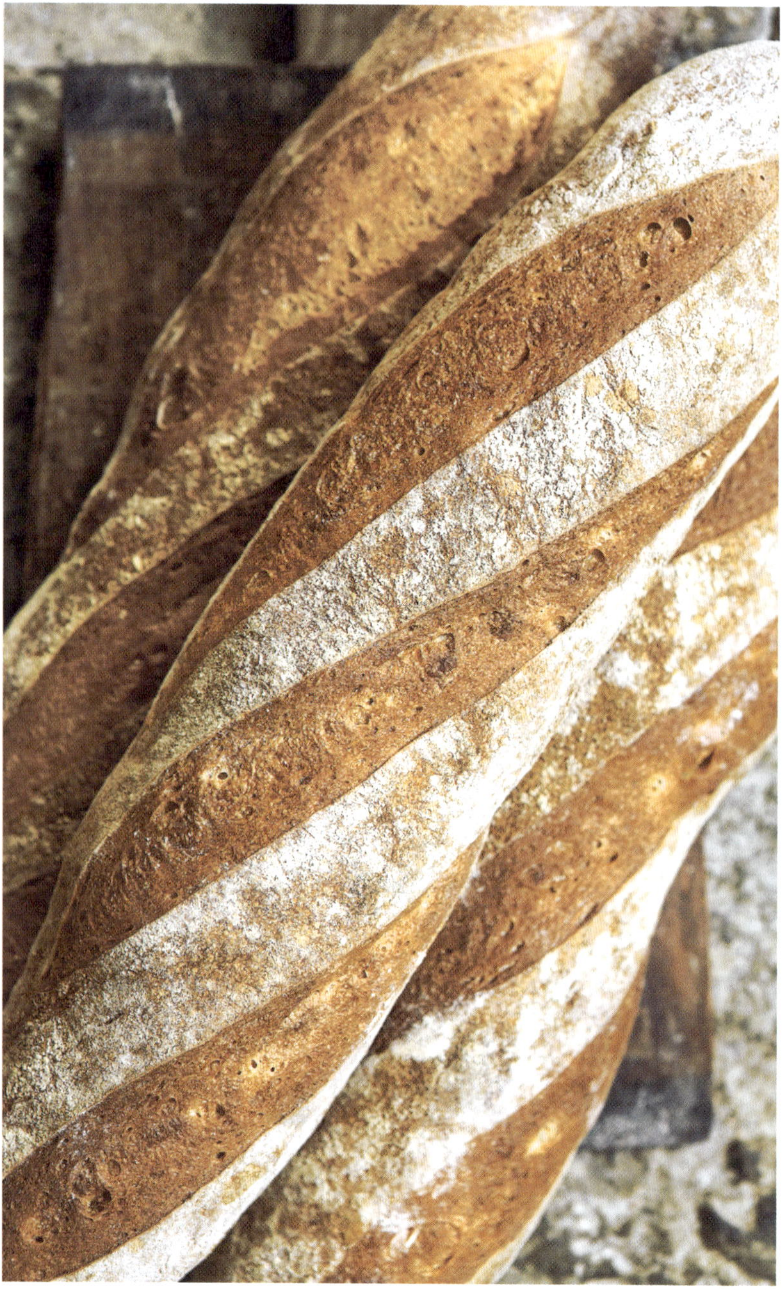

Index

acetic acid 28
additives
    in mass-produced bread 10
    in salt 31
alfalfa seeds
    festival bread 81
apple juice 31
    hazel maizel bread 82

bacon
    cornbread 167
    migas 176
bagels 96
baguettes, shaping 55
bakeries 12
baking bread 66
    in clay oven 209
    timings 66
    see also bread making
baking powder, self-raising flour 22
baking stones 17, 53
    baking bread 66
    pizza 104
    transferring loaves for baking 63–4
baking trays 17, 53
    transferring loaves for baking 63–4
bannocks 137
barbecue breads 107
barley flakes 32
    festival bread 81
basic bread recipe 72–7
    variations 78–83
basil
    panino 91
baskets, proving 16, 63
batons, shaping 56
beer 31
beetroot houmous 178
bin liners 50
biscuits
    poppy and caraway crackers 163
    River Cottage shortbread 158
    Scottish oatcakes 164
    spelt digestives 161
bleaching flour 19
blinis 168
boards 16
bowls 17
bran 19, 20
bread and butter pudding 186
bread flour 20
bread making 34–70
    baking bread 66
    coating the outside 61

cooling bread 68
deflating dough 50
dividing dough 54
kneading dough 44–7
leaving dough to ferment 50
leaving dough to prove 63
measuring ingredients 39–40
mixing dough 42
preparing dough for baking 53–4
shaping dough into a round 48–9
shaping loaves 55–9
slashing the tops 64
transferring loaves for baking 63–4
troubleshooting 70
bread sauce 176
breadcrumbs 176–7
breadsticks 92
breakfast 167
breakfast rolls 80
bricks, building a clay oven 197, 205
brioche 95
brown bread ice cream 189
brown flour 19, 20
brown soda bread 130
buckwheat 32
buns
    Chelsea buns 154
    hot cross buns 152
buttermilk
    soda bread 130

calcium 24, 31
Canadian wheat 21
candied peel
    lardy cake 151
caraway seeds
    poppy and caraway crackers 163
carbon dioxide 28
    see also gas bubbles
carbonic acid 28
cheese
    nettle pesto 181
    panino 91
    pizza 104
Chelsea buns 154
chickpea flour
    socca 172
chimney, clay oven 196, 205, 208
Chorleywood Bread process 10–12
churros 144
ciabatta 86, 90–1
cider 31
    festival bread 81
clay
    for clay oven 197, 198
    clay slip 206

INDEX   219

clay ovens
    building 192–208
    using 209
cling film 50
cloths 16
containers, oiling 50
conversion charts 214
cooling bread 68
corn tortillas 134
cornbread 167
cornmeal 32
crackers, poppy and caraway 163
cream
    bread and butter pudding 186
croissants 147–9
croûtons 176
crumpets 165
crust
    coating 61
    'flying crust' syndrome 63, 70
    slashing tops 64
    steam and 53
    troubleshooting 70
    using as a plate 176
cucumber
    panzanella 182
currants
    Chelsea buns 154
    hot cross buns 152
    lardy cake 151

deflating dough 50
digestives, spelt 161
digital scales 17, 40
dips
    beetroot houmous 178
    taramasalata 179
dividing dough 54
doors, clay ovens 208
dough
    coating the outside 61
    deflating 50
    dividing 54
    intermediate shaping 54
    kneading 44–7
    mixing 42
    'oven spring' 53, 66
    preparing for baking 53–4
    proving 63
    rising 28–9, 48, 50, 53
    shaping into a round 48–9
    shaping loaves 55–9
    slashing tops 64
    starter 40
dough scrapers 17
doughnuts 142–3

dried fruit 32
    adding to dough 40
    festival bread 81
    hot cross buns 152
    lardy cake 151
dried yeast 26, 28
durum wheat 22

eggs
    bread and butter pudding 186
    migas 176
    pain perdu 184
    scotch eggs 176
empty-the-shelf bread 82
endosperm 20
English muffins 99
equipment 16–17
esters 28

fan-assisted ovens 66
fat 31
    quantities 39–40
fermentation 28–9
    rising dough 48, 50
    sourdough starter 112
festival bread 81
fire, in clay oven 209
fish, coating with breadcrumbs 176
fish fingers 177
flambéed pain perdu 184
flatbread 103
    roti 133
    tortillas 134
flour 19–24
    coating loaves 61
    gluten-free bread flour 23
    hydration 39
    kamut flour 23
    leaving dough to ferment 50
    milling 24
    quantities 39, 40
    rye flour 23
    spelt flour 23
    wheat flour 20–2
Flour Milling and Baking Research Association 10
'flying crust' syndrome 63, 70
focaccia 86, 89
food mixers 17
    kneading dough 47
former, for clay oven 198–201
freezing
    bread 68
    breadcrumbs 176
    dough 29
    yeast 28
fresh yeast 26–8

fridges, storing bread in 68
fruit
  summer pudding 190
  see also dried fruit

garlicky olive oil 104
gas bubbles
  'oven spring' 53, 66
  rising dough 28–9, 48
germ 20
gluten 24
  effect of salt on 29
  gluten intolerance 10
  kneading dough 44
  proving dough 63
  relaxing 54
  rising dough 48, 50
  slashing tops 64
  in spelt flour 23
  in wheat flour 20–2
gluten-free bread flour 23, 24
goat's cheese
  panino 91
grains
  adding to dough 40
  coating loaves 61
Granary flour 22

hazelnuts 32
  festival bread 81
  hazel maizel bread 82
hemp seeds
  spelt sourdough 122–3
honey 31
  walnut and honey bread 131
hot cross buns 152
houmous, beetroot 178
hydration 39

ice cream, brown bread 189
ingredients 19–32
  basic bread recipe 75
  measuring 39–40
insulation, clay ovens 206
intermediate shaping 54

kamut flour 23, 24
kneading dough 44–7
knives
  bread knife 16
  slashing tops 64
  slicing bread 68
'knocking back' 50

lactic acid 28
lardy cake 151

leftover bread 174–91
  beetroot houmous 178
  bread and butter pudding 186
  breadcrumbs 176–7
  brown bread ice cream 189
  nettle pesto 181
  pain perdu 184
  panzanella 182
  summer pudding 190
  taramasalata 179
levain 110
linen cloths 16
liquids 31
loaf tins 55
loaves
  coating the outside 61
  shaping 55–9
  size 54
  slashing the tops 64
  transferring for baking 63–4
low-gluten breads 64

magnesium 24, 31
maize meal 32
  corn tortillas 134
  cornbread 167
  hazel maizel bread 82
malted and seeded loaf 80
malted grain bread 78
malted grain flour 22
mass-produced bread 10–12
measuring ingredients 39–40
migas 176
milk 31
millet 32
mineral water 24
'mini-blinis' 168
mixing bowls 17
molasses
  pumpernickel 124–5
monastery bread 81
muffins, English 99
my sourdough 117–19

nachos 134
nettle pesto 181
nuts 32
  adding to dough 40
  festival bread 81
  hazel maizel bread 82
  walnut and honey bread 131

oats and oatmeal 31
  bannocks 137
  coating loaves 61
  festival bread 81

monastery bread 81
oaty wholemeal 79
Scottish oatcakes 164
spelt digestives 161
Staffordshire oatcakes 171
oil 31
  leaving dough to ferment 50
  in wheat flour 20
olive oil
  ciabatta 90–1
  focaccia 89
  garlicky olive oil 104
one-stage mixing method 42
onions
  migas 176
  panzanella 182
organic flour 19
'oven spring' 53, 66
ovens 53
  clay ovens 192–209
  for pizza 104
  preparing for baking 53–4
  refreshing bread 68
  steam 53
  temperatures 53, 66, 215

pain perdu 184
pancakes
  blinis 168
  socca 172
panino 91
panzanella 182
Parmesan, 'poor man's' 176
peels 17, 53, 66
  transferring loaves for baking 64
pesto, nettle 181
pikelets 165
pizza 104–6
plain flour 22
plinth, clay oven 195–6
poolish 110
'poor man's Parmesan' 176
poppy and caraway crackers 163
proteins 20–1
proving baskets 16, 63
proving dough 63
pumpernickel 124–5

racks, cooling 68
raising agents, self-raising flour 22
raisins
  bread and butter pudding 186
  festival bread 81
  hot cross buns 152
refreshing bread 68
refrigerators, storing bread in 68

rising dough 28–9, 48, 50, 53
  'oven spring' 53, 66
  proving dough 63
  slashing tops 64
River Cottage shortbread 158
River Cottage sourdough 116
rock salt 29
roe
  taramasalata 179
roller milling, flour 19
rolls
  breakfast rolls 80
  refreshing 68
  shaping 59
  size 54
roof, clay oven 196
rosemary
  focaccia 89
roti 133
rye berries
  pumpernickel 124–5
rye flour 23, 24
  blinis 168
  coating loaves 61
  pumpernickel 124–5
  sour rye bread 120

salads
  panzanella 182
salami
  panino 91
salt 29–31
  focaccia 89
  quantities 39, 40
sand
  for clay oven 197, 198
  former 198–201
sandwiches
  panino 91
sauces
  bread sauce 176
  nettle pesto 181
  roast tomato sauce 104
sausage meat
  scotch eggs 176
scales 17, 40
scones 156
scotch eggs 176
Scottish oatcakes 164
sea salt 29–31
seeds 32
  adding to dough 40
  coating loaves 61
  malted and seeded loaf 80
sel gris 31
self-raising flour 22

semolina 32
    ciabatta 90–1
shaping, intermediate 54
shaping loaves 55–9
shortbread, River Cottage 158
slashing tops 64
slicing bread 68
slip, clay 206
smoked pollack roe
    taramasalata 179
socca 172
soda bread 130
    walnut and honey bread 131
'soggy tea towel' technique 107
sour rye bread 120
sourdough 115–16
    my sourdough 117–19
    pumpernickel 124–5
    River Cottage sourdough 116
    sour rye bread 120
    spelt sourdough 122–3
    sponge method 42
    starter 40, 110–13
spelt flour 23, 24
    festival bread 81
    spelt bread 79
    spelt digestives 161
    spelt sourdough 122–3
sponge method, mixing dough 42
spray bottles 17, 53
spring water 24
Staffordshire oatcakes 171
staling 68
starter 40
    sourdough 110–13
steam
    cooling bread 68
    in oven 53
stoneground flour 19
stones *see* baking stones
storing bread 68
strong flour 20–1
stubby cylinders, shaping 56–7
sultanas
    hot cross buns 152
    lardy cake 151
summer pudding 190

tapered batons, shaping 56
taramasalata 179
temperature
    in clay oven 209
    dough 28, 29
    oven 53, 66, 215
texture, troubleshooting 70
thermometers 17, 209

tin loaves, shaping 58
tins 55
toast 177
tomatoes
    panino 91
    panzanella 182
    roast tomato sauce 104
toppings, pizza 104, 106
tops, slashing 64
tortillas 134
trays, baking 17, 53
troubleshooting 70
two-stage mixing method 42

vetkoek 100

walnuts 32
    walnut and honey bread 131
water 24
    quantities 39, 40
water spray bottles 17, 53
weighing scales 17, 40
wheat 20–1
    flour 20–2, 24
    wheat intolerance 12, 22
wheat berries
    pumpernickel 124–5
white bread 78
white flour 19
wholemeal flour 19
    hydration 39
    oaty wholemeal 79
wild yeasts 26, 108–25
wood-fired ovens, pizza 104
wood shavings, for clay oven 197
wooden boards 16
work surfaces, kneading dough 44
wort 26

yeast 26–9
    how yeast works 28–9
    quantities 39, 40
    rising dough 50, 53
    sourdough starter 110–13
    wild yeasts 26, 108–25
yeast-free breads 126–37
yoghurt 31
    blinis 168
    cornbread 167
    flatbread 103
    my sourdough 117–19

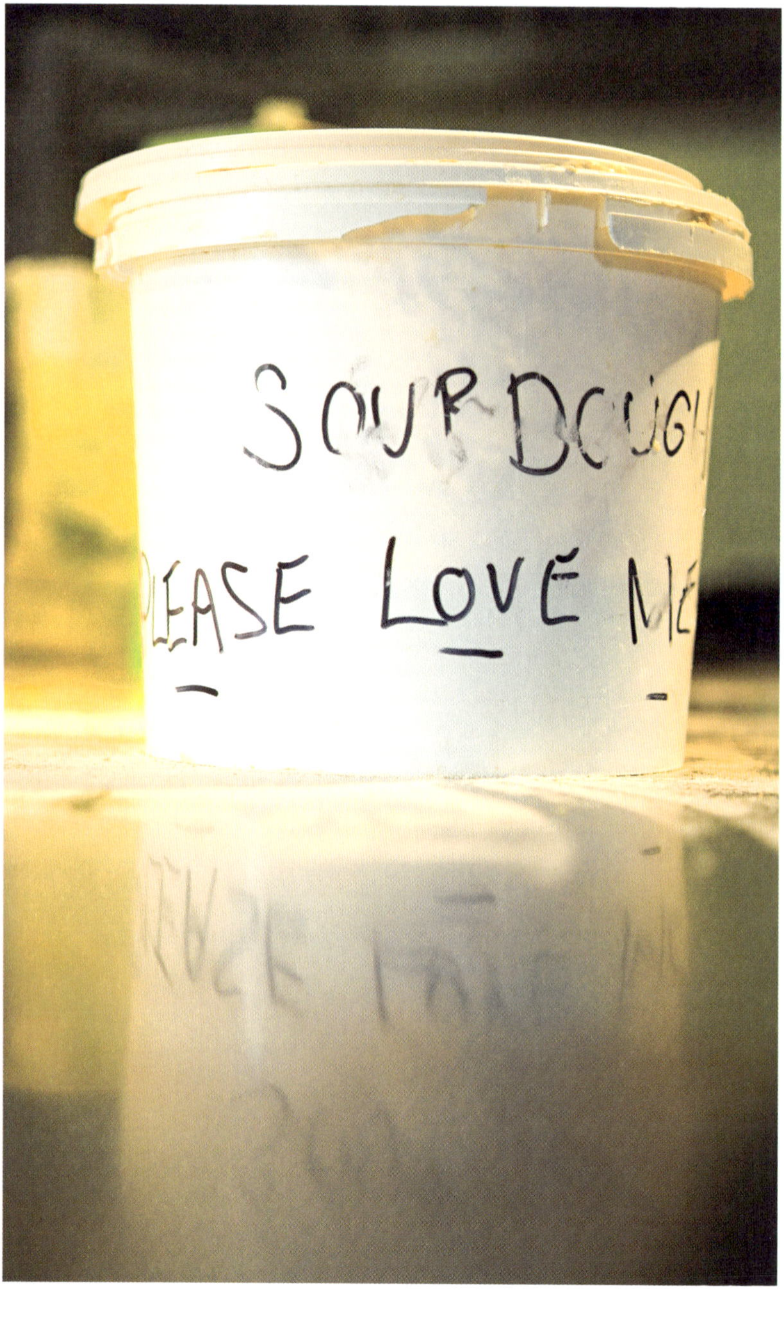

SOURDOUG
LEASE LOVE ME

River Cottage Handbooks

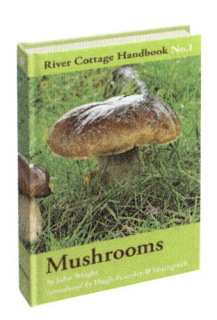

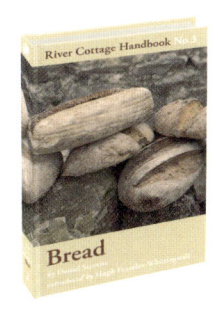

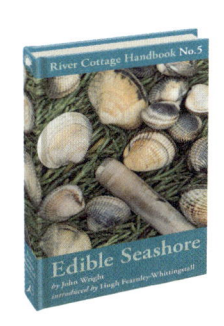

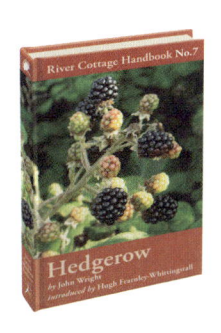

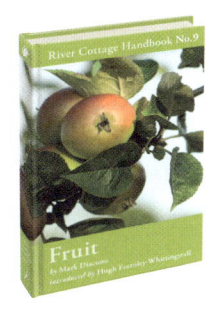

Seasonal, Local, Organic, Wild

FOR FURTHER INFORMATION AND
TO ORDER ONLINE, VISIT
RIVERCOTTAGE.NET